The Enterprise Engineering Series

More information about this series at http://www.springer.com/series/8371

Boris Shishkov

Designing Enterprise Information Systems

Merging Enterprise Modeling and Software Specification

 Springer

Boris Shishkov
Faculty of Information Sciences
University of Library Studies
and Information Technologies
Sofia, Bulgaria

Institute of Mathematics and Informatics
Bulgarian Academy of Sciences
Sofia, Bulgaria

Interdisciplinary Institute for Collaboration
and Research on Enterprise Systems and Technology
Sofia, Bulgaria

ISSN 1867-8920   ISSN 1867-8939   (electronic)
The Enterprise Engineering Series
ISBN 978-3-030-22443-1   ISBN 978-3-030-22441-7   (eBook)
https://doi.org/10.1007/978-3-030-22441-7

This Springer imprint is published by the registered company Springer Nature Switzerland AG.
The registered company address is: Gewerbestrasse 11, 6330 Cham, Switzerland

Prologue

We arrive at the truth not by the reason only but also by the heart
—Blaise Pascal

I have written this book for:

- Analysts who are interested in the construction and the operation of enterprises.
- Enterprise engineers who are challenged by the needs for adequate models to be used either as a basis for enterprise engineerings/reengineerings and/or in support of software specifications.
- IT architects who are inspired to improve the way in which they are specifying enterprise information systems.
- Software engineers who are aware of the necessity for better establishing the computation-independent models that concern the software system-to-be.

Even though delivering adequate enterprise models used to be a challenge, the emerging enterprise engineering discipline and its underlying social theories seem to be giving a good basis for modeling complex real-life (organizational) processes. Next to that, software engineering and corresponding computing paradigms have advanced and represent a good basis for developing software, starting from a computation-independent model of the software system-to-be. Nevertheless, bringing together enterprise modeling and software specification is still a challenge, although the enterprise-software gap has been broadly discussed for more than 15 years already. For this reason, it is not surprising that currently many software projects are reaching failure and/or going overbudget and/or bringing insufficient satisfaction to users and so on. Hence, the modeling featuring enterprises and their processes (on the one hand) and the software specifications (on the other hand) need to be better aligned and considered as one integrated task. Otherwise, computation-independent software models that lack adequate enterprise modeling background would keep on leading to the development of software that would only partially fit its real-life (enterprise) environment. I provide further elaboration and justification concerning those claims in the following two paragraphs.

THE IMPORTANCE OF ENTERPRISE MODELING

For centuries already, business processes of different kinds have been part of our societies. For decades already, global enterprises have been offering products and services around the globe. Currently, organizations are experiencing increasing needs for adequate ENTERPRISE MODELING because of the following: (1) Often (distributed) organizational processes are becoming too complex to be grasped intuitively. (2) Change impact analysis is often needed, but it requires structured enterprise data as input. (3) Enterprise innovations are considered of key importance for gaining competitive advantages, but this would often assume enterprise reengineering activities that in turn "ask" for legacy models and corresponding information. (4) Introducing new technology and/or accommodating automations can only be really successful if the technology is well aligned with the original business processes; this in turn can only be possible if we are able to adequately describe and model those processes, such that we know the "design restrictions" with regard to the introduced technology. Those are only four claims justifying the importance of enterprise modeling; I can provide even more justification in that direction. Nevertheless, we observe insufficient maturity as it concerns enterprise modeling: (a) Many analysts conduct intuitive enterprise modeling that is not scientifically justified—this often leads to modeling of low quality. (b) They often fail to be exhaustive in their modeling—some of them would only focus on modeling behavior and others would only focus on modeling data, and so on. (c) Some analysts would mix up essential business things (e.g., John paid for his service subscription) with information exchange that is not featuring essential business things (e.g., John entered his PIN incorrectly while using an ATM). (d) Other analysts would be unaware of the importance of communicative acts in real-life communication, through which commitments are generated, that are in turn crucially important with respect to the processes within an organization. (e) Many analysts would overlook regulations and public values as key restrictors with regard to the functioning of an organization. Hence, a sound and exhaustive conceptual reference is needed and the emerging ENTERPRISE ENGINEERING discipline is expected to be the solution.

USING ENTERPRISE MODELS AS A BASIS IN GENERATING SOFTWARE SPECIFICATIONS

Businesses changed when computers first appeared on the scene and enterprises had to accommodate (partial) automation of their business processes. Businesses changed again when web services and cloud infrastructures appeared, and enterprises faced the challenge of making (some) internal business processes external. Nothing was the same anymore—two "worlds" emerged: the domain experts, "playing on the enterprise field," and the technical experts, "playing on the software field." Nevertheless, more than 15 years of discussions (as mentioned above) featuring the mismatch between enterprise modeling and software design did not help—the two "worlds" are still separated. The hopes for changes are justified by the rapid enterprise-technological developments (see the beginning of the current paragraph) and it is expected that it will be those developments that would make the abovementioned mismatch socially unacceptable anymore. Said otherwise, the abovementioned developments have been justifying more and more the necessity for bringing together enterprise modeling and software specification since a domain (enterprise) expert alone is insufficiently capable of grasping the technical complexity of the enterprise's IT system and its reach outside through software services, while a software engineer would only have superficial enterprise-specific domain knowledge. What complicates things further is that software engineering and the emerging enterprise engineering discipline have developed separately. Most enterprise modelers would not "step in the shoes" of software designers, while most software engineers would not "broaden their horizon" beyond the software artifact being developed—even the computation-independent modeling of MDA (model-driven architecture) is just about the software system-to-be. Anything outside it would often be considered by software engineers as an "abstract environment," and the only thing to do about it is specifying "interfaces." Many software engineers would be insufficiently focused on questions, such as: What is the construction of the broader enterprise environment? How can the software system under development be adaptable with regard to possible environmental changes? How can the software system-to-be achieve user-perceived effectiveness? How can the software system-to-be be adequately aligned with the enterprise norms and broader societal regulations? How can human responsibility and authority be aligned to what the software system-to-be actually does? How can public values (such as privacy, accountability, and transparency) be properly "translated" into (software) requirements? The lack of adequate "answers" to those questions justifies the claim that the alignment between enterprise modeling and software specification is still uncertain, and this in turn often leads to enterprise information systems of low quality—software applications and information systems are not as effective as they should be; this leads to software failures as mentioned above. It is therefore not surprising that the latest technological innovations (e.g., innovations concerning Internet-of-things and machine learning) are only partially "brought" to enterprises via software applications. I argue that only the ENTERPRISE-MODELING-DRIVEN SOFTWARE GENERATION could be the solution as it concerns the mismatch between enterprise engineering and software design.

Bridging that gap is thus considered important as it concerns enterprise information systems, inspiring me to propose a modeling approach. For this reason, on the one hand, the proposed approach steps on a conceptual invariance (embracing concepts whose essence goes beyond the barriers between social and technical disciplines), while, on the other hand, the approach builds upon that "common ground" to accommodate a modeling duality featuring (1) technology-independent enterprise modeling that is rooted in social theories and (2) software specifications that are rooted in computing paradigms. On top of that, the approach's guidelines and related notations further grease such an enterprise-software modeling by facilitating modeling generations and transformations: starting from unstructured business information, coming through enterprise models, and reaching as far as the specification of software. The alignment between enterprise modeling and software specification is realized in a component-based way, featuring a potential re-use of modeling constructs, such that the modeling effectiveness and efficiency are stimulated. Finally, I provide a case study and illustrative examples for the sake of "grounding" my studies and demonstrating some strengths and limitations of the proposed modeling approach.

Nevertheless, this book is not about the approach itself. This book is about bringing together enterprise modeling and software specification (maybe also by using another approach and/or other notations) such that an enterprise-modeling-driven software generation is achieved. Even though the book is supposed to be telling you how to sort this out, it does not give you an "A to Z" recipe as in cooking. Instead, it raises awareness and provides directions. I have stressed upon the mismatch between enterprise modeling and software design, and I have proposed solution directions accordingly, featuring on the one hand a conceptual invariance and on the other hand a modeling duality (see above). I believe that reading this book will inspire thoughts and ideas that are useful as it concerns YOUR way of analyzing enterprises and/or YOUR way of specifying software. Hence, I have not only presented social theories (Chap. 4) and computing paradigms (Chap. 5), but I have also introduced a common conceptual background for them, touching upon systemics (Chap. 2) on the one hand and context-awareness (Chap. 3) on the other hand. Further, by introducing (in Chap. 6) an approach (see above), namely the SDBC approach, and by considering accordingly a case study and illustrative examples, I have brought forward some justification on the adequacy and feasibility of merging enterprise engineering and software engineering. It is up to you to reflect those ideas, guidelines, and examples in your work, such that you usefully enrich the approaches you follow as it concerns enterprise modeling and/or software specification.

As it concerns readability, I have emphasized issues through various fonts and styles, for example: <Courier New 9 Points, bold>emphasis</Courier New 9 Points, bold>, <bold>emphasis</bold>, <underlined>emphasis</underlined>, <uppercase>emphasis</uppercase>, and so on. This allows me to emphasize in different "levels" distinguishing, for example, between different parts, then between key issues concerning each of the parts, then between different concepts considered accordingly, and so on.

This book is based on my previous book *Enterprise Information Systems - A Modeling Approach* which was published in 2017 but has never been really distributed and is no longer available. Even though the current book is essentially based on the 2017 book, it also contains new and reworked material, and is the only one that now counts as a summary of my work over the last years.

Anyway, more effort is still needed as concerns the mismatch between enterprise modeling and software design—this has been a challenge for many years already (as mentioned above), and bridging that gap is not just a matter of innovative ideas but also of changing attitudes. This challenge is of an interdisciplinary essence and it needs bringing together enterprise engineers and software developers, inspiring them to join interdisciplinary projects and discussions. I believe that the current book represents a small contribution in that direction. Hopefully, such efforts would be embraced by relevant communities and adequate solutions would be materialized. If you want to join activities in that direction, visit the website www.is-bmsd.org

featuring BMSD—the international symposium on business modeling and software design.

In carrying out those studies, I have been inspired by joint work and collaborations with my colleagues from Delft University of Technology, the University of Twente, the University of Reading, and IICREST, to whom I am happy and honored to extend my gratitude and compliments. Further, I am privileged as well to be leading for 9 years already (as General Chair + Program Chair) the prestigious BMSD symposium (see above), whose community's feedback is always so stimulating. Finally, I dedicate this book to the memory of my father, Blagovest; it is really special to me that it would have been my dad's 82nd birthday today. He used to be a wonderful father and a brilliant scientist, always inspiring!

I hope you will find the current book interesting and will consider it a helpful reference with regard to enterprise information systems.

Sofia, Bulgaria   Boris Shishkov
6 April 2019

Contents

Chapter 1
Introduction

How did *enterprises* look *40–50 years ago today*? What were then the *rudimentary business process automations* [1] and how is this different from the current *business process automations that go beyond conventional data manipulation and record-keeping activities* [2]? How did enterprises exchange information then, not counting on the *global telecommunications* and the *digital multimedia* [3] and what are the differences now when a *cell phone* alone seems to be capable of supporting video communication, answering complex questions, and providing satellite navigation [4]? Was it possible then (without *web services* [5] and *cloud infrastructures* [6]) for associations between different enterprises to combine manufacturing, assembly, wholesale distribution, and retail sales in what is currently called *business process externalization* [7]? Were software technologists able then to develop really *adaptable information systems* [8], not counting on *sensor technology* [9]? We argue that answering those questions would bring us to the conclusion that over the past several decades enterprises have been shifting to experience a growing dependency on **ICT** (**I**nformation and **C**ommunication **T**echnology) [10]. For this reason, it is not surprising that **SE** (**S**oftware **E**ngineering) [11] gets increasingly relevant with regard to enterprise developments. Hence, even though **EE** (**E**nterprise **E**ngineering) [12] and *SE* have developed separately as disciplines, it is currently important to bring together *enterprise modeling* and *software specification*; we argue that this would allow enterprises to adequately utilize current technology.

There have always been *business activities*—from ancient times [13] to the present day [14]. Referring to the observations and conclusions presented above, it is interesting to particularly consider those business activities whose realization requires *ICT*, pointing to technical developments that had originated in the previous century, when *computers* first appeared on the scene [15]. Hence, for around 50 years already, we have enjoyed business activities of another kind—business activities that are *supported by ICT* (we call them *ICT-supported business activities*). Finally, it is interesting to discuss how has technology (and *ICT*, in particular) changed over the past 50 years when we have reached as far as business activities that are *essentially driven by ICT* (we call them *ICT-enabled business activities*).

© Springer Nature Switzerland AG 2020

B. Shishkov, *Designing Enterprise Information Systems*, The Enterprise Engineering Series, https://doi.org/10.1007/978-3-030-22441-7_1

Hence, we call *"traditional business activities"* those business activities that are neither *ICT-supported* nor *ICT-enabled*. For instance:

- Business activities such as paid consultancy (we mean the mere intellectual work on delivering an advice) and haircut delivery (we mean the mere physical trimming of the customer's hair) are examples for **traditional business activities**—*(i)*.
- Business activities such as the delivery of automated brokerage instructions and the delivery of automatically generated documents are examples for **ICT-supported business activities**—*(ii)*.
- Business activities such as web trading and e-transportation (using unmanned ground/aerial vehicles [16]) are examples for **ICT-enabled business activities**—*(iii)*.

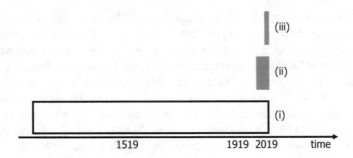

Fig. 1.1 Business activities over time

As illustrated in Fig. 1.1, it is only for several decades that *ICT*-supported/enabled business activities have been possible. Hence, this is a matter of emerging knowledge, new disciplines, and ongoing technical and technological developments that all concern what we label as **EIS—Enterprise Information Systems** [17]. Further, the rectangles that are next to the labels "(ii)" and "(iii)" are colored in gray to indicate that the current book's *EIS* focus is dominated by the consideration of *ICT*-supported business activities and *ICT*-enabled business activities. Nevertheless, (i) should not be ignored because traditional business activities concern the broader real-life environment in which enterprises and *EIS* are to operate. Still, it is for sure that the *EIS* developments should assume bringing together past and emerging knowledge and best practices. Finally, we argue that no matter if we are considering (ii) or (iii), it is essential bringing together *EE* and *SE*. This is obvious for (iii) when *ICT* (software)-driven activities would have to be given a business realization and not so obvious for (ii) where it may seem that SE only would be relevant to the process automation challenge; we claim however that automated processes need to be perfectly aligned and integrated with the other business processes (otherwise, the enterprise would not be a coherent whole), and this could only be achieved if *EE* and *SE* are brought together.

The remaining of the current chapter is organized as follows: In *Sect. 1.1*, we provide an analysis of the technological progress over time, as a justification for the importance of *ICT* as one of the foundations of the currently evolving *EIS* discipline. In *Sect. 1.2*, we consider the public drive towards bringing together *EE* and *SE* for the sake of an adequate utilization of current technology by enterprises. Several identified important challenges relevant to the *EE–SE* merging are presented and discussed in *Sect. 1.3*. The abovementioned *EIS* discipline is introduced and discussed in *Sect. 1.4*, while corresponding essential concepts are presented in *Sect. 1.5*. In *Sect. 1.6*, we bring forward a modeling perspective over *EIS* that is dominant within the current book. Finally, *Sect. 1.7* is featuring an outlook with regard to the remainder of the book.

1.1 Retrospection

Even though more than 500 years back from now *Leonardo da Vinci* and *Michelangelo* have inspired amazing achievements in civil engineering, mechanical engineering, and architectural engineering [18, 19], it is the eighteenth century that marks the beginning of *industrialization* and corresponding enterprise developments [20]. Crucial in this regard was the *Industrial Revolution* (*IR*) marked by key inventions and developments, such as the spinning jenny, the power loom, the steam engine, and the internal combustion engine [21]. The period up to the twentieth century was also marked by other key developments: the invention of the *telegraph* and the invention of the *telephone* [22]; also the *electric power* was introduced [23]. Next to that, it was at the end of the nineteenth century when the first *automobile* was created [24]; nevertheless, it was only at the beginning of the twentieth century when cars had become widely popular (mainly in Europe and USA), inspired by the affordable *Ford Model T* that was characterized by efficient fabrication, including assembly line production instead of individual hand crafting [25]. This was followed by impressive industrial developments in the USA, marked by the "Rockefeller Era" when oil was used throughout the country as a light source until the introduction of electricity and as a car fuel [26]. This has boosted the railroad industry with trains transporting oil around the country. Both *auto transportation* and *rail transportation* have inspired *infrastructure developments* that in turn have opened up new horizons for enterprise developments [27]. In parallel, the first *radio* has appeared, changing everything with intangible signals being transmitted through the air over long distances, this giving birth to *telecommunications* and *electronics* [28]. All those developments have led to an apogee—the first television coming out in the 1920s [29]. This was the time when nothing was the same anymore because businesses were no longer physically restricted in the distribution of immaterial products, such as commercial music and movies—they could instantly reach many audiences all around the globe; this has boosted marketing, advertising, and mass media [30]. Even though those huge developments were "used" in the Second World War, they were also used in the postwar period, inspiring the quick recovery of Europe [31]. Emblematic in this regard is *The Beatles* phenomenon, demonstrating for the first time how talented musicians can de facto "reach" millions of neighborhoods on the planet through television and radio (next to the records distribution channel), challenging as "industry" any other form of business established by then [32]. This power was mainly associated with the *television communication channel* and with the essence of the product—songs: a song is dominated by the power of creativity (no matter if it is authored by *Mozart* [33] or *John Lennon* [34]); still, in the 1960s, The Beatles were empowered by technology to transmit their songs as "information" in an effective and efficient manner, such that millions of people would be able to hear The Beatles' new song minutes after its release. Nevertheless, even though amazing, that *post-IR progress* was limited with its assuming only the production and distribution of material and immaterial goods. What about *virtual communities, remote activities, real-time global collaborations*, and *artificial agents*? They were impossible in the 1960s. Mankind required new developments and the *Digital Era* began with advancement of technology *from analog electronic and mechanical devices to digital electronics* [35].

Hence, businesses changed when *computers* firstly appeared on the scene and enterprises had the chance to accommodate (partial) *automation* of their business processes; *mainframe computers* were used in enterprises, representing large-scale systems designed for processing and storing huge amounts of data [1]. For example, such computers could facilitate logistically warehouses and inventory, by controlling supplies and orders. Being computationally powerful, mainframe computers were used for data processing. Next to that, they were enabling trans-manipulators to effectively realize automated warehouse operations [36]. Nevertheless, it was only possible for larger enterprises to purchase and maintain mainframe machines, and it was the appearance of smaller ones in the early 1970s that has made computers really popular. It was firstly the office/bookkeeping computer the size of a table that has brought real benefits to small and medium-sized enterprises; it was possible to easily connect such a computer to a printer. This could be of much help to the administrative facilitation of businesses. For example, using an invoicing program, one would manually enter order header data, a customer number, and order line data (item number—quantity—unit price) to produce a paper invoice. Master data for the customers and items were retrieved from a mini-cassette tape. Saving administrative work and reducing the risk of errors were among the benefits from using such computers. Nevertheless, memory technologies were yet insufficiently mature and this was a drawback, with such computers counting on a working memory of 6 kB or less, with the option to use the mini-cassette drive for external memory (disk storage was rarely an affordable option for those computers). Later, floppy disks (360 kB storage capacity) were an affordable option for external data storage as well as hard disks (up to 20 MB storage capacity); in the late 1980s, hard disks of much greater storage capacity (of several hundred MB) were an affordable option. Still up to the 1980s, computers had a limited impact—they have only been *facilitating data processing and enabling rudimentary automations* [15].

It was during the 1980s when something crucially important has happened: The *Advanced Research Projects Agency Network* (*ARPANET*) adopted *TCP* (*Transmission Control Protocol*)/*IP* (*Internet Protocol*) as a suite of communication protocols used to *interconnect network devices*, and this has de facto introduced:

- *Internet* as a loose confederation of independent yet interconnected networks that use the TCP/IP protocols for communications.
- The *Client-Server Communication* that enables *client* (computer) devices to communicate via Internet with a *server* computer (examples of computer applications that use the client-server model are *e-mail*, *network printing*, and the *World Wide Web*) [37].

That is how computers have become powerfully enriched from a networking perspective. This has further increased the popularity of the computers of that time (the desktop personal computer and the laptop) through which people were benefitting from:

- The global telecommunications.
- The digital multimedia [10].

This has led to significant societal changes, as acknowledged by the Interdisciplinary Institute for Collaboration and Research on Enterprise Systems and Technology (IICREST) [38]:

- Enabling scientists to carry out remote experiments, accessing and manipulating lab facilities from a distance.
- Making it possible for many workers to work from home, using connected computers and exchanging work results via Internet.
- Allowing people who are not physically together to carry out virtual video "meetings."

Those changes have led to an increased importance of the service sector in industrialized economies, with an emphasis on *IT-enabled services*. This brings us to the current years.

Hence, businesses changed again when *web services* and *cloud infrastructures* appeared and enterprises faced the challenge of making (some) internal business processes external, as already mentioned.

Current web services with their underlying *ICT components* count on advanced *context-aware ICT applications* that adapt their operation to context changes, achieving accordingly (1) *optimization of their internal processes*, (2) *maximization of the user-perceived effectiveness*, and (3) *conformance to relevant public values* [39]. Nevertheless, the levels of trust are insufficient with regard to the corresponding enabling environments and this has inspired solutions related to *blockchain technology* that allows for trusted data exchange [40].

Our conclusion is that even though in the past it was possible to separate ICT (software) activities from the other activities concerning an enterprise, this is not possible anymore because many enterprise processes are already essentially enabled by software. For this reason, at the beginning of the twenty-first century, it is demanded that EE and SE are brought together; this will be the focus of the following section.

1.2   Enterprise Engineering (EE), Software Engineering (SE)

Numerous researchers and practitioners are currently inspired by the goal of proposing innovative ideas and solutions about a better *utilization of advanced ICT by
enterprises*. That goal is reflected in the *evolution of business processes*: Considered
as an essential enterprise asset, *business processes* used to receive much attention,
for the sake of improving the enterprise performance, decreasing the enterprise costs,
increasing the satisfaction of customers, and so on. Hence, it was (and it is) widely
agreed that by improving business processes, enterprises could substantially increase
their value. Many years ago, improving business processes was a matter just of
enterprise engineering—then the big challenge was how to organize ordering,
accounting, shipping, etc., such that all the different tasks are in synch while the
business processes are as simple as possible, leading to effectiveness and efficiency
in serving the customer. Nevertheless, changes in business processes came *when
computers first appeared* on the scene and it was possible to replace paper streams
by databases, to re-use content, and to quickly find needed information, as discussed
already—then the big challenge already was how to make better use of computers
that are in turn heavily dependent on corresponding *software*: this was a matter also
of software engineering (next to *enterprise engineering*). Hence, *enterprise engineering* and *software engineering* had to be brought together [41]. However, those
two disciplines had developed separately because the so-called "computerization"
was simply about *automation*—the same tasks realized by human entities had to be
"given" to computers. *Automation* indeed allowed many companies to tremendously
bring down their workforce but the quality of the IT support delivered to *enterprises*
used to be low exactly because of the mentioned "separation": *Enterprise engineers*
would only superficially redesign their *business processes* (when bringing in computers) because they lacked deep IT knowledge, while *software engineers* would
only partially respond to the original business *requirements* because they lacked
deep domain knowledge. This was labelled as a "*mismatch (or gap) between
enterprise modeling and software design*" [17]. Since the new millennium, we
have been witnessing more and more efforts directed towards *bringing together
EE and SE*, for the sake of bridging the abovementioned *gap*. This would mean *de
facto* bringing together:

(a) Social theories, such as *enterprise ontology, organizational semiotics, theory of
    organized activity*, etc. (see Chap. 4).
(b) Computing paradigms, such as *component-based software development, ser-
    vice-oriented computing, model-driven engineering*, etc. (see Chap. 5).

However, this appeared to be a nontrivial task because:

• Within the scope of *enterprise engineering*, as according to [12], used to be the
  creation of enterprise models capable of usefully restricting the software system-
  to-be, but this only reached the level of software functionality specification,

leaving ambiguity with regard to the implementation choices, platform choices, networking choices, and their impact with regard to the business processes.

- Within the scope of *software engineering*, as according to [42], used to be the development of software, based on computation-independent models and/or the composition of software services (considered at high level and pointing to underlying technical complexity), but all those issues stemmed from a view on the software itself, not assuming an enterprise-modeling-driven derivation of software.

Hence, not bridging that *gap* has led and is currently leading to *failures* of many software projects as well as to *projects going over budget*, and we often observe evidence of *low levels of customer satisfaction* with regard to software applications and/or (enterprise) information systems [17].

Further, the abovementioned *gap* is pointing not only at the *creation of software* as a way of allowing enterprises to utilize advanced IT but also at the *integration of already created (legacy) IT systems in enterprises*. We observe that many software systems being developed need to be adequately *integrated* in a (new) enterprise context and sometimes already running software applications are "part" of that enterprise context. For this reason, it is essential to have *alignment* and *traceability* between the enterprise level and the software level, and therefore it seems logical to try to identify *enterprise systems* and *software systems* and bridge the two on that basis [41]. As is well-known, when speaking of a system, we are interested in what the system components are (*composition*), how they are related to each other (*structure*), how they are related to the *environment*, and what the principles are that guide the system evolution. We need an integrated view of the system under consideration and for an enterprise this would point at a coherent whole of principles, methods, and models that are used in the design and realization of the enterprise's structure, processes, (possibly) information systems, and infrastructure. Even though *structure, processes*, and *data* are essential for software development as well, *more complexities occur when developing software* (coming through analysis, design, and implementation)—what lags behind is managing system complexity expressed in terms of *dependencies between system elements*. Finally, current enterprises and software applications both need to be *adaptable* because of the constantly changing real-life environment to which they should conform [17].

This all inspires us to pose several **research goals** (see below) that are about enabling developers both conceptually and methodologically:

- Identifying the enterprise system(s) and/or the software system(s) to be considered.
- Building aspect models accordingly, including models that reflect structure, processes, data, and so on.
- Establishing inter-model consistency.
- Capturing the granularity levels that feature the enterprise models and the (corresponding) software models, acknowledging that it is possible that the particular enterprise models and software models point at different levels of granularity.

- Establishing alignment and traceability between enterprise models and corresponding software models.
- Addressing possible dependencies between system elements.
- Allowing for ways to model adaptability.

In the following chapters, we address those goals, also acknowledging their relevance to several essential challenges (presented in the following section) as considered in [17].

1.3 Challenges

EE and SE would assume applying different **viewpoints** not only to each of them but also to both of them; achieving an overall consistency is hence an important challenge. Further, it is challenging to consider **data** accordingly since to date EE and SE are both counting on data analytics as an important input. Finally, **adaptability** is considered to be crucially important for any enterprise and also for any ICT application because currently it is often that environments are much dynamic and different environmental states require different enterprise/software behaviors.

Design-wise, we have identified two key challenges, namely, (1) achieving **re-use** of modeling/design artifacts, as a way of stimulating engineering effectiveness and efficiency and (2) sticking to **service orientation** as a design choice that is considered adequate with regard to the current user demands for flexible, composable, and service-driven enterprise/ICT solutions.

Fig. 1.2 EE-SE challenges

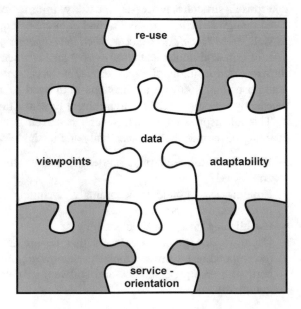

Those five challenges (presented and discussed further in the current section) are illustrated in Fig. 1.2, suggesting that each of them is important by itself but it is also important that they are considered together in their interrelationship.

Modeling Viewpoints and Overall Consistency Applying a modeling approach in closing the EE–SE gap would assume establishing a *common enterprise-software conceptual foundation*; abstract models can essentially capture entities, processes, and regulations, no matter if this concerns software or an enterprise (this would mean emphasizing the similarities between enterprise systems and software systems, despite their specific differences). Such a common foundation would be useful in achieving enterprise-software alignment and traceability because *enterprise models and software models would be "written in the same language."* Nevertheless, *challenges* would be popping up, related to the numerous enterprise-software-modeling *perspectives* (`viewpoints`): (1) *No matter if one would model an enterprise or software, one would need to be able to model structure, dynamics, and data and still keep all as a coherent whole*; modeling structure with no grasp on behavioral aspects or modeling behavior with no grasp on data issues (for example) would be of limited use. (2) *In considering enterprise information systems, one would face the specific EE vs. SE viewpoints (even if enterprise models and software models would be "written in the same language," there would be issues that are enterprise-specific and issues that are software-specific), needing nevertheless to keep the software under development consistent with its surrounding enterprise environment.* (3) *In modeling an enterprise/software system, one may take a black-box (functional) or a white-box (operational) perspective (this will be discussed further in the current chapter), but it is necessary to keep the white-box models consistent with regard to the corresponding black-box models.* (4) *In specifying a context-aware enterprise information system, one should decide whether this is about a context-driven optimization of system-internal processes or about a context-driven maximization of the user-perceived effectiveness; hence, balancing between the (software) system perspective and the user perspective is required.* (5) *In specifying software, one may need to weave in public values (such as privacy, transparency, accountability, and so on) that are essentially non-functional (hence, assuming a non-functional perspective) but they need to be operationalized (hence, assuming a functional perspective), in order to be actually reflected in the system's functionality.* Thus, we have many *MODELING VIEWPOINTS* and we need an *OVERALL CONSISTENCY* in order to be able to effectively *bring together enterprise modeling* (which is mainly rooted in social theories) *and software specification* (which is mainly rooted in computing paradigms), such that the specification of software is properly restricted by corresponding enterprise models. We argue that only then it would be possible to develop software that adequately meets the original *business requirements*. For this reason, *consistency* is to be aimed not only within a system *(among the different aspect models characterizing the system under study)* but also across systems (in our case—*between the enterprise models and their corresponding software models*).

Integrating Data Analytics in Enterprise Modeling and Software Development Current information system development assumes an *increasing importance of data analytics*. With regard to enterprise modeling and software specification, `data` has always been important both functionally and non-functionally: *at design time*, *statistical data* may help building "realistic" models, while *at run time*, "incoming" *environmental data* may help adapting the system behavior accordingly. Nevertheless, it is a question what makes difference today, compared to several years ago. Why is *data science* so increasingly popular to date? Is a reason for that the current *abundance of (sensor) data* showering us every day, and if yes, how are we coping with this abundance—distinguishing between the really useful data and the data that may be ignored? Further, it is important to know how we translate *low-level (sensor) data* into *higher-level information* that is a basis for *reasoning* and as well how we know which data to *trust*. Currently, those questions are even more important than in the past [17]. The *integration of data analytics* in *enterprise modeling* and *software development* is hence not only about establishing the context situation or providing a statistical data modeling background, but it is also about other issues, such as *quality of data*, *occurrence probabilities*, *data formats*, and so on. Hence, in aligning enterprise modeling and software specification, it is important to take those issues into account.

Supporting Adaptability When developing an information system, we usually aim at making it `adaptable` with regard to environmental changes. At the same time, there are restrictions which are twofold: *(1)* the system behavior "patterns" through which adaptability would be realized need to be foreseen and "prepared" at design time and *(2)* environmental changes are not always trivial to "sense"; hence, it is important to know to what and how an information system should *adapt* and also if this is concerned with predefined (at design time) scenarios and/or with the run-time (intelligent) behavior of the information system. Further, if we assume that *adapting* means *adjusting behavior to a changing environment*, it would be interesting to also consider how we capture those changes (probably through *sensors*) and how we process and interpret this information (see above). Finally, all those issues point to `context-awareness`, assuming that *the system "switches" to a particular behavior variant based on the appearance of a particular context state*. Thus, *context-awareness* (i.e., explicitly addressed in Chap. 3) is to be considered in the enterprise perspective, in the software perspective, and also with regard to the alignment between *enterprise modeling* and *software specification*.

Considering Re-use in Modeling It is widely agreed that if possible modeling should be based on `re-usable modeling building blocks`, such that the modeling itself is more *effective* and *efficient* [41]. For this reason, in aligning *enterprise modeling* and *software specification*, it would be useful to identify enterprise modeling building blocks and consider corresponding mappings towards software models—this would allow for bridging the abovementioned gap in a `component-based way`. Nevertheless, it is a question how to methodologically identify enterprise modeling building blocks and reflect them in corresponding software components, as it will be further discussed in the current book. Also, exhaustive guidelines are needed on how to realize this, taking into account *granularity concerns*, *traceability concerns*, and *re-use concerns*. Further, a shift to service-based systems (to be explicitly addressed in the following paragraph) is often the case since currently more and more ICT applications provide support to their users through *web services* (running software instances), as will be discussed in Chap. 5. This in turn leads to questions because developers are often with limited or no control over the *software components* that are "underlying" with regard to the *web services* that are used (composed); but still developers should keep the ICT applications (that may be (partially) based on such *web services*) aligned with corresponding enterprise models. Hence, those concerns need to be reflected in the way we look at the enterprise-software relationship: enterprise modeling building blocks would be related to corresponding models featuring software components that may in turn be related to corresponding web service models. Thus we argue that *aligning enterprise modeling and software specification in a component-based way* is a key challenge with regard to the goal of effective software development.

Enabling Service Orientation As mentioned above, it is often that customers utilize *Information Technology—IT* / software, by composing web *services* (or `services`, for short)—this allows for letting the *users* consider *services* at high level, not being burdened by their underlying technical complexity, while at the same time, *developers* consider the corresponding software components (which are running the *services*). That is how *services* relate to both *enterprise engineering* and *software specification*. For this reason, in aligning *enterprise modeling* and *software specification*, it is important to assume the possibility that the resulting software would be *service-oriented* and if necessary carry out redesigns accordingly.

   As studied in [17], those five challenges are of key relevance to the goals presented at the end of the previous section. Nevertheless, just formulating and discussing those challenges would be of limited use without more thorough theoretical studies and corresponding methodological proposals. For this reason, further on in this book, we will consider concepts and theories, and we will also propose methodological solutions.

   Finally, those goals, the five challenges and the two above considered disciplines (EE and SE), are all "intersecting" somewhere "on the territory" of an emerging discipline, labelled "EIS—*Enterprise Information Systems*" (Fig. 1.3); see the following section.

1.4 Enterprise Information Systems (EIS)

As it is seen from Fig. 1.3, there are labels pointing at different relevant disciplines or areas—some more widely accepted than others. Still, questions arise in this regard:

- Is "computer science" covering only software-development-related issues or also enterprise modeling that may be relevant to the software development?
- What is the difference between "computer science" and "data science," and is "computer science" not covering data analytics or is "data science" focused on data aspects only, not touching upon other related issues [43]?
- Should we consider "requirements engineering" as a part of "enterprise engineering" if we stress upon the original business requirements or should we consider "requirements engineering" as a part of "software engineering" if we stress upon the user-defined technical requirements that straightforwardly concern the specification of software [44]?
- Is "cloud computing" only about the utilization of cloud resources or is it also about the software-related issues concerning this [45]?
- Is the label "management information system" referring to the management of information systems, assuming a technical-independent view [35]?

Those are just some of the questions concerning those labels and inspiring a discussion on how to position and label our work whose focus is on enterprises and the software support they are utilizing. We realize that there are two disciplines essentially underlying the issues discussed above:

- ENTERPRISE ENGINEERING.
- SOFTWARE ENGINEERING.

Enterprise engineering: It is about analyzing, modeling, and (re)designing an enterprise without considering anything in a technology-specific perspective. Said otherwise, we are interested in the entities (observed within the enterprise under study), their relations, and corresponding processes, no matter if the entities are human beings or technical devices (we may consider technical devices but we abstract from their internal technical complexity).

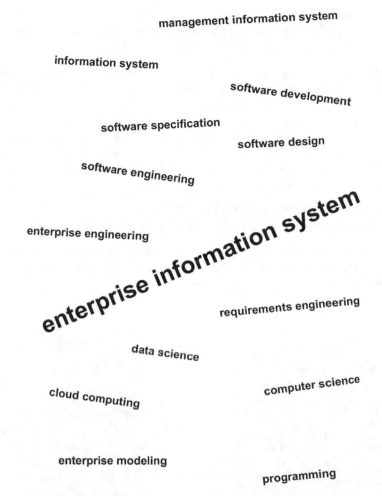

Fig. 1.3 Labels of disciplines and areas (©2017, The Author, reprinted with permission)

Software engineering: Firstly, it should have a focus—there may be software developed for cars or software developed for hospital equipment or software embedded in devices and so on; we particularly focus on *enterprise software*. Further, the software engineering scope is the *software system-to-be*. Finally, with regard to the software system-to-be, we take a *technology-specific perspective*. Said otherwise, we are interested in the technical complexity inside the software system-to-be.

Our bringing together <u>enterprise engineering</u> and <u>software engineering</u> would point at what we label as:

ENTERPRISE   INFORMATION   SYSTEMS.

We therefore make a clear distinction between issues that concern the enterprise-engineering aspects of *Enterprise Information Systems (EIS)* and issues that concern the software-engineering aspects of such systems. For this reason, any relevant discipline or area of interest, as the ones presented in Fig. 1.3, is to be "positioned" with regard to either <u>enterprise engineering</u> or <u>software engineering</u>. Bridging the two is a matter of a dedicated approach, as it will be studied in the current book.

Further, enterprise engineering concerns *enterprise systems*, while software engineering concerns *software systems*:

- The former we consider as SOCIAL SYSTEMS.
- The latter we consider as TECHNICAL SYSTEMS.

This inspires our viewing enterprise information systems as socio-technical systems [45] (as illustrated in Fig. 1.4) and taking an abstract perspective accordingly.

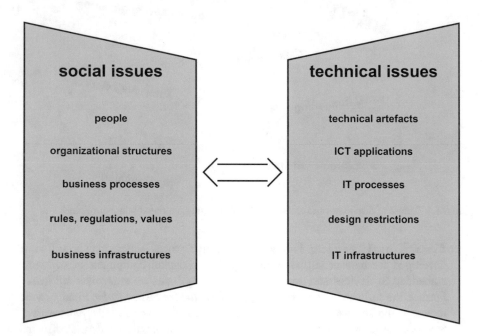

Fig. 1.4   Viewing an enterprise information system as a socio-technical system

In line with this and as suggested by the figure, we may distinguish between **social issues** and **technical issues**:

- The *social issues* are all about PEOPLE who initiate <u>business processes</u> individually and/or through organizations and corresponding *organizational structures*, being restricted by *rules* and *regulations* [46] and also being addressed by societal expectations for sticking to particular *public values* [47]; for this, a *business infrastructure* is needed, including a *legal environment* [48], *accounting adjustments* [49], *financial/credit instruments* [50], *logistics channels* [51], *marketing options* [30], and so on.
- The *technical issues* concern TECHNICAL ARTEFACTS that are used through *ICT applications* [41]—they in turn trigger <u>IT processes</u> that are restricted by the *application designs* [17]; for this, an *IT infrastructure* is needed, including a *networking facilitation* [37], *middleware* [52], *cloud facilities* [45], and so on.

As also suggested by Fig. 1.4, social issues and technical issues should not be considered separately. We argue that this is especially valid for most current complex enterprise systems where business processes, IT processes, people, and technical artifacts are all mixed together. The rules that concern business processes have also indirect impact on the technically enabled actions related to those processes. Organizational structures are facilitated by ICT. Many legal, accounting, and other actions that concern a business infrastructure are implemented electronically. Many design restrictions over technical artifacts and ICT applications straightforwardly stem from corresponding societal regulations. Thus, all those social issues and technical issues are to be brought together as part of a SOCIO-TECHNICAL SYSTEM, and we consider enterprise information systems as socio-technical systems.

Hence, all those issues must be balanced and "work together" such that the information processing functionalities required by an enterprise to fulfill its information needs are adequately delivered. And the corresponding "driving forces," as already discussed, are:

- The HUMAN ELEMENT of an enterprise information system, concerning the <u>people</u> and corresponding (organizational) <u>structures</u>.
- The TECHNICAL ELEMENT of an enterprise information system, concerning the <u>IT resources + services</u> as well as corresponding IT (software) <u>processes</u>.

Thus, *IT services* and *technical processes* are supporting not only particular *human entities* but also *organizational units* as such. At the same time the *human entities* are functioning within corresponding *organizational units*. Further, *IT services* and *technical processes* are essentially "fueled" by actions realized by particular *human entities* and also by collective actions realized by particular *organizational units*; in this the *IT services* and the corresponding *technical processes* are to be in synch.

Since the application area concerning *enterprise information systems* is the area of *enterprises* [53] and *enterprises* in turn represent ORGANIZATIONS [54], we

need to have a good *overall organizational perception*, and inspired by [17, 45], we
consider accordingly three essential perspectives, as depicted in Fig. 1.5:

- The HIERARCHICAL PERSPECTIVE (assuming a centralized organization)
  features three primary levels in an organization where specific to each level of
  activity and decision-making events take place: *(1)* At the operational level, short-
  term, highly structured activities are performed and the objective is efficient
  processes under a limited degree of uncertainty (hence, recurring operations
  allow to be conveniently automated, assuring in this way speed, accuracy, and
  precision in their execution). *(2)* At the management level, semi-structured
  (decision-making) activities are performed, mainly related to functional areas,
  and focused on the execution and control over processes, based on adopted
  patterns and proven models (hence, the typical IT support in this context would
  come through decision-support systems that are founded on enterprise-internal
  operations and resources). *(3)* The executive level handles all strategic planning
  and *ad hoc* circumstances, prioritizing long-term and wide-range decisions
  (hence, their typical IT support in this context would come through executive
  information systems that are capable of collecting, analyzing, and synthesizing
  organizational and external trend data).

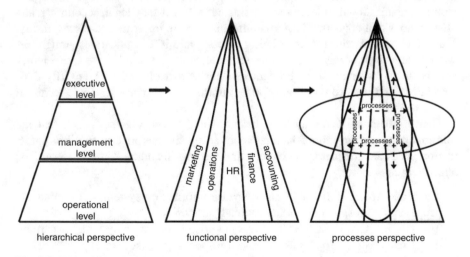

Fig. 1.5 Hierarchical, functional, and process organizational perspectives

- The FUNCTIONAL PERSPECTIVE (assuming a decentralized organization)
  features business entities based on distinct functional areas such as *marketing*
  [30], *operations, human resources* [55], *finance* [50], *accounting* [49], and so on.
- The PROCESSES PERSPECTIVE utilizes *top-down* methodology to achieve
  internal business integration, *activities rationalization*, and *duplications elimi-
  nation* across functional areas and managerial levels.

Also, the two left-to-right arrows in the figure suggest an evolution over time from *hierarchical* organizations through *functional* organizations to *process-oriented* organizations, each of which has advantages and limitations. Still, we consider the *processes perspective* as most appropriate with regard to *enterprise information systems* because structures of processes are considered proper as a basis for utilizing software support.

1.5   Essential Concepts

Furthering the discussion from the previous sections, we come to the point of introducing the basic *EIS* concepts considered in the current book, inspired by Shishkov et al. [39]; they are presented in Fig. 1.6, using the *MOF/UML* (*Class Diagram*) notations [56, 57], noting nevertheless that in this section, we are only briefly introducing the concepts. They will be addressed in more detail in the following chapters.

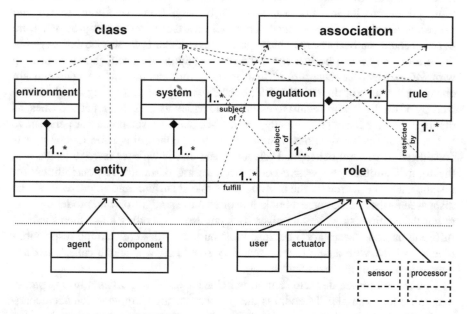

Fig. 1.6 Basic EIS concepts (inspired by: [39], p. 197; ©2018, Springer, reprinted with permission)

As the figure suggests, we always consider a **system** of some kind and what does not belong to the system belongs to the system **environment** (see Chap. 2). Therefore, there should be an explicit *boundary* delimiting the two—anything that is "inside" with regard to the boundary belongs to the system and anything that is "outside" with regard to the boundary belongs to the environment. For example, if a

university is considered in general and its Computer Science department, in particular, then anything that is internal with regard to the department is part of the system
and anything else is part of the environment. With regard to both (system and
environment), their *composition elements* are **entities** that in turn can be either
components, part of the whole ((software) components will be extensively
discussed in Chaps. 2 and 5), or **agents**—unlike components that are just parts
of the system/environment and can be "triggered" through their interfaces, agents are
mobile, proactive, and autonomous [58]; nevertheless, *considering agents is left
beyond the scope of the current book*. Entities can fulfill different **roles** and from
the perspective of their positioning with regard to the system under consideration
those could be **user** (the one using what the system is delivering, e.g., the customer
in a shop), **actuator** (the one acting on behalf of the system, e.g., the pizza
deliverer at a pizza restaurant), **sensor** (the one capturing contextual data, e.g., the
event officer who is monitoring the incoming cars, prior to a rock concert, such that
the acquired information is used by the arena car park operators to decide which
parking sectors to close and to which ones to keep on directing cars), and **processor** (the one processing information, e.g., the receptionist at a sport center who
is calculating the available training "slots" at a moment, in order to decide how many
more persons to let in). Further, as it can be seen from the figure, *sensor* and
processor are dashed-line-outlined. This indicates that sensing and processing are
not only about realized essential business actions (for example: service delivery), but
those roles might also be just about the data manipulation itself, therefore dealing
with *informative "conversations"* that are only reproducing known facts and not
changing the state of the object world; hence, sensing and processing are characterized by a "duality" with regard to essential activities vs. informational activities, as
distinguished by Dietz [12]. Finally, the user-actuator-sensor-processor perspective
is just one of the possible abstraction perspectives concerning roles (actually, it is
considered of general conceptual relevance and that is why we have reflected it in
the figure); another perspective could be featuring particular responsibilities, for
instance, the role secretary, the role cook, the role chauffeur, and so on; as it will be
discussed further in the current book, it is often more straightforward modeling roles
rather than entities (e.g., if at a university a professor is sending a fax, then she/he is
fulfilling the role "secretary") because most business rules concern the responsibilities associated with a role (e.g., a secretary should answer phone calls, introduce
new employees to the team, and so on).

Hence, **rules** are de facto restricting behavior-wise the entities fulfilling particular roles; for example: If Sandra is the secretary of the Computer Science department of a university, then she is allowed to book appointments in the agenda of her
boss but she is not allowed to approve business trips of employees. Thus, the
behavior concerning one role is restricted by one or more rules, as Fig. 1.6 suggests.
Further, it is often that several rules in combination are governing a particular
behavior type—this we refer to as **regulation** [46]. As represented in the figure,
the composition elements of a regulation are rules; also, one or more roles (or even
one or many systems) may be subject of a particular regulation, and this is
established through the behavior restrictions discussed above.

As already mentioned, those are just the basic EIS concepts that we consider in the current book and they will be further discussed and elaborated in the following chapters.

1.6   The Modeling Approach

Even though we acknowledge the *socio-technical issues* and corresponding *driving forces* (as featured in Fig. 1.4) and the *organizational perspectives* (as featured in Fig. 1.5), we claim (inspired by [17]) that a sound approach to *enterprise information systems* should assume a reference to the underlying disciplines (namely, *enterprise engineering* and *software engineering*) and corresponding theories/paradigms (namely, social theories and computing paradigms), as exhibited in Fig. 1.7.

As it is seen from the figure, we observe both *human entities* and *technical entities* not only within any *enterprise information system* but also within its *environment*. Further, *human entities* as well as their relations and behavior are to be addressed through *social theories* (as it will be discussed in Chap. 4); *technical entities* and their operation are to be addressed through *computing paradigms* (as it will be discussed in Chap. 5).

Inspired by [41] and acknowledging the *gap* between *enterprise modeling* and *software specification* (as discussed already in the current chapter), we consider a *modeling approach* towards *enterprise information systems*, grounding it in the disciplines and corresponding theories/paradigms, as mentioned above and adding further elaboration in terms of *modeling viewpoints*, as follows:

- Enterprise engineering is instrumental with regard to real-life enterprise processes while software engineering is instrumental with regard to related technical (IT) issues; requirements engineering concerns both since there are not only (original) business requirements but also technical (user-defined) requirements.
- Especially (social) theories are to be considered, touching upon human entities and corresponding real-life behavior and in particular:

  - Human relativism (featuring human centricity in enterprise modeling).
  - Theory of organized activity (useful in modeling human behavior).
  - Language-action perspective (useful in modeling language-driven communicative acts).
  - Enterprise ontology (useful in modeling coordination and production).
  - Organizational semiotics (useful in modeling signs and business rules).
  - Probabilities and statistics (useful in modeling surrounding context).

- Especially computing paradigms are to be considered, touching upon technical entities and their operation and in particular:

  - Component-based development (useful in specifying component-based software applications).
  - Service-oriented architecture (useful in specifying web services).

- Model-driven engineering (useful in abstractions-based modeling).
- Cloud computing (useful in modeling utilization of distant resources).
- Aspect-oriented software development (useful in modeling crosscutting non-functional concerns).

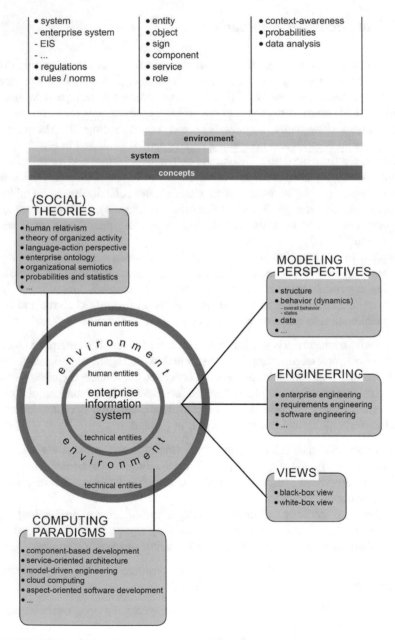

Fig. 1.7 Enterprise information systems—a modeling approach (©2017, The Author, reprinted with permission)

- Several modeling perspectives are to be considered, regarding enterprise/software engineering, namely:

  - Structure (how different entities are related to each other).
  - Dynamics:

    What the overall behavior of the considered entities is
    What the states an entity comes through are

  - Data.

- Depending on the purpose of modeling:

  - A functional (black-box) view would be appropriate if establishing what the system should do.
  - A constructional (white-box) view would be appropriate if establishing how the system should realize its functioning.

- In considering all this, a systemics approach is to be followed (see Chap. 2), such that the modeling focus is put on either of the following:

  - The system itself.
  - The system environment.

- The concepts to be considered in this regard (in line with what was already discussed in Sect. 1.5 and also with the study presented in Chap. 2) are:

  - Concepts relevant to the system scope:

    System:

      Enterprise system.
      Enterprise Information System (EIS).

    Regulations.
    Business rules (also labelled "norms").

  - Concepts relevant to the environment scope:

    Context-awareness.
    Occurrence probabilities.
    Data analysis.

  - Concepts relevant to both:

    Entity.
    Object.
    Sign.
    Component.
    Service.
    Role.

Hence, taking a *modeling approach* with regard to *enterprise information systems* requires *interdisciplinary* efforts and *multiple perspectives* that are to be applied in synch.

This book tells you how to *bring together enterprise modeling and software specification*, such that an *enterprise-modeling-driven software generation is achieved*—this is considered crucial with regard to the development of *enterprise information systems*.

1.7   Outlook

The remainder of the current book is structured as follows:

Chapter 2 will introduce our systemics views, touching upon systems and their composition.

Chapter 3 will consider the system environment and context of users, extending this to enterprise systems and enterprise information systems and introducing a number of concepts accordingly, also touching upon public values and their operationalization often needed by the user and/or environmental third parties.

Chapter 4 will present relevant social theories (as according to Fig. 1.7), including human relativism, theory of organized activity, language-action perspective, enterprise ontology, and organizational semiotics.

Chapter 5 will present relevant computing paradigms (as according to Fig. 1.7), including component-based development, service-oriented architecture, model-driven engineering, cloud computing, and aspect-oriented software development.

Chapter 6 will introduce the SDBC approach, presenting its foundations, outline, and notations, driven by the goal of proposing a way to bring together enterprise modeling and software specification for the sake of bridging the enterprise-software gap (as discussed already in the current chapter).

Chapter 7 will feature one case study and two illustrative examples, in order to demonstrate how (1) enterprise engineering and software engineering can be brought together, supported by SDBC and enriched by an explicit consideration of user-defined requirements, and also how (2) this can be extended to accommodate service orientation and middle-out modeling.

References

1. Ammons JC, Govindaraj T, Mitchell CM (1988, Sep/Oct) Decision models for aiding FMS scheduling and control. IEEE Trans Syst Man Cybernet 18(5):744–756
2. Javaid S, Sufian A, Pervaiz S, Tanveer M (2018) Smart traffic management system using internet of things. In: 20th International conference on advanced communication technology (ICACT), Chuncheon-si Gangwon-do, Korea (South), 2018, pp 393–398

3. Zerbiec TG (1992, March) Considering the past and anticipating the future for private data networks. IEEE Commun Mag 30(3):36–46

4. Wang Q, Pan W, Li M (2012) Robot's remote real-time navigation controlled by smart phone. In: IEEE international conference on robotics and biomimetics (ROBIO), Guangzhou, pp 2351–2356

5. Papazoglou M (2008) Web services: principles and technology. Prentice Hall, Upper Saddle River, NJ

6. Colman-Meixner C, Develder C, Tornatore M, Mukherjee B (2016) A survey on resiliency techniques in cloud computing infrastructures and applications. IEEE Commun Surv Tutor 18 (3):2244–2281. thirdquarter

7. O'Hara B (2012) Approach to information management in an externalized business environment. In: 2012 IEEE international conference on bioinformatics and biomedicine, Philadelphia, PA, pp 1–2

8. AWARENESS (2008) Freeband AWARENESS project. http://www.freeband.nl/project.cfm? id=494&language=en

9. Kopják J, Sebestyén G (2018) Comparison of data collecting methods in wireless mesh sensor networks. In: IEEE 16th world symposium on applied machine intelligence and informatics (SAMI), Kosice and Herlany, Slovakia, 2018, pp 000155–000160

10. Wu J, Guo S, Huang H, Liu W, Xiang Y (2018) Information and communications technologies for sustainable development goals: state-of-the art, needs and perspectives. IEEE Commun Surv Tutor 20(3):2389–2406. thirdquarter

11. Brambilla M, Cabot J, Wimmer M (2012) Model-driven software engineering in practice. Morgan & Claypool, New York, NY

12. Dietz JLG (2006) Enterprise ontology, theory and methodology. Springer, Heidelberg

13. Manning JG (2018) The open sea: the economic life of the ancient Mediterranean world from the iron age to the rise of Rome. Princeton University Press, Princeton, NJ

14. Urien P (2018) Towards secure elements for trusted transactions in blockchain and blockchain IoT (BIoT) Platforms. Invited paper. In: 4th International conference on mobile and secure services (MobiSecServ), Miami Beach, FL, USA, 2018, pp 1–5

15. Suurmond C (2018) IT systems in business: model or reality? In: Shishkov B (ed) Business modeling and software design. BMSD 2017. Lecture notes in business information processing, vol 309. Springer, Cham

16. Shi C, Lan X, Wang Y (2017) Motion planning for unmanned vehicle based on hybrid deep learning. In: International conference on security, pattern analysis, and cybernetics (SPAC), Shenzhen, 2017, pp 473–478

17. Shishkov B (2017) Enterprise information systems, a modeling approach. IICREST Press, Sofia

18. Laurenza D (2006) Leonardo's machines: secrets and inventions in the Da Vinci Codices. Giunti, Florence-Milan

19. Ackerman J (1961) The architecture of Michelangelo. University of Chicago Press, Chicago

20. Bloom RL et al (1958) The beginnings of industrialization in England. Pt XIV: The industrial revolution, classical economics, and economic liberalism. Ideas and Institutions of Western Man, Gettysburg College, pp 1–5

21. Landes DS (2003) The unbound prometheus: technical change and industrial development in Western Europe from 1750 to the present. Cambridge University Press, Cambridge

22. Flood JE (1976, December) Alexander Graham Bell and the invention of the telephone. Proc Inst Electr Eng 123(12):1387–1388

23. Parker S (1992) Electricity. Dorling Kindersley, London

24. Parissien S (2014) The life of the automobile: the complete history of the motor car. St. Martin's Press, New York, NY

25. Ford (2018) The website of the Ford Motor Company. http://www.corporate.ford.com

26. Knowles JC (1973) The Rockefeller financial group. Warner Modular Publications, Andover, MA

27. Petroski H (2016) The road taken: the history and future of America's infrastructure. Blooms-
    bury Publishing, London
28. Pierce J (1977) Electronics: past, present, and future. Science 195(4283):1092–1095
29. Greenfield J (1977) Television: the first fifty years. Harry N. Abrams, New York, NY
30. Kotler P, Turner R (1995) Marketing management: analysis, planning, and control. Pearson,
    New York, NY
31. Lowe K (2013) Savage continent: Europe in the aftermath of world war II. St. Martin's Press,
    New York, NY
32. Millard A (2012) Beatlemania: technology, business, and teen culture in cold War America
    (Johns Hopkins introductory studies in the history of technology). John Hopkins University
    Press, Baltimore, MD
33. Johnson P (2014) Mozart: a life. Penguin Books, London
34. Norman P (2009) John Lennon: the life. Ecco Press, New York, NY
35. Laudon K, Laudon J (2017) Management information systems: managing the digital firm.
    Pearson, New York, NY
36. Shishkova T (1986) Exploring the possibilities for creating and implementing high-level
    programming languages specific to the domain of warehouse management, PhD thesis. Tech-
    nical University Press, Sofia
37. Tanenbaum AS (1996) Computer networks. Prentice Hall, New Jersey, NJ
38. IICREST (2019) The website of the International Institute for Collaboration and Research on
    enterprise systems and technology. http://www.iicrest.org
39. Shishkov B, Larsen JB, Warnier M, Janssen M (2018) Three categories of context-aware
    systems. In: Shishkov B (ed) Business modeling and software design. BMSD 2018. Lecture
    notes in business information processing, vol 319. Springer, Cham
40. Huang Z, Su X, Zhang Y, Shi C, Zhang H, Xie L (2017) A decentralized solution for IoT data
    trusted exchange based-on blockchain. In: 3rd IEEE international conference on computer and
    communications (ICCC), Chengdu, China, 2017, pp 1180–1184
41. Shishkov B (2005) Software specification based on re-usable business components. Delft
    University Press, Delft
42. Stahl T, Völter M, Bettin J, Haase A, Helsen S (2006) Model-driven software development—
    technology, engineering, management. Wiley, Heidelberg
43. Hirschheim R, Klein H, Lyytinen K (1995) Information systems development and data model-
    ing—conceptual and philosophical foundations. Cambridge University Press, Cambridge
44. Kotonya G, Sommerville I (1998) Requirements engineering. Wiley, New York, NY
45. Ivanov I (2012) Cloud computing in education: the intersection of challenges and opportunities.
    In: Filipe J, Cordeiro J (eds) Web information systems and technologies 2011. LNBIP, vol 101.
    Springer, Heidelberg, pp 3–16
46. Lang J, Pigozzi G, Slavkovik M, van der Torre L (2011) Judgment aggregation rules based on
    minimization. In: Proceedings of the 13th international conference on theoretical aspects of
    rationality and knowledge, ACM
47. Friedman B, Hendry DG, Borning A (2017) A survey of value sensitive design methods. In: A
    survey of value sensitive design methods, vol 1. Now Foundations and Trends, Hanover, MA, p
    76
48. Avgousti AA (2007) Regulating convergence in Europe. In: ITI 5th International conference on
    information and communications technology. Cairo, Egypt, pp 325–325
49. Eisen PJ (2013) Accounting. Barron's Educational Series Inc, New York, NY
50. Nikbakht E, Groppelli AA (2012) Finance. Barron's Educational Series Inc, New York, NY
51. Versteegt C, Verbraeck A (2002) Holonic control of large-scale automated logistic systems. In:
    Proceedings of the IEEE 5th international conference on intelligent transportation systems, pp
    898–903
52. Caminha J, Perkusich A, Perkusich M (2018) A smart middleware to detect on-off trust attacks
    in the Internet of things. In: 2018 IEEE international conference on consumer electronics
    (ICCE), Las Vegas, NV, USA, pp 1–2

53. Ross JW, Weill P (2006) Enterprise architecture as strategy: creating a foundation for business execution. Harvard Business Press, Boston, MA
54. Sousa HPdS, Leite JCdP (2017) Requirement patterns for organizational modeling. In: IEEE 25th international requirements engineering conference workshops (REW), Lisbon, 2017, pp 252–259
55. Mathis RL, Jackson JH (2016) Human resource management. Cengage Learning, Boston, MA
56. MOF (2018) The website of the meta-object facility. http://www.omg.org/mof
57. UML (2018) The website of the unified modeling language. http://www.uml.org
58. Wooldridge M (2009) An introduction to multiagent systems. Wiley, New York, NY

Chapter 2
Systems

There are numerous scientific disciplines: some are purely scientific, such as *mathematics*, *physics*, and *biology*, while others are applied, such as *computer science* and *engineering* [1]. In considering any discipline nevertheless, the notion of **system** is an important one [2]; in *physics*, they study *physical systems*; in *biology*, they study *biosystems*; in *sociology*, they study *social systems*; and so on. Hence, the development of the *General Systems Theory* has been inspired [3, 4], referred to as **systemics**. *Systemics* focuses on the characteristics of systems across the barriers between scientific disciplines. Such a perspective is considered important with regard to *EIS* since in approaching *EIS*, one would have to deal with *social systems* (because there are human entities, human behavior, and so on, in any enterprise) and also with *technical systems* (because there are technical devices, software applications, and so on, in any information system). Hence, both social systems and technical systems would not only need to be studies in isolation but it is also necessary to understand their interrelationship.

For this reason, firstly in the current chapter, we will clarify what we mean by "*system*" and then we will touch upon *enterprise systems* and (*enterprise*) *information systems*—all considered essential with regard to the focus of this book. Secondly, we will explicitly discuss not only the *construction* of any system, by considering ontological systems, but also its *function*, emphasizing as well on the distinction between the two, reflected in two essential perspectives on system behavior: (a) the *black-box perspective* considering what the system is delivering to its environment (functionally) and (b) the *white-box perspective* considering how the system is delivering this. Finally, we will touch upon the *evolvability* of any technical (software-intensive) (sub-)system, part of an *EIS*, by considering *combinatorial effects*, in general, and the *Normalized Systems Theory*, in particular.

© Springer Nature Switzerland AG 2020

B. Shishkov, *Designing Enterprise Information Systems*, The Enterprise Engineering Series, https://doi.org/10.1007/978-3-030-22441-7_2

2.1 The System Concept

The *General Systems Theory* (already mentioned) proposes a unified approach in considering a system, based on the (justified) claims that there are some:

- Concepts and structural principles that seem to hold for systems of many kinds.
- Modeling strategies that seem to hold everywhere.

That has inspired Bunge [5] to consider theories that focus on the structural characteristics of systems and can therefore cross the "largely artificial" barriers between disciplines. Such efforts have triggered interest to discover similarities among systems of many kinds despite their specific differences, such that studying current (complex) enterprises would become easier [6]—this often assumes de-emphasizing the aspects concerning the particular scientific discipline, focusing instead on the *structure* and the *behavior* of the system as such. This even goes beyond systemics and points to the broader notion of **system analysis**, as defined by Bunge: the essential goal behind system analysis is to enable one understand how a system operates.

Since those views are considered relevant to our focus on systems in general and enterprise systems (and *EIS*), in particular, we have adopted the *system definition* proposed by Bunge [5]:

Definition 1 Let T be a nonempty set. Then the ordered triple $\sigma = \langle C, E, S \rangle$ is **system** over T if and only if C (standing for *Composition*) and E (standing for *Environment*) are mutually disjoint subsets of T (i.e., $C \cap E = \varnothing$) and S (standing for *Structure*) is a nonempty set of active relations on the union of C and E. The system is *conceptual* if T is a set of conceptual items and *concrete* (or material) if $T \subseteq \Theta$ is a set of concrete entities, i.e., things.

The *system definition* of Dietz [2] is consistent with the above definition, acknowledging that among the *properties* of a system are:

- *Composition*: a set of elements of some category (physical, social, biological, etc.).
- *Environment*: a set of elements of the same category; the composition and the environment are disjoint.
- *Structure*: a set of influence bonds among the elements in the composition and between the elements in the environment.

Nevertheless, Dietz considers one more property, namely, *production*, pointing that:

- The elements in the composition produce things, such as goods, services, and so on, that are delivered to elements in the environment.

For us, the *composition–environment–structure system view* is appropriate because even though production characterizes most systems, we claim that it is also possible that the composition elements of a system stay inactive (for a period of time or forever), still being part of the system.

Next to that, in line with the systemics views, we would consider further system categorizations depending on the (research) area of interest; some examples of such categories are:

- *Legislative system*—a system concerning legal norms and acts.
- *Planet system*—a system concerning planets.
- *Political system*—a system concerning political subjects.

Since our focus is on enterprises and information systems supporting enterprises, we are interested in two system categories, namely:

- *Enterprise system.*
- *EIS.*

As for the *enterprise system concept*, it should correspond to a view on business, in general, and for this we refer to [6]: by *"business thing"*, it is not meant only things concerning trade/commerce but also all things that refer to any *organized activity* which is driven by a particular *goal*. Next to that, businesses are envisioned as *human-driven* since humans are those through whom businesses operate. Hence, inspired by the views of Shishkov and Dietz [7], we propose the following definition:

Definition 2 A system should be considered being an **enterprise system** if and only if it is composed of *human entities* collaborating among each other through *actions* which are driven by the *goal* of delivering *products* to entities belonging to the environment of the system.

By *"product"* we mean anything that is or can be delivered to a customer, no matter if it is a material thing (often called *product* or *goods*) or an immaterial thing (often called *service*), and this is referred to as a *production fact*.

In the same spirit and inspired by [6], we propose the following *EIS definition* where *"ICT"* stands for *"Information and Communication Technology"*:

Definition 3 A system should be considered being an **EIS** if and only if it is composed of *human entities* (often facilitated by ICT applications as well as by technical and technological facilities) collaborating among each other driven by the *goal* of *supporting informationally* a corresponding enterprise system.

Definitions 2 and 3 both reflect the *ontological* (constructional) essence of the addressed system categories. This is claimed to be insufficient nevertheless with regard to EIS because an enterprise information system is not only about structurally bringing together different human and technical entities, but it is also about enabling technical entities, such as devices, ICT applications, and so on, to support corresponding human entities accordingly. We argue that in order to achieve deep understanding on this, one would also need a *functional view* as well, such that one could "step in the shoes" of a particular human entity and understand the way this human entity is supported functionally by a device and/or ICT application. For this reason, we propose also another *EIS definition* (also inspired by [6]) that assumes a *functional perspective*:

Definition 4 Concerning its *functional characteristics*, an **EIS** is a system which *manipulates data* and normally serves to *collect, store, process,* and *exchange* (or *distribute*) *data* among users within or between enterprises, or among people within wider society.

In the following two sections, we will subsequently consider enterprise systems and EIS.

2.2 Enterprise Systems

In considering *enterprise systems*, we stick to *Definition 2*, according to which the goal of delivering products to the environment is essential and for this reason we take this as an important criterion for determining whether or not a particular entity belongs to an enterprise system. Only entities driven by the same *goal* would be considered belonging to the same enterprise system. If a consultancy company is also dealing with property rental, for example, then the human entities and activities about property management should not be considered belonging to the consultancy enterprise system since they are irrelevant with respect to the consultancy goal, and similarly, the human entities and activities about consultancy should not be considered belonging to the property renting enterprise system. Hence, this is all about the role and behavior that a particular human entity takes, not about the formal belonging of the entity to one organization or another. Further, this goal-driven criterion is not in conflict with our adopting a *composition-environment-structure system view* (as discussed already) since the goal itself (e.g., delivering consultancy) may be existing and entities in relevant roles may be existing but this does not mean that those entities are active.

Fig. 2.1 A simplified view on an enterprise system (Source: [6], p. 21) (©2005, The Author, reprinted with permission)

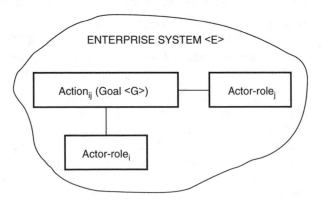

Hence, although it does not directly concern the composition and structure of an enterprise system, the **goal** driving it has to be taken into account when considering such a system.

Further, in identifying an enterprise system, it is important being aware of the *actions* and *human entities* (as well as the *roles* in which they appear) that are relevant to the system.

As for **actions** that may take place in an enterprise system, we distinguish between two action types, namely, *production* and *communicative* (*coordination*) *ones*: *Production actions* (or *acts*) concern a particular output in the form of a material product or an immaterial product while *communicative* (*coordination*) *actions* (or *acts*) concern the collaboration within the enterprise system; this collaboration is in support of the realization of (corresponding) production actions [6].

As for **human entities** and the **roles** in which they appear, we consider just the *actor-roles*: the roles being fulfilled by corresponding human entities; this we consider adequate for enterprise analyses because otherwise it would be confusing considering some entities who may appear in different roles, including nontypical ones (e.g., a professor sending a fax, thus fulfilling the role *secretary*). Hence, we are interested in the role and not in the particular (human) entity fulfilling it.

We thus view an enterprise system (inspired by [6]) as a collection of actions and corresponding actor-roles: the actor-roles are the composition elements of the system, while the actions concern its structure, as depicted in Fig. 2.1.

As seen from the figure, within an enterprise system, one could identify *actions* whose realization relates to corresponding *actor-roles*.

In order to bring a deeper clarification regarding enterprise systems, we need to further elaborate on the notion of action (as mentioned already, we distinguish between *production actions* (or *acts*) and *communicative* (*coordination*) *actions* (or *acts*), and this also needs to be considered). We reflect this in the **transaction** concept [2] because of its capabilities to grasp those two aspects, namely, production and coordination. Further, this concept is well aligned with the *actor-role* notion, assuming the possibility that not only a particular human entity could fulfill more than one actor-role but that a particular actor-role could be fulfilled by more than one human entity. If nevertheless one particular actor-role is being fulfilled by one particular human entity, then the combination of the human entity and the actor-role is called **actor**. Hence, we consider the following definition [6, 8]:

Definition 5 A **transaction** is a finite *sequence of coordination acts* between two actors, concerning the same *production fact*. The actor who starts the transaction is called the *initiator*. The general objective of the initiator of a transaction is to have something done by the other actor, who therefore is called the *executor*.

Hence, *transactions* should be considered as the elementary building blocks of an enterprise system. As studied by Dietz [9], transactions are related to each other in a tree structure. The top of the tree is called the *starting transaction* [10]—it is a transaction that is not caused directly by another transaction (from the particular tree) but triggers the execution of other transactions (within the tree).

Considering *transaction trees* (as a level of granularity) rather than transactions is more appropriate to be done in modeling enterprise systems because at the granularity level of transactions, the complexity is often rather big: even a simple enterprise system would contain a great number of transactions, making it difficult for modelers to grasp precisely and describe those transactions [6]. Thus, the consideration of transaction trees would help partitioning somehow the multitude of transactions, grouping them into segments. We hence introduce the **business process** concept in this regard [10]:

Definition 6 A **business process** is a *structure of* (*connected*) *transactions* that are executed in order to fulfill a starting transaction.

Thus, in our view, the operation of enterprise systems concerns business processes (which are driven by the goal characterizing the system). Each business process consists of transactions, including a starting transaction [6]—as exhibited in Fig. 2.2. Transactions in turn relate to initiators and executors.

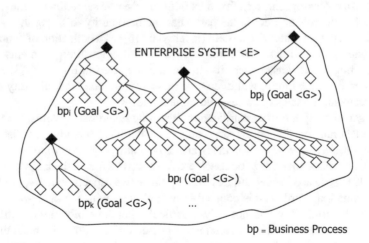

Fig. 2.2 Visualizing the operation of an enterprise system (Source: [6], p. 23) (©2005, The Author, reprinted with permission)

The figure exhibits a particular example of an enterprise system operation, featuring many *business processes*; four of them are depicted in the figure, namely, bp_i, bp_j, bp_k, and bp_l. As seen from the figure, each of the business processes (generally driven by the *goal* $\langle G \rangle$) consists of transactions (with a starting transaction on top). The transactions are presented by white diamonds while the starting transactions are presented by black diamonds. A *starting transaction* could be activated in any of the following three ways: *outside cause* (activation from a customer), *periodic activation* (usually concerning payment activities), and *activation resulting from a waiting relation* (a transaction could start only after another one is completed) [11].

Summarizing so far, we have presented our viewing the operation of enterprise systems as concerning a number of business processes driven by a common general goal. We have also elaborated on our defining a business process.

A further consideration of enterprise systems should touch upon decomposition: firstly because as it is well known, decomposition reduces complexity in considering any system and secondly because addressing particular parts of an enterprise system could allow for treating them separately and also for re-using them. Hence, we will consider the notion of **enterprise sub-system**, by putting forward the following definition inspired by [6]:

Definition 7 An **enterprise sub-system** is a *system* which is a *part of an enterprise system*.

Based on *Definition 7*, it becomes clear that if W is the *set* containing all the *transactions* and *actors* included in an *enterprise system*, any *sub-set* $W^i \subseteq W$ which satisfies the system definition would represent an *enterprise sub-system*.

Nevertheless, considering the enterprise sub-system concept without any other restrictions makes little use because of the *non-determinism of the concept*: any combination of transactions and actors could be an enterprise sub-system. Hence, we argue that making use of the mentioned concept should assume the application of clear criteria when deciding what enterprise sub-systems to use, and here the *re-use potential* is claimed to be of importance—this includes a clear *granularity positioning* of the enterprise sub-systems which an analyst is to consider [6].

A possible and logical way of defining an enterprise sub-system is to consider corresponding *business processes*, because:

• The issues related to a particular business process are distinguishable from all other issues that belong to the corresponding enterprise system.
• Business processes relate to a *useful granularity level* (between the *transaction level* and the *enterprise system level*).

Hence, we will consider such enterprise sub-systems that relate to particular business processes. We will call such enterprise sub-systems **business components**, bringing forward the following definition [7]:

Definition 8 A **business component** is an *enterprise sub-system* that *comprises exactly one business process*.

If more business processes are to be considered, for example, three, then this would point to three corresponding business components. If it would then be necessary to bring two of them together (for example), this would mean just bringing together two business components, ending up in a *component of components*. This is certainly possible if: (1) the interrelations concerning those components (two in our example) are well-defined, (2) the relations with the environment are well-defined also, since this would not necessarily mean just "putting together" the relations of one of the components with its environment and the relations of the other one with its environment—possible conflicts, redundancy, and so on should be avoided.

We have now introduced and clarified some basic *EIS*-relevant notions, paying special attention to the concept of *business component*. *Definition* 8 positions this concept within the *enterprise engineering* area unlike other definitions according to which *business component* is a *software engineering* concept [12, 13].

Still, the consideration of the notion of **component** vs. the notion of **system** requires further discussion because in our view touching upon those issues is not only a matter of *granularity* but also a more general thing pointing to basic terminology currently used in *systems engineering*, *software engineering*, and so on. It would often be the case that our system of consideration is pointing to a particular enterprise but this may also depend on the viewpoint, as discussed already. *Business processes* are identified within the enterprise and on that basis we identify *business components*. Hence, it might be (although not necessarily) that an *enterprise system* is decomposed in terms of *business components* which are nevertheless not the *atomic* entities within the enterprise—the *business components* could be **decomposed** themselves.

In *programming*, *components* are *decomposed* in terms of *objects* [12], but what is **object** in *enterprise engineering*? According to Dietz [2], an *object* is an *observable* and *identifiable* individual *thing*, for example, a person or a car. Hence, we observe different ways of defining *object* in different disciplines— *software engineering* and *enterprise engineering* in this case. Since *EIS* relates to both of those disciplines, we need to go deeper in discussing that notion, such that we position it correctly among the other concepts we are considering in the current chapter. To do this, we note the word *observable* from the definition of Dietz, and this brings us to *organizational semiotics* [14] where **sign** is defined as *something that stands for something else in some respect or capacity*. *Organizational semiotics* brings useful value to *enterprise engineering*, by its theoretically relating the notions of *object* and *sign* through the so-called *meaning triangle*, as depicted in Fig. 2.3.

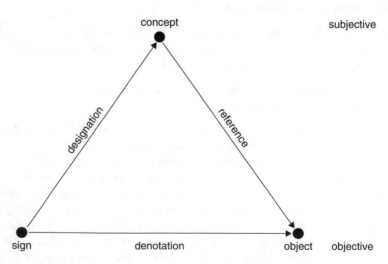

Fig. 2.3 The meaning triangle (Source: [2], p. 36; ©2006, Springer-Verlag Berlin Heidelberg; reprinted with permission)

As the figure suggests, people use *signs* as *representations of objects* in order to be able to communicate about those objects, and here the notion of *concept* is to be considered as well—this notion is **subjective** (unlike the notions of *object* and *sign* which are **objective**). Hence, a *sign* is an *object* that is used as a *representation of something else*. A well-known class of signs are the *symbolic signs*, as used in all natural languages, for example, the name *"John Atkinson"*—we may write this name many times without the corresponding person named *John Atkinson* to be present, and we use this *sign* in support of our communicating about the mentioned person. When it comes to the *object* *"John Atkinson,"* this assumes our being *physically* able to perceive *John*, his face, and so on. This corresponds to the notion of *concrete object*—observable by human beings, unlike objects that are not observable by human beings, for example, *"number three"*, called **abstract objects**. Further, the properties of an object collectively constitute the "form" of the *object* [2]. *Objects* may be **composite**: *an aggregation of two or more objects* is also an *object*; for example, a car as a whole is an *object* but also the back seat of the car (or any other (*composite*) detail) is an *object* by itself.

What about *business components* and how does the notion of *business component* relate to the notion of *object*, as above presented? Let us take as an example a tourist enterprise, dealing with vacations' organization, accommodation bookings, flight bookings, and so on, and let us consider different *business processes* there, such as the accommodation booking business process and the flight booking business process. Hence, those two business processes would point to corresponding *business components*, namely, accommodation booking and flight booking. As it is clearly seen from the example, we may consider those *business components* as:

- *Abstract objects* since they are not observable by human beings.
- *Composite objects* because we can go to *finer granularity*, for example, splitting the accommodation booking into the booking itself and the payment that goes as part of the booking.

Even though many examples one could think of point to *abstract composite objects*, it would not be justified claiming that all *business components* represent *abstract composite objects*. Still, being considered as an *object*, a *business component* represents a useful *enterprise modeling unit*, yet not the *atomic* modeling unit because, as discussed above, most *business components* could undergo further decomposition. This is logical because a *business component* points to a corresponding *business process* and the *business process* in turn represents a structure of *transactions*, as according to *Definition* 6. For this reason, we consider transactions as the *atomic enterprise modeling units*.

Still, at a *higher level* (with regard to elaboration), one could consider *business components* that give the right perspective for grasping the *enterprise* while at a *lower level*, where a more elaborated view is needed, considering *transactions* would be better.

Furthermore, when considering *actor-roles*, *transactions*, *business components*, and so on, it is necessary to establish what *governs* their (complex) *interrelationships* and *behavior*. For this reason, we consider as well **regulations** in general, as important with regard to *behavior orchestration*, and in particular (*aggregation*) `rules` that help introducing *behavior restrictions* [15]. We find *organizational semiotics* useful in this regard and particularly its *norm analysis method* reflected in the widely popular *rule (**norm**) pattern* [14]:

```
whenever <condition>
if <state>
then <agent>
is <deontic operator>
to <action>
```

We will not go discussing the *norm pattern* in more detail in this chapter—we only justify the need for *regulations* and *rules* in *analyzing* and/or modeling an *enterprise system*.

Finally, valid challenges in the context of what has been presented so far in the current chapter could hence be (1) realizing an enterprise model that may help in better *understanding the enterprise under consideration* and/or *reengineering* the enterprise, and/or *engineering a new enterprise*, and so on and (2) delivering an enterprise model to be used as *basis for software specification* that may help if automation is to be introduced within the enterprise, running software is to be updated, and so on. Thus, (2) is especially relevant with regard to *EIS*. As studied by Shishkov [6], the `enterprise-modeling-driven software specifi-cation` is a complex task that could usefully be accomplished in a *component-based way*, such that *re-use*, *traceability*, and *evolvability* are possible.

Hence, an *enterprise-modeling-driven software specification* would assume using *business components* (and possibly *transactions* and corresponding *rules*) as *basis for specifying software*. This represents therefore a `model-driven` *enterprise-software alignment*, and elaborating on what we mean by `model` is necessary in this regard.

As considered by Shishkov [6] and Dietz [2], a *model* of *system A* is a *system* used to acquire knowledge about *system A*. Those views are consistent with the definition of Apostel [16], which we use:

Definition 9 Any subject using a *system A* that is neither directly or indirectly interacting with a *system B* to obtain information about the *system B* is using *A* as a `model` for *B*.

Moreover, realizing that a *model* of anything gives usually a "partial picture," we need to define what should be considered as a *complete model*, and for this we firstly consider the notions *composition* and *structure* of an (*enterprise*) *system*; those notions are essential. They both concern two things: one of them is how the entities belonging to the system are positioned among each other and the other one is what are the (business) processes realized accordingly; the former is referred to as *structure* and the latter is referred to as *behavior* (or *dynamics*). We secondly consider *data* because any *system* (possibly an *enterprise system*, an *EIS*, or any other one) holds the need for storing, processing, and communicating data (it is always that things are counted, (statistical) data analysis is applied) and so on, no matter if this concerns biology, politics, or enterprises, to give just three examples of system domains. On that basis, we define **complete model** as follows:

Definition 10 A **complete model** is a *model* that is elaborated at least in three perspectives, namely, *structural perspective*, *dynamic perspective*, and *data perspective*.

We will also present (below) the **business coMponent** concept denoting a *complete model* of a *business component* where the word *"component"* is with a capital *"M"* to indicate the relation to the word *"model"* [6]:

Definition 11 A **business coMponent** is a *complete model* of a *business component*.

Hence, if we know the *structure* of an enterprise unit, the *processes* over this structure, and the related *data flows*, we claim to have a somehow *"complete"* perception of the enterprise unit, but is this always the case? What about situations in which complicated human-to-human communication goes beyond the mere business processes and data flows? We may consider two examples: (1) A holder of a debit card tries several times unsuccessfully to withdraw money from a cash machine, entering wrong personal identification number $\Rightarrow$ we observe a process and data flows but nothing actually happens between the bank and its customer. (2) As a result of a simple conversation between a pizza restaurant waiter and a customer, a commitment appears for delivering a pizza to the customer $\Rightarrow$ even though this is just a simple conversation, it brings in an obligation that has actual business sense. Thus, *EIS* as *systems* consisting of *human entities*, *technical entities*, and so on are often characterized by **human-to-human communications,** and those are to be considered as part of the *enterprise modeling* since such *communications* bring in *promises*, *commitments*, *negotiations*, and so on, and those issues may have impact on particular *business processes* and corresponding *enterprise (information) systems*. For this reason, in [6] this has especially been labelled as **communication perspective**. We have not considered such a perspective explicitly because according to *Definition 6*, *business processes* are considered as structures of *transactions* and transactions in turn are not only about the *production acts* but also about the *communicative (coordination) acts*—we believe that this already gives good reference to *human-to-human communication* and represents a guarantee that when considering *business processes* from a *dynamic* perspective, such *communications* would be adequately reflected.

And in the end, in Fig. 2.4, we outline (inspired by [6]) our view on how to use those concepts for *modeling*.

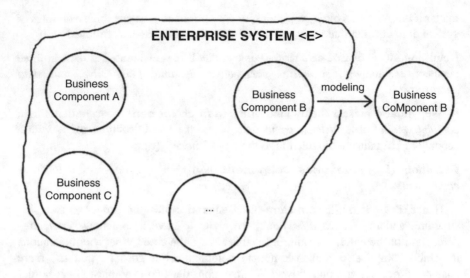

Fig. 2.4 The component-coMponent relation (Source: [6], p. 24) (©2005, The Author, reprinted with permission)

As seen from the figure, we view an *enterprise system* as composed of *business components*. We could represent such *components* in terms of *business coMponents* via *modeling*. Those *coMponents* could be used either as *enterprise modeling units* or as input for further *software specification* tasks.

2.3   Enterprise Information Systems

As mentioned at the beginning of the current chapter, after discussing *systems* and *enterprise systems*, we are addressing (in this section) particularly *EIS*, noting nevertheless that (1) *enterprise systems are a well-known class of systems* and (2) *enterprise information systems are a class of enterprise systems*. Thus, all characteristics of *systems* and *enterprise systems*, as discussed already, are to conform to *EIS* as well. For this reason, we will only focus on the distinctive features of *EIS* in this regard. Further, we make the assumption that ICT in general and **ICT applications** in particular represent an important part of any *EIS*—by "*ICT application*" we mean a *software application* that is nevertheless operating in a distributed networked environment and may thus benefit from current mobile and cloud technologies [17]. Still, no matter if we consider a *software application* or (more broadly) an *ICT application*, the **software specification** task is claimed to play a crucial role [6]. For this reason, we outline two important challenges, namely:

- The *software specification* task and its role in the creation of *EIS*.
- The *relation* between *business coMponents* and *software specification*.

Further, being an *enterprise system* itself, an *EIS* has the following properties:

- Its compositional elements are *human entities*.
- Human entities fulfill particular *actor-roles* in realizing activities within the EIS.
- The *EIS* structure concerns *inter-role relations* which are in turn driven by *goals*.

However, with regard to *enterprise systems*, the *goal* is the *delivery of business products and/or services* to entities belonging to the *system environment*, while with regard to *EIS*, the *goal* is the **informational support to a corresponding enterprise system**. As for *environments*, the *environment* of an *enterprise system* consists of *actor-roles* (those *actor-roles* may be fulfilled by human entities, but they may also be fulfilled by technical entities) and *actions*, and those are external with regard to the enterprise of consideration; the *actor-roles* and *actions* that belong to the *environment* of an *EIS*, in contrast, are usually internal with regard to the *enterprise* of consideration, and the reason for this is the role of an *EIS* as *supporting* a corresponding *enterprise system* [6].

Thus, an *enterprise system* exploits an *EIS*, benefitting from corresponding *EIS services*. Said otherwise, an *EIS* supports a corresponding *enterprise system*, by providing *services* to it.

As mentioned already, such kind of support is usually realized by means of *ICT applications* which allow *enterprise systems* to utilize current possibilities that are related to ICT. With regard to this, we consider the following definition for "*ICT application*", adapted from [6], that is consistent with the definitions and assumptions put forward in the current chapter:

Definition 12 An **ICT application** is an *implemented software product* realizing a particular *functionality* for the benefit of entities that are part of the composition of an *enterprise system* and/or a (corresponding) *EIS*.

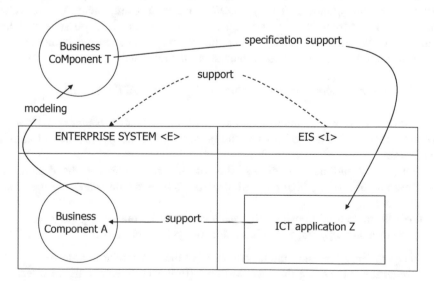

Fig. 2.5 Business coMponents supporting the applications' specification (Source: [6], p. 26) (©2005, The Author, reprinted with permission)

Hence, *ICT applications* are largely instrumental with regard to the way in which *enterprise systems* are supported informationally, and in many cases, this is about the (1) *automation of business processes belonging to an enterprise system* (e.g., part of what human insurance brokers are doing is being automated, such that this same work is realized in an automated way, by means of software) and (2) *enrichment of existing business processes for the sake of utilizing new technological possibilities* (e.g., moving storage to the Cloud would assume additional efforts on coping with information security, possible latency, and so on, to mention just two possible implications in such a context). Therefore, an ICT application is to be "covering" either a whole enterprise system (this is obviously rare because as above suggested, the delivered ICT support is most often focused on a particular issue(s) within the enterprise under consideration) or part(s) of it corresponding to particular business processes—this makes *ICT applications straightforwardly aligned to business components* or components consisting of business components. Since this is a matter of *granularity*, we would not distinguish between the cases when an ICT application points to one particular business component and the cases when an ICT application points to a group of (several) interrelated business components (which we called *component of business components*)—we will speak of an *ICT application* pointing to a *business component* and mean both. Such a relationship should (logically) assume that the business component would have to be precisely reflected in the **specification** of the corresponding *ICT application*; otherwise, the *ICT application* support would be inconsistent with regard to the *enterprise* context. For this reason, we propose using *business coMponents* as source for the derivation of *ICT applications' specification*, as shown in Fig. 2.5 (inspired by [6]).

As seen from the figure, the support (indicated by the dashed line) that an *EIS* realizes to an *enterprise system* is facilitated (actually driven) by *ICT applications*. As it is also seen from the figure, a *business coMponent* might support the *specification* of a corresponding *ICT application* (Business Component A is reflected in Business CoMponent T in the figure, to indicate that it is possible that the Business CoMponent supporting the application's specification is a component of CoMponents). Hence, of particular interest are the relations:

business component − business coMponent − ICT application.

Said otherwise, we are interested to know how a (re-usable) *business coMponent* could be identified and also how it could be reflected in the *specification* of an *ICT application*.

Thus, we would need to discuss the role of *specification* in the design and development of *ICT applications* and also possibilities for decomposing the specification model.

We will hence firstly position the *specification task*, considering the *three-phase software creation process*, following Atkinson and Muthig [18]:

- *Specification*, addressing the functionality of the software artifact-to-be.
- *Realization*, addressing the specification's (further) refinement and also technological aspects.

- *Implementation*, addressing the model-based coding bringing about the final software application output.

Hence, according to [6], the *modeling support* that is provided by a *business coMponent* affects the *specification* phase as depicted in Fig. 2.6:

Fig. 2.6 A business coMponent supporting an application's specification (Source: [6], p. 26) (©2005, The Author, reprinted with permission)

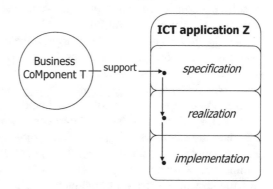

As far as *ICT applications* are concerned, we take also into account the current software development standards, as discussed at the Panel of BMSD'14—the international symposium on Business Modeling and Software Design (BMSD) [19]—according to which the **component-based software specification and development** are largely recognized.

Usually, within the software community, the term *software component* is associated with the *component-based development of ICT applications*, which is characterized by assembling re-usable software components [6]. They represent prefabricated, configurable, and independently evolving building blocks which provide some functionality that can be used separately or in composition with the functionality provided by other software components.

According to the *middleware* perspective [20], which does not necessarily envision a software component in the context of the development of an ICT application, software components are blocks of code ready to be deployed on top of a suitable execution environment (often called *container*) which provides a number of generic services for the execution of components, such as *event notification*, *authentication*, and so on.

We hence conclude about several essential characteristics of *software components*, also referring to MDA (see Chap. 5) [21], relevant to the *software engineering* domain:

- Any *software component* is characterized by a particular *functionality* and is driven by the *goal of providing service(s) to its environment*.
- In its providing service(s), a *software component* could *collaborate* with other *software components*.
- The *environment* of a *software component* may consist of other *software components*, *ICT applications*, supporting platforms, and so on.

Hence, in addressing *software components*, we consider it necessary paying attention to the *interface specification*, *component dependencies*, *deployment*, and *granularity*—those issues are briefly discussed below. This is in tune with related studies reported in [20].

An *interface specification* can be seen as a contract which is established between a software component providing (implementing) a service and the component's environment using (invoking) it.

The *component dependencies* comprise the events that can be either produced or consumed by a software component, in its providing service(s).

Given its binary representation, a software component is a self-contained building block which could be *independently deployed* in a variety of environments.

Noting *composability*, a software component should not necessarily be a complete ICT application; it may be a part of the whole. It is well known, nevertheless, that there are examples of large software components that could be envisioned either as components or as applications. Thus, considering the *granularity* of a software component under development is of significant importance. In our view, in specifying the size of a software component, the modeler should take into account the fundamental requirement that a software component should be general enough to be re-usable in a number of ICT applications [22].

Hence, on the basis of the above analysis, we consider a relevant **software component** *ontological definition* [10]:

Definition 13 Software components are *implemented pieces of software*, which represent *parts of an ICT application* and which *collaborate among each other* driven by the *goal* of *realizing the functionality of the application*.

Since the *software component* concept concerns the implementation phase, we would need to propose also a *functional definition*, inspired by Szyperski [23]:

Definition 14 A **software component** is *functionally* a *part of an ICT application*, which is *self-contained*, *customizable*, and *composable*, possessing a *clearly defined function and interfaces* to the other parts of the application, and which can also *be deployed independently*.

Thus, by creating an instance of a *software component*, we do actually deploy it. We could view, therefore, such a component instance as an *object*. However, there is little agreement on the differences between *software components* and *objects* [20]. For this reason, we will not enter this discussion within the current chapter.

Since any support from a *business coMponent* would concern the *specification* phase, we should consider another relevant concept referring to the logical building blocks of an ICT application (in contrast to software components representing the physical application building blocks, in the sense of *physical* component technologies, such as CORBA [24], .NET [13], EJB [25], and so on). We hence introduce the term **software coMponent** to reflect the abovementioned *logical* aspects:

Definition 15 A **software coMponent** is a *conceptual specification model* of a *software component*.

Summarizing our views and referring to Shishkov [6]:

- An *enterprise system* consists of *business components*.
- An *ICT application* consists of *software components*.
- The creation of a *software component* is supported conceptually by a corresponding *software coMponent*.
- The identification of the *software coMponents* is supported conceptually by a corresponding *business coMponent*.

Figure 2.7 illustrates this:

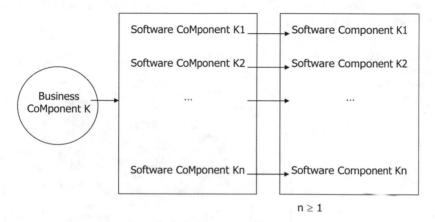

Fig. 2.7 Business coMponent, software coMponent, and software component (Source: [6], p. 28) (©2005, The Author, reprinted with permission)

As seen from the figure and as already stated, a *business coMponent* supports conceptually the identification of at least one *software coMponent*. A *software coMponent* in turn supports conceptually the creation of a corresponding *software component*.

We hence claim that the concepts introduced so far in the current chapter allow for deriving a (component-based) *software specification model* on the basis of a corresponding *enterprise model*, realizing in this way a (component-based) *business-IT alignment*.

Construction is crosscutting with regard to all this—by *construction* we mean the ontological dependencies and relations among system elements, relevant to the question: *How is the system realizing its functionality?* (as opposed to the question *What is the system realizing as functionality?*). And this will be considered in the following section. Still, it is to be noted that we have been consistent with such an ontological perspective in this chapter so far—what we will do in the following section is to consider those issues more explicitly.

2.4   Ontological Systems and Function

Referring to the notions addressed in the previous sections, we consider a *system* and its *environment*, and we may like to also be explicit about the **system boundary**—the *system boundary* separates the *system* from its *environment*. Let us then consider together the *system*, the *system boundary*, and the *system environment*, calling this collectively **Universe of Discourse** or *UoD*, for short. Then, according to Dietz [2], the *system composition*, the *system*, the *environment*, and the *structure* (spanning over them) are collectively called the *UoD construction*. The *UoD construction* can thus be described by enumerating the entities within the *system*, the entities of the *environment*, as well as the relationships in the *structure*—this is illustrated in Fig. 2.8:

Fig. 2.8 TheUoD construction (©2017, The Author, reprinted with permission)

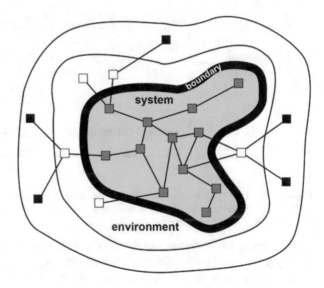

On the figure: the *composition* of the *system* consists of the gray-colored elements; the *environment* consists of the white-colored elements; as for the black-colored elements, since they do not have influencing bonds with elements of the system, they are considered *UoD* external; the black line separating the *system* elements and the *environment* elements represents the *boundary*; and the lines represent the structural bonds between elements. Thus, only the bonds among the system-internal elements and the bonds between system elements and environment elements belong to the *UoD structure*. Finally, the *UoD composition* together with the *UoD* structural bonds is called the *UoD kernel*.

An identical but more precise formal definition of the **UoD construction**, following Bunge [5], is presented below, using two special symbols, namely, (1) ≺ meaning *is part of* and (2) ▷ meaning *acts upon*, and particularly **x** acts upon **y** if and only if **x** influences the *behavior* of **y**; if both **x** ▷ **y** and **y** ▷ **x** hold, we say that **x** and **y** *interact*.

Let **σ** represent our considered *UoD* and **Γ** a class of things, called the *category* of **σ**. Then, the *composition* **C** of **σ** is defined as:

$$C(\sigma) = \{x \in \Gamma | x \prec \sigma\},$$

the *environment* **E** of **σ** is defined as:

$$E(\sigma) = \{x \in \Gamma | x \not\subseteq C(\sigma) \wedge \exists y : y \in C(\sigma) \wedge (x \triangleright y \vee y \triangleright x)\}$$

and the *structure* **S** of **σ** is defined as:

$$S(\sigma) = \{\langle x, y \rangle | (x \triangleright y \vee y \triangleright x) \wedge (x, y \in C(\sigma) \vee (x \in C(\sigma) \wedge y \in E(\sigma)))\}.$$

As for the notion of *sub-system* that has been already considered in this chapter, we are now revisiting this notion, providing below a precise definition from an *ontological perspective* [2].

Let there be a *system* **σ₁** with the *construction*:

$$<C(\sigma_1), E(\sigma_1), S(\sigma_1)>$$

and a *system* **σ₂** with the *construction*:

$$<C(\sigma_2), E(\sigma_2), S(\sigma_2)>.$$

Then *system* **σ₂** is a *sub-system* of *system* **σ₁** if and only if:

$$C(\sigma_2) \subseteq C(\sigma_1)$$
$$E(\sigma_2) \subseteq (C(\sigma_1) \backslash C(\sigma_2) \cup E(\sigma_1))$$
$$S(\sigma_2) \subseteq S(\sigma_1)$$

Further, with regard to a *UoD*, the collective activity of the *system* elements and the *environment* elements is called **operation**. Even though this concerns not only the *system* but the whole *UoD*, the *operation* is essentially initiated and driven by the *system* (and possible contribution from elements that belong to the *system environment* is triggered by *system* elements). For this reason, we may say that the *operation* of a *system* is the manifestation of its *construction* in the course of time— this encompasses both the *production actions* and the related *coordination actions*, preformed accordingly [2].

And in the end, heterogeneous systems (e.g., a car where one could identify (1) a mechanical system, (2) an electrical system, and so on) are more complex than homogenous systems (just the mechanical system, for instance, if we take the above example), and the above definitions and discussion apply straightforwardly to *homogenous systems*. When one would address a *heterogeneous system*, nonetheless, one would have to reflect such a system in *a number of homogenous systems which are related to each other in a layered nesting* [5]. The way in which a collection of *homogenous systems* constitutes a *heterogeneous system* is nontrivial, and this holds particularly for *enterprises* since *enterprise systems* are *heterogeneous systems* [2].

However, we will not go deeper in this discussion in the current chapter. Instead, we will touch upon another important perspective over a system, namely, the *functional perspective* (as opposed to the *constructional perspective* considered above). Below, we will explicitly discuss each of those two perspectives and will emphasize on the distinction between them.

2.4.1 Construction vs. Function

When modeling a *system*, one could take a **white-box** perspective that is closest to the *ontological* view considered above—this is about capturing the *construction* and the *operation* of the *system* while abstracting from implementation details which are assumed to be irrelevant; the *white-box model* is hence adequate for *building* or *changing* a *system*. Contrary to this, taking a **black-box** perspective is about capturing the *interactions between the system composition and the environment*—this conveys the *functional* perspective on a *system* and a *black-box model* hence has no direct relation with the *construction* and *operation* of the *system* under consideration [2].

To illustrate this, inspired by Dietz [2], we consider, for example, a car, and we take a *white-box view* over the car as well as a *black-box view*, as shown in Fig. 2.9.

As seen from the figure, the white-box view is close to the mechanic's perspective—the mechanic being interested in HOW the components of the engine, the components of the suspension, the components of the electric system, and so on work (each one and in combination among each other), such that the desired performance is realized. In contrast, the black-box view is close to the driver's perspective—the driver being interested in WHAT the car can do for him/her in terms of *an input triggering corresponding output*—whether or not pressing the inside lamp button would lead to illumination inside the coupe, whether or not turning on the car key would lead to noise from the engine, whether or not pressing the brake pedal (while the car is moving) would stop the car, and so on.

Hence, taking a white-box perspective would lead to a constructional decomposition into engine, wheels, exhaust, and so on, while taking a black-box perspective would lead to a functional decomposition into the power system, the brake system, the audio system, and so on, as suggested by the figure.

After having discussed the *construction* and *function* of a *system*, we will turn to another important issue concerning *systems*, namely, *evolvability*. In the following section, we will consider *combinatorial effects*, as strongly relevant to the mentioned concern, addressing this from the perspective of the *Normalized Systems Theory*.

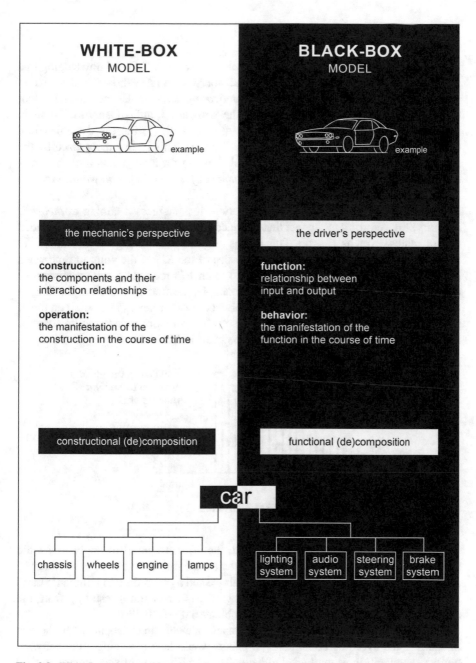

Fig. 2.9 White-box view vs. black-box view (©2017, The Author, reprinted with permission)

2.5 Normalized Systems

We consider the *Normalized Systems Theory*, referring to [26], acknowledging that *EIS* should be able to *evolve* over time; said otherwise, an *EIS* should be designed in such a way that it is *capable of accommodating change*. Hence, such kind of evolution concerns the maintenance of the software "part" of an *EIS*. *Software maintenance* is not only expensive but it also leads to (1) increased architectural complexity and (2) decreased software quality [27]. This is also recognized by the *Lehman's Law of Increasing Complexity*, indicating for a degradation of the structure of an EIS over time [28]. Thus, *the impact of a single change would increase over time*.

In order to avoid such quality degradation, it is suggested aiming at *theoretic stability* [29], referring to the fact that bounded input to a function results in bounded output values, even as $t \rightarrow \infty$. This means that a specific change to an *EIS* should require the same effort, irrespective of the size of the *EIS* or the point in time when being applied. Each change that is applied to an *EIS* requires a certain amount of effort. This effort can be measured in, for example, the amount of time or the lines of code needed to apply the change. This effort would nevertheless increase if on top of this intrinsic amount of effort, additional software components need to be adapted. How such effort increases over time is illustrated in Fig. 2.10:

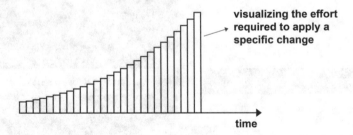

Fig. 2.10 Visualizing the impact of combinatorial effects

When an "ideal" system is considered, the effort required to apply a specific change does not increase over time. However (as the figure suggests), this effort will actually increase over time (as mentioned above and as according to Lehman's Law) in a "real" system, leading to deteriorating effects (over time) resulting from the applied changes and this concerns the combinatorial effects [30].

Combinatorial effects occur when the impact of a change is dependent on the size of the *EIS* and avoiding *combinatorial effects* would lead to avoiding the software quality deterioration as explained already. The identification of such *combinatorial effects* assumes that software is considered as a *modular structure*.

Huysmans [26] considers the *inter-module EIS dependencies* as causing *combinatorial effects*, claiming that in such cases, realizing a change in a specific module would lead to *impact on other modules* that are (in principle) unrelated to the original change. Such dependencies can be *introduced at design time* while the vision on stability requires that *not a single dependency is introduced*, even when an unlimited amount of modules would be added—this is called *the assumption of unlimited systems evolution* [31]: thus, *only when no combinatorial effects occur while the EIS grows, it is considered to be evolvable.*

An *EIS* would be considered as a **normalized system**, if exhibiting *stability* with respect to a defined set of changes and the *Normalized Systems Theory* deduces a set of *four design theorems* that act as *design rules* to identify and circumvent most *combinatorial effects* [31], claiming that any failure to adhere to one of those theorems would result in the introduction of *combinatorial effects*.

With regard to this, considering *modular structures*, taking a basic view, assumes the consideration of *action modules* and *data modules* only, called "*entities*". Hence, our simplified view assumes considering *action entities* which perform certain operations on *data entities* (*action entities* also receive input in the form of *data entities*). A *data entity* thus contains *attributes*—concrete values or links to other *data entities*. An *action entity* in turn represents an *operation* at a given modular level and this would concern (several) tasks—a *task* is a *set of instructions* performing a certain functionality. Such a conceptualization is consistent with *Definition 10* where *structure*, *behavior*, and *data* are considered essential with regard to an *EIS*.

The first theorem, *separation of concerns*, implies that every change driver or *concern* should be separated from other *concerns*. The theorem allows for the isolation of the impact of each change driver; this means that each *module* can contain only one sub-modular *task* (which is defined as a change driver) but also that workflow should be separated from functional sub-modular *tasks*.

The second theorem, *data version transparency*, implies that data should be communicated in *version-transparent* ways between components. This requires that introducing the *data* change (e.g., sending additional data between two components) should take place without having an impact on the components and their interfaces.

The third theorem, *action version transparency*, implies that a component can be upgraded without impacting the calling component(s).

The fourth theorem, *separation of states*, implies that actions or steps in a workflow should be separated from each other in time, by keeping *state* after every action or step. This suggests an *asynchronous and stateful way of calling other components*.

Hence, those theorems show at which point in the modular structure of an *EIS* combinatorial effects occur and that the only *modular structures* free from *combinatorial effects* are the fine-grained structures. Especially the principles of *separation of concerns* and *separation of state* indicate that *modules* have to be *separated both functionally and in time*.

We are not going in more detail on discussing those four theorems and we are also not elaborating further on the *Normalized Systems Theory* because our goal in this section is to only consider the impact of *combinatorial effect* with regard to the *evolution* of an *EIS*.

In the following chapter, we will shift focus from the *system* to the *environment*—considering the challenge of adapting the behavior of an EIS to the surrounding *context*.

* * *

IN SUMMARY, in the current chapter, we introduced our systemics views, touching upon systems and their composition, extending this to enterprise systems and EIS. In the following chapter, we will explicitly focus on the system environment and context of users.

References

1. Wikipedia. The free encyclopedia. http://en.wikipedia.org
2. Dietz JLG (2006) Enterprise ontology, theory and methodology. Springer, Heidelberg
3. von Bertalanffy L (1968) General systems theory. Braziller, New York
4. Weinberg GM (1975) An introduction to general systems thinking. Wiley, New York
5. Bunge MA (1979) Treatise on basic philosophy, vol 4, A world of systems. D. Reidel Publishing, Dordrecht
6. Shishkov B (2005) Software specification based on re-usable business components. Delft University Press, Delft
7. Shishkov B, Dietz JLG (2005) Applying component-based UML-driven conceptual modeling in SDBC. In: Proceedings of the 7th international conference on enterprise information systems (ICEIS), 24–28 May 2005. SCITEPRESS, Miami, FL, USA
8. Dietz JLG (2003) The atoms, molecules and fibers of organizations. Data Knowl Eng 47:301–325
9. Dietz JLG (2004) Basic notions regarding business processes and supporting information systems. In: Proceedings of the CAiSE'04 workshops in connection with the 16th international conference on advanced information systems engineering, Riga, Latvia, 7–11 June 2004
10. Shishkov B, Dietz JLG (2004) Design of software applications using generic business components. In: Proceedings of the 37th Hawaii international conference on system sciences (HICSS), IEEE, Big Island, Hawaii, USA, 5–8 Jan 2004
11. Dietz JLG (2003) Generic recurrent patterns in business processes.In: Proceedings of the international conference on business process management (BPM), Springer—LNCS, Eindhoven, The Netherlands, 26–27 June 2003
12. Abolhassani M (2003) Business objects: from definition to application. Delft University Press, Delft
13. Atkinson C, Bayer J, Bunse C, Kamsties E, Laitenberger O, Laqua R, Muthig D, Paech B, Wust Z, Zettel J (2001) Component-based product line engineering with UML. Addison-Wesley, Boston, MA
14. Liu K (2000) Semiotics in information systems engineering. Cambridge University Press, Cambridge
15. Lang J, Pigozzi G, Slavkovik M, van der Torre L (2011) Judgment aggregation rules based on minimization. In: Proceedings of the 13th international conference on theoretical aspects of rationality and knowledge, ACM
16. Apostel L (1960) Towards the formal study of models in the non-formal sciences. Synthese 12 (2–3):125–161. https://doi.org/10.1007/BF00485092
17. CLOSER. The international conference on cloud computing and service science. http://closer. scitevents.org

18. Atkinson C, (1960) Towards the formal study of models in the non-formal sciences. Synthese 12(2–3):125–161. https://doi.org/10.1007/BF00485092
19. Panel Discussion of BMSD'14. In: The international symposium on business modeling and software design. http://www.is-bmsd.org/Panel_2014.htm
20. de Farias CRG (2002) Architectural design of groupware systems: a component-based approach. University of Twente, Enschede
21. MDA. The OMG model driven architecture. http://www.omg.org/mda
22. Shishkov B (2002) Business engineering building blocks. In: Proceedings of the 9th doctoral consortium of CAiSE—international conference on advanced information systems engineering, Toronto, ON, Canada, 27–28 May 2002
23. Szyperski C (1998) Component software, beyond object-oriented programming. Addison-Wesley, Boston, MA
24. CCM. The OMG CORBA component model. http://www.omg.org/spec/CCM/
25. EJB. The ORACLE enterprise JavaBeans technology. http://www.oracle.com/technetwork/java/javaee/ejb/index.html
26. Huysmans P (2011) On the feasibility of normalized enterprises: applying normalized systems theory to the high-level design of enterprises, PhD thesis. University of Antwerp
27. Eick SG, Graves TL, Karr AF, Marron J, Mockus A (2001) Does code decay? Assessing the evidence from change management data. IEEE Trans Softw Eng 27(1):1–12
28. Lehman MM, Ramil JF (2001) Rules and tools for software evolution planning and management. Ann Softw Eng 11(1):15–44
29. Mannaert H, Verelst J, Ven K (2011) The transformation of requirements into software primitives: studying evolvabilitybased on systems theoretic stability. Sci Comput Program 76 (12):1210–1222
30. Mannaert H, Verelst J, Ven K (2011) Towards evolvable software architectures based on systems theoretic stability. Softw Pract Exp 42(1):89–116
31. Mannaert H, Verelst J (2009) Normalized systems—re-creating information technology based on laws for software evolvability. Koppa, Kermt

Chapter 3
System Environment and Context-Awareness

Referring to the previous chapter, whenever a group of entities (actor-roles) collectively realize a goal, we consider them to belong to a **system**. What has not been discussed in the mentioned chapter nevertheless is **adaptability**—we observe that in their behavior, humans are adapting every minute and every second to what is happening around (a human would often do this intuitively), and for this reason it makes sense considering this issue with regard to systems and especially enterprise systems (and EIS) which are human-driven. An **adaptable system** has the ability to adjust to new conditions [1]. An essential feature of adaptable systems is **context-awareness** [2]—this is *adjusting the system behavior depending on the situation at hand* (**context state**) [3]. As studied in [2], **context-aware systems** are all about adjusting "something" to the *context state*; however, what is adjusted differs: (1) Some context-aware systems optimize system-internal processes based on the context state at hand [4, 5], for example, *regulating the electro-consumption of home appliances for the sake of keeping the overall building consumption within some boundaries*. (2) Other context-aware systems maximize the user-perceived effectiveness of delivered services, by providing different *service variants* depending on the situation of the user [6], for example, *treating a distantly monitored patient in one way when his/her condition is normal and in another way in case of emergency*. (3) Still other context-aware systems are about offering value sensitivity when the society demands so [7], for example, *in the case of supporting judiciary processes, different levels of transparency are to be provided to different categories of stakeholders*. We do not claim exhaustiveness with regard to those three *context-awareness perspectives*. At the same time, as studied in [2], those three perspectives "cover" a broad range of currently relevant applications, especially as it concerns real-life (business) processes. For this reason, we will elaborate and discuss those perspectives in the first section of the current chapter. Then in Sect. 3.2 we will conceptualize context-awareness (considering it in general). In Sect. 3.3, we will consider the operationalization of context-awareness—by means of context-aware applications. In Sect. 3.4, we will address the potentials of (statistical) data analysis [8] with regard to context-aware applications. Finally, in Sect. 3.5 we will briefly

© Springer Nature Switzerland AG 2020
B. Shishkov, *Designing Enterprise Information Systems*, The Enterprise Engineering Series, https://doi.org/10.1007/978-3-030-22441-7_3

discuss the relevance of *classification* (and *decision trees*, in particular) as a prediction "instrument" [9] in the cases when sensing technology [10] is inapplicable.

3.1 System Behavior Perspectives

Referring to the notions considered above and also referring to [2], we will firstly elaborate on the context-driven optimization of system-internal processes, secondly on the context-driven maximization of the user-perceived effectiveness, and finally on the context-driven value sensitivity. It is often that context-awareness is enabled by sensor technology [11] allowing us to "know" what is happening around; alternatively, there should be other ways of "sensing" the environment [6] or "predicting" the environment [9]. As it concerns (1), (2), and (3)–see above–this counts for all of them. Further, considering the essence of their underlying system behaviors, we use the following labels: SELF-MANAGING CONTEXT-AWARE SYSTEM for (1), USER-DRIVEN CONTEXT-AWARE SYSTEM for (2), and VALUE-SENSITIVE CONTEXT-AWARE SYSTEM for (3). Finally, even though most often context-aware systems are "sensitive" to changes in the system environment, it is also possible that the "sensitivity" is towards internal issues (things happening inside the system (not in the environment) may trigger either internal optimizations, or changes in the services delivered to the user, or a reconsideration of the "covered" values). Especially in the current section, we are not restrictive with regard to "sensitivity" (whether it concerns the system or the environment).

3.1.1 Self-Managing Context-Aware Systems (SMCAS)

SMCAS' context-awareness is directed towards **internal (system) optimization purposes** [12]. Such **autonomic** solutions [5] are proposed as a way to reduce the cost of maintaining complex systems and to increase the human ability to manage these systems properly, by automating (part of) their working. In essence, **self-managing** systems can be characterized by a **feedback loop mechanism** that allows them to optimize their working based on input from the environment. For the basic *feedback loop*, the system receives *input from the environment* (monitor) and can change its behavior which in turn has an *effect on the environment* (effector). In **Autonomic Computing** [13] this basic loop is extended into *four components*, resulting in the **MAPE Cycle**; see Fig. 3.1 (left). Next to the "monitor" and "effector" phases, the system internally has an analyze phase that *processes environmental input* and a plan phase that *changes the internal and external working of the system*.

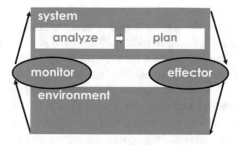 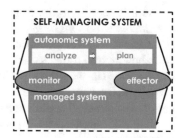

Fig. 3.1 *Monitor-Analyze-Plan-Effect* (MAPE) cycle (left). A *managed system* and an *autonomic system* that together form a *self-managing system* (right) (Source: [2], p. 188; ©2018, Springer, reprinted with permission)

Taking this one step further, an **autonomic system** can manage another system (the **managed system**) by placing it in the *MAPE cycle* as shown in Fig. 3.1 (right). Placed in such a configuration, the *autonomic* and *managed* systems together form a **SELF-MANAGING SYSTEM** or *self-adaptive system* [14].

Internally, *self-managing systems optimize their behavior based on inputs to and outputs from the managed system*. Such state updates can range from simple **if-then rules** (e.g., *if the temperature is below zero degrees, then preheat the car*) to more sophisticated approaches such as those based on **machine learning techniques** [9] (e.g., *neural networks* or *inference engines that determine the best action based on a large internal knowledge base*). Thus, the main **objective of self-managing systems** is to optimize their internal working based on inputs from the environments.

3.1.2   User-Driven Context-Aware Systems (UDCAS)

The UDCAS' context-awareness is directed towards the **maximization of the external (user) satisfaction** [6]. Hence, such systems should be able to (1) identify the situation of the user (possibly through *sensors* or *predictions*) and (2) deliver a service to the user that is suited for the particular situation, as illustrated in Fig. 3.2 (left).

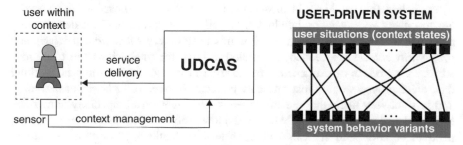

Fig. 3.2 The UDCAS vision (inspired by [3, 15]): a schematic representation (left); context-states-driven system behavior variants (right) (Source: [2], p. 189; ©2018, Springer, reprinted with permission)

As it is seen from the figure, a **service** is delivered to the **user** and *the user is considered within his or her context*, such that *the service is adapted on the basis of the context state* (or situation) the user finds himself/herself in. That state is to be somehow *sensed* (often technical devices, such as sensors, are used for this purpose) or *predicted* (in the figure, we have only visualized the sensing "option"). UDCAS actually deliver services to the user by means of ICT (Information and Communication Technology) applications [16] (**applications**, for short). Hence, unlike "traditional" applications assuming that users would have common requirements independent of their context, *user-driven context-aware* applications are **capable of adapting their behavior to the situation of the user** (this is especially relevant to services delivered via mobile devices). Hence, such applications are, to a greater or lesser extent, **aware of the user context situation** (e.g., *user is at home*, *user is traveling*) and **provide the desirable services corresponding to the situation at hand**. This quality points also to another related characteristic, namely, that *user-driven context-aware* applications must be able to capture or be informed about information on the context of users, **preferably without effort and conscious acts from the user part** [15]. Hence, a basic *assumption* underlying the development of *user-driven context-aware* applications is that **user needs are not static**, however partially dependent on the particular situation the user finds himself/herself in, as already mentioned. For example, depending on his/her current *location*, *time*, *activity*, *social environment*, *environmental properties*, or *physiological properties*, the user may have different *interests*, *preferences*, or *needs* with respect to the *services* that can be provided by *applications*.

User-driven context-aware applications are thus primarily motivated by their **potential to increase the user-perceived effectiveness**, i.e., to *provide services that better suit the needs of the user, by taking account of the user situation*. We refer to the collection of parameters that determine the situation of a user and which are relevant for the application in pursuit of user-perceived effectiveness, as *user context*, or **context** for short, in accordance to definitions found in literature [17]. We will discuss context-aware applications in more detail in Sect. 3.3.

Finally, UDCAS are hence about delivering **behavior variants** to corresponding user situations (**context states**), as illustrated in Fig. 3.2 (right). The idea is that for each *context state*, the system has a *behavior variant*. Nevertheless, this would not be always realistic because if the possible *context states* are too many (e.g., tens or hundreds), the effort for "preparing" (at design time) *behavior variants* would be huge. For this reason, *statistical data analysis* and *probability studies* are needed, as studied in [16], for establishing the **context states of high occurrence probability** (e.g., during a normal working day, an employee would most probably be either *at work* or *at home*, or *traveling*, and it is not very likely that the employee is somewhere else, especially during day hours). Hence all other (possibly hundreds) low probability *context states* would not need to be addressed at design time; instead, a "collecting" *context state* (e.g., labelled OTHER) may be considered at design time, assuming a more *generic* *behavior algorithm*, such that the behavior is "tuned" at real time (possibly in a *rule-based way*). This would of course lead to lower quality of service which is nevertheless justified since it would be very rare that the OTHER behavior variant is triggered. Thus, this is a matter of "trade-off" between *quality of service* and *resources*. Those issues will be further elaborated in Sect. 3.4.

3.1.3 Value-Sensitive Context-Aware Systems (VSCAS)

VSCAS' context-awareness is directed towards a **sensitivity to public values** [7]. *Public values* (**values** for short) like *privacy* and *data protection*, *security*, *accountability*, *integrity* and *provenance*, and *sustainable data storage* often need to be incorporated in the functionalities of *information systems*. Hence, the first question to be answered is: How do values relate to requirements [18] (we mean particularly *non-functional requirements* because values are essentially *non-functional*)? In answering this question, we refer to Shishkov and Mendling who argue that values are desires of the general public (or public institutions/organizations that claim to represent the general public) that are about properties considered societally valuable, such as *respecting the privacy of citizens* or *prohibiting polluting activities* [19]. Even though values are to be broadly accepted (that is why they are **public**), they may concern individuals (e.g., considering privacy). Hence, put broadly and referring to [19], values concern the *societal expectations with regard to the way services should be delivered* and with regard to the above question: *values* are *desires* or *goals*, not *requirements*. Values are abstract and not directly related to an enterprise or software system, as opposed to requirements. Moreover, values are a construct by and for society and not by and for the enterprise domain in which a specific system will be used. Those domains may overlap but are not the same. Values that are adopted as goals by an enterprise would therefore affect the requirements on a system that the enterprise wants to introduce in order to realize its goals. For this reason, *the impact of values cannot be limited to non-functional requirements*. It is therefore considered important to clearly distinguish *values* from *requirements* and acknowledge the limitations of requirements engineering with regard to the development of value-sensitive (software) systems.

Hence, the development of systems should take into account the objective, the user needs, but also the operating and societal context. In this way *values* can be used as a *guidance for making choices when developing systems*; looking at possible *tensions* among values is an issue as well. Thus, we consider challenges in several directions, as identified by Shishkov et al. [2].

Firstly, values are normative by nature and different stakeholders might prefer different values; also, values might differ among countries and cultures.

Secondly, even though different societies may agree on a value at high level, their cultural and other differences may "push" for different value "realizations." This may result in different operationalizations and implementations of the same value.

Thirdly, values may be conflicting to each other (e.g., fulfilling two values at the same time may be impossible); searching for criminals might lead to violating the privacy of innocent people, for example.

Thus, in considering VSCAS, it is important to be aware that **different context states may assume the consideration of different values**, which in turn would mean **different system functionality variants**. Nevertheless, this goes beyond a mapping just between *values* and *non-functional requirements* and would assume a *broader consideration of the software functionalities specification*.

Overall, *computing power becomes larger, wireless telecommunications are advancing*, and *sensor technology is developing fast* [16]; this allows for *ubiquitous network connectivity* and numerous *capabilities of smart devices*, as a basis for developments in at least two directions: (a) **Systems that are traditionally designed for one specific situation and task can be augmented to become "smarter," being able to operate in complex environments.** (b) **Systems are empowered to "sense" what is going on inside them and also what is going on with the end-user while she/he is utilizing corresponding services.** This concerns the system-internal processes, the way services are delivered to users, and the way values are considered.

3.2 Context-Awareness

Let us consider again the constructional UoD view presented in Fig. 2.8, elaborating the view on the *environment* and also on those entities using the system products and/or services (called **users**); in Fig. 3.3, we have explicitly depicted the user(s). The following is visualized on the figure:

- A *system* comprising entities and corresponding relationships.
- An *environment* comprising other entities and their corresponding relationships.
- A *boundary* separating the two (the *system* and its *environment*).
- A *user* comprising some entities (e.g., in the figure they are two) and their corresponding relationships.
- The broader *universe* where the UoD (the *system* and its *environment*) belongs.

Fig. 3.3 Modeling the user

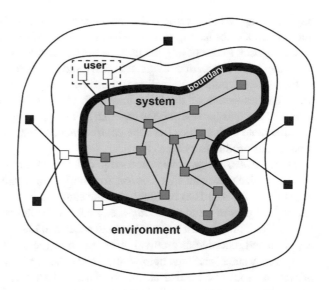

We would avoid discussing whether the user belongs to the system or to the environment: from one point of view, the system is driven by the goal of delivering something to the user and hence, the user is to be considered part of the system; nevertheless, from another point of view, the user is not among the entities who are delivering the product/service because the user is consuming it and hence the user is not to be considered part of the system (and is thus part of the environment). We therefore observe lack of consensus about how the user is to be considered. For this reason, we clearly distinguish between what belongs to the system, what belongs to the environment, and the user.

As it concerns the *environment*, it may look as if we are "establishing" limits on it—see Fig. 3.3. This is certainly not true because we engineer *enterprises/EIS*, and in doing that, we are certainly limiting the *system*, establishing what is to belong to the *system* but we are not engineering the *environment* and thus we are not in a position to say what belongs to the *environment* and what does not belong to the *environment*. It is, for this reason, more straightforward to consider as *environment* anything that is outside the *system*. Still, this would be an obstacle to distinguish between those entities (outside the *system*) that are somehow interacting with the *system* and those entities (outside the *system*) that are not interacting with the *system*. Said otherwise, we position as belonging to the *environment* anything that is not only *system*-external but is also concerned with interaction(s) with the *system*, and this goes beyond our control—the designer cannot establish who and how may happen to be interacting with the *system*. For this reason, the separation between what belongs and what does not belong to the *system environment* remains abstract.

Going back to discussing the user, as the figure suggests, there is always a *user*— no matter what a system delivers, it is delivered to a *user* (otherwise, the functioning of the system would be unjustified). Further, the system *user* may comprise one or more entities—each of them [or they both (e.g., if they are two)] could consume different *services* (or one *service* together). Finally, it might be that the *system* needs to collaborate with entities from the *environment*, such that it is capable of delivering a particular product/service to the *user*.

Hence, a *user perspective* is needed in order to capture such a delivery of products and/or services (we call this *service*, for short). Further, it is often that the *service* delivered to the *user* is to be adapted to the situation of the *user* (see Sect. 3.1.2). For example, a person wearing a body-area network [6] through which body vital signs are captured, may appear to be at "normal state" and then, for example, vital signs are captured and recorded as archival information or the person may appear to be in an "emergency state" and then help would need to be urgently arranged. Thus, one kind of *service* would be needed at *normal state* and another kind of *service* would be needed at *emergency state*. This is illustrated in Fig. 3.2 (left).

It is important to note that even though the current discussion and example seem "closer" to UDCAS (compared to SMCAS and VSCAS), all of them (SMCAS, UDCAS, and VSCAS) are about CONTEXT-AWARENESS, only the perspectives are different, and in the current section we are addressing *context-awareness* in general.

Hence, we summarize that as it concerns service delivery, currently it is often the case that context-awareness is desired. This means that whenever a service is being delivered to the user, the service delivery is to be adjusted to the situation at hand - if this is the case, then adaptability is achieved.

3.3   Context-Aware Applications

As mentioned in Sect. 3.1, traditional ICT application development methods do not consider the *context* of individual users of applications, assuming that *end-users* would have common requirements independent of their context. This may be a valid assumption for applications running on and accessed at desktop computers but would be less appropriate for applications whose *services are delivered via mobile devices*. Ignoring the dynamic *context* of users may lead to suboptimal applications, at least for a subset of the *context situations* the *end-user* may find himself/herself in. Hence, *context-aware applications* (discussed already in Sect. 3.1) have emerged, driven by the successful uptake of *mobile telephony* and *wireless telecommunications* [20]. Such *applications* are, to a greater or lesser extent, *aware of the end-user context situation* (e.g., *user is at home, user is traveling*) and provide the desirable services corresponding to the situation at hand [21]. As mentioned already, this quality points also to another related characteristic, namely, that *context-aware applications* must be able to capture or be informed about information on the *context* of *end-users*, preferably *without effort and conscious acts from the user part* [3].

Developing *context-aware applications* is hence a nontrivial task; inspired by the above discussion, we suggest considering the following related *challenges*: (1) Properly deciding what *physical context* to *sense* and what *high-level context information* to pass to an application and also *bridging the gap between raw context data and high-level context information*, (2) deciding which potential *end-user context situations* to *consider* and which ones to *ignore*, and (3) modeling *context-aware behavior variants* including *switching* between *alternative ones* [21].

Context-aware applications can be particularly effective if the *end-user* is *mobile* and uses a personal handheld device for the delivery of services. The mobile case is characterized by *dynamic context situations* often dominated by changing location (however not necessarily restricted to this). Different locations may imply different social environments and different network access options, which offer opportunities for the provision of *adaptive or value-added services* based on *context sensitivity*. Especially in the mobile case, context changes are continuous, and a *context-aware application* may exploit this by providing *near real-time context-based adaptation* during a *service* delivery session with its *end-user*. The adaptation is *near real-time* because *context information is an approximation* (not exact representation) of the real-life *context* and thus there may be a time delay [20].

Hence, through *context-awareness*, *applications* can be proactive with respect to *service* delivery, in addition to being just reactive, by detecting certain *context situations* that require or invite the delivery of useful services which are then initiated by the application instead of by a *user request*. Said otherwise, traditional *applications* provide *services* in reaction to *user requests* (<u>reactive</u>), whereas *context-aware applications* have also the possibility of initiating a *service* when a particular *context situation* is detected, without a *user input* (<u>proactive</u>).

In summary, *context-awareness* concerns the possibility of delivering effective personalized *services* to the *end-user*, taking into account his/her particular *situation* (it can also be labeled "context state"). Technological advances enable better and richer *context-awareness*, beyond mere *location sensitivity*.

With regard to the design implications concerning *context-aware applications*, those *applications* require knowledge on *context* and exploit this knowledge to provide the best possible *service*, as mentioned above. This concerns, for example, the *end-user context*, i.e., the *situation of a person who is the potential user of services offered by an application*. Examples of end-user context are the *location of the user*, the *user's activity*, the *availability of the user*, and the *user's access to certain devices or facilities*. The *assumption* we make is that the *end-user is in different context situations over time*, and as a consequence, she/he has *changing preferences or needs with regard to services*.

This corresponds to what is exhibited in Fig. 3.2 (left), limited to the UDCAS perspective and assuming sensing (not prediction): the *application* is *informed by sensors* of the *context* (or of *context changes*), where the *sensing* is done as *unobtrusively* (and *invisibly*) for the *end-user* as possible. *Sensors sample the user's environment and produce (primitive) context data*, which is an *approximation* of the *actual context*, suitable for *computer interpretation* and processing. *Higher-level context information* may be derived through *inference* and *aggregation* (using input from *multiple sensors*) before it is presented to *applications* which in turn can decide on the current *context* of the *end-user* and the corresponding *service(s)* that must be offered. Further, according to Shishkov and Van Sinderen [21], *the design, implementation, deployment, and operation of context-aware applications have many interesting concerns*, including:

- *Social / economical*: how to determine *useful context-aware services* where *useful* can be defined in terms of *functional and monetary value*?
- *Methodological*: how to determine and model the *context* of the *end-user* that is relevant to the *application*; how to relate the *context* to the *service* of the *application* and how to *model* this *service*; and how to *design* the *application* such that the *service* is *correctly implemented*?
- *Technical*: how to represent *context* in the *technical domain*; how to *manage context information* such that it is useful to the *application*; and how to *use context information* in the *provisioning* of *context-aware services*?

Addressing the last two concerns (especially the last one) starts with considering possible *IT architectures* and according to Shishkov and Van Sinderen [21], *two principle architectures* could be appropriate, namely:

- **Context-aware selection**: *end-user request(s)* and *end-user-related context information* are used to *discover a matching service* (or *service composition*). *Discovery is supported by a repository of context-enhanced service descriptions.* A *context-enhanced service description* not only specifies the *functional properties* (goals, interactions, input, output) and *non-functional properties* (performance, security, availability) but also the *context properties* of the *service*. *Context properties* indicate what *context situations* the *service* is targeting. For example, a service could provide information which is region-specific (such as a sightseeing tour), and therefore the context properties could indicate the relevance for a particular geographical area.
- **Context-aware execution**: after the end-user request(s) has been processed and a matching service(s) has been found (possibly in the same way as described above), the *service delivery* itself would *adapt* to *changing context* during the *service session* with the *end-user*. When the *context* of the *end-user changes* in a relevant (to the application) way, the *service* provided is *adapted* to the *situation* at hand. For example, the user may move from one location to another while using a service that offers information on objects of interest, which are close by (e.g., such as historic buildings within a radius of 5 km).

In both *context-aware selection* and *context-aware execution*, a new role is introduced, namely, the role of **context provider**. A *context provider* is an information service provider where the information is context information. *A context provider captures raw context data and/or processes context information with the purpose of producing richer context information which is of (commercial) interest.* Interested parties could be other context providers or application providers. Further, a context-aware application obviously requires an *adaptive service provisioning component* and a *context information provisioning component*.

As far as the design of *context-aware applications* is concerned, we follow an approach that is a partial refinement of an existing one considered in [22] that concerns a general *design life cycle* comprising among other phases:

- **Enterprise modeling**: during that phase, the *end-user* is considered in relation to *processes* that either support him/her directly or the goal(s) of related business (es). Those *processes* have to be *identified*, *modeled*, and *analyzed* with respect to their ability to (collectively) achieve a stated goal(s). Modeling in this way processes and their relationships represents actually *enterprise modeling*.

- **Application modeling**: during that phase, the attention is shifted from the business to the IT domain. The purpose is to derive a *model of the application*, which can be used as a blueprint for the *software implementation* based on a target *technological platform*. A model of the application, whether as an integrated whole or as a composition of application components, is called an *application model*. Enterprise models and application models should certainly be *aligned*, in order to achieve that the application properly contributes to the realization of the business/user goals. As a starting point for achieving proper alignment, one could delineate in the final enterprise model which (parts of) processes are *subject to automation* (i.e., are considered for replacement by software applications). The most abstract representation of the delineated behavior would be a *service specification of the application* (as an integrated whole), which can be considered as the initial application model.

- **Requirements elicitation**: both the enterprise model and the application model have to meet certain *requirements*, which are captured and made explicit during the phase called *requirements elicitation*. Application requirements can be seen as a *refinement* of part of the business requirements, as a consequence of the proposition that the initial application model can be derived considering (parts of) the business processes (within the final enterprise model), especially those processes selected for automation.

- **Context elicitation**: an important part of the design of a context-aware application is the process of finding out the *relevant end-user context from the application point of view*; we will refer to that phase as *context elicitation*. End-user context is relevant to the application *if a context change would also change the preferences or needs of the end-user, regarding the service of the application*. Context elicitation can therefore be seen also as the process of determining an *end-user context state space*, where each *context state* corresponds to an *alternative desirable service behavior variant*. Since relevant end-user context potentially has many attributes (location, activity, availability, and so on), a context state can relate to a complex end-user situation, composed of (statements on) several context attributes. Moreover, context elicitation relates to requirements elicitation in the sense that *each context state is associated with requirements* (i.e., preferences and needs of the end-user) on desirable application behavior. Context elicitation can best be done in the final phase of enterprise modeling and the initial phase of application modeling, when the role and responsibility of the end-user and the role and responsibility of the application in their respective environments are considered.

Figure 3.4 depicts those different phases and activities:

Following [3], *we assume that an end-user context space can be defined and that*

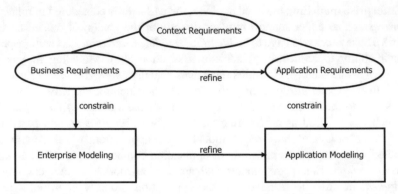

Fig. 3.4 Application design life cycle (Source: [21], p. 26; ©2008, SCITEPRESS, reprinted with permission)

each context state within this space corresponds to an alternative application service behavior variant. In other words, the application service consists of several sub-behaviors or variants of some basic behavior, each corresponding to a different context state. Any service behavior model would have to express the context state dependent *transitions* from one sub-behavior (or behavior variant) to another one.

With respect to those issues, the following *challenges* have been identified:

- Properly deciding what to *sense* and how to *interpret* it in adapting application behavior can be problematic since the interpreted sensed information must be a valid indication for a change in the situation of the end-user, and it is not always trivial to know *how context information is to correspond to a user situation.*
- Deciding *which potential end-user context situations to consider and which ones to ignore* is challenging because there may be tens or even hundreds of possible end-user situations, with only several of them with high probability to occur, and therefore considering the others at design time is not sensible (if an adequate resources expenditure is to be observed).
- Modeling the application behavior including the *switching* between *alternative desirable application behavior variants* can be complicated because alternative behavior variants are behaviors themselves which also are to be considered in an integrated way, allowing for modeling the *switching* between them, driven possibly by *rules.*

Those challenges will be discussed below.

With regard to ***deriving context information***, an adequate decision about what should be *sensed* and how it is to be *interpreted* concerns the extraction of context information from raw data, which relates broadly to *context reasoning* [6].

Context reasoning is concerned with *inferring context information from raw sensor data* and *deriving higher-level context information from lower-level context information*. As for the extraction of context information from raw data, related *algorithms* are needed to support it, and two main concerns are to be taken into account:

- The ability of specific target applications, e.g., in domains such as healthcare or finance (for example), to use the *output* of the algorithms.
- The availability of sensors providing *input* to the algorithms.

Current standard mobile devices can already operate as sensors, e.g., they can gather *GPS* info, *Wi-Fi* info, cellular network info, *Bluetooth* info, voice call info, and so on. In addition, dedicated sensors (e.g., which measure vital signs) can be integrated with existing mobile networked devices. Next to that, future standard mobile devices may even include other types of sensors, e.g., measuring temperature.

Hence, it is considered crucial developing *efficient context reasoning algorithms*, by investigating whether it is possible to derive certain specific *context information* from certain specific *sensor data*. In order to adequately refine such algorithms, additional restrictions would need to be taken into account: (1) restrictions concerning *the (specific) processing environments of mobile devices*; (2) restrictions on *memory usage, processing power, battery consumption, and wireless network usage*; and (3) restrictions that concern *real-time versus delayed availability of extracted context*.

In order to develop adequate algorithms that extract context from raw sensor data, it is therefore important to appropriately consider *gathering raw sensor data which is augmented with user input*. Concerning the sensor data, it should be *preprocessed and filtered*, in order to be properly structured as input for the context reasoning algorithms which in turn would be expected to *automatically yield the desired output*. The (delivered) context information must be of certain (minimal) quality in order to be useful; said otherwise, certain *quality-of-context* levels should be maintained.

Finally, some issues that have indirect impact need also to be taken into account:

(a) The delivered context information would often be applied in real-time environments where failures, performance requirements, available interfaces, and operational environments are to be taken into careful consideration.
(b) In order new applications to be enabled, it is important to investigate how the algorithms could be integrated in the "infrastructure" for context-awareness.

With regard to ***context situations***, it may be the case that there are many (tens, hundreds, and even more) possible end-user situations, for example, user is at home, user is driving, user is busy, user is out of battery, user is on holiday, user is in emergency, and so on. Situations are situations but *which situations are relevant, how many of them have high occurrence probability*, and which situation corresponds to the so-called *main success scenario*? Those questions points to the following claims:

- The application designers should only consider *relevant* context situations (also labeled "context states," as already mentioned). For example, if a phone call with John is being arranged, then "John is at home" or "John is driving," or "John is in a meeting," and so on are relevant context states, but "John is insured" is irrelevant.
- Out of all possible relevant context states, there should be several ones that are of *high occurrence probability* and thus all other ones are of lower occurrence probability (see Sect. 3.4).

    - The *high-probability context states* could be reflected at design time; this makes sense because the applications developers are preparing a "solution box," such that upon identifying a particular high-probability context state, the application "takes" a system behavior variant out of the box—a behavior variant that matches the context state; this would lead to adequate system behavior, carefully "prepared" at *design time*.
    - The *low-probability context states*, in contrast, may be ignored at design time because spending time and resources for specifying system behavior variants that are not expected to occur is considered inappropriate. Still, it is possible (even though not very probable) that such context states occur. For this reason, we argue that even though not considered at design time, such context states are to be addressable at *run time*, through intelligent algorithms.

- There should always be a *default behavior* because in our view, the application behavior modeling needs a *main success scenario* to serve as the "behavior back" for the system—then, any possible deviations from the main success scenario could be modeled as extensions [23].

This is illustrated in Fig. 3.5.

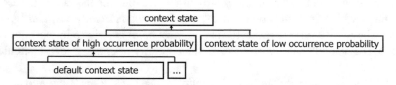

Fig. 3.5 Classification of context states (©2017, The Author, reprinted with permission)

As seen from the figure, from the perspective of developing a context-aware application, one is to distinguish between *context states of high occurrence probability* and *context states of low occurrence probability*, and the *default context state* is certainly one of the context states of high occurrence probability.

Switching between application behavior variants is important as well: Even if context states are identified properly and also matched to corresponding desired behavior variants (or addressed by intelligent algorithms), *it is a challenge to handle the mere switching between one (<u>current</u>) desired behavior (behavior variant) of the application and another one (<u>upcoming</u>)*. Let us take, for example, the case of supporting a person wearing a *body-area network*, by means of a *context-aware e-health application* [6]; let us take for simplicity just two of the possible context states, namely, *"normal"* (the person is being just monitored, by transmitting (to a hospital) data that concerns vital signs) and *"emergency"* (the person urgently needs medical help, and the goal is that the person sees a medical specialist as soon as possible, no matter who the medical specialist is or which the hospital is where the medical specialist stays, or if this would be arranged by an ambulance reaching the person). Then, if there is a context state change, for example, from *"normal"* to *"emergency"*, how would this be realized? If the application would stop the data transmission and start searching for the closest medical specialist, would the data (featuring vital signs) still be recorded such that it is possibly used by the medical specialist? In the opposite case, if there is a context state change, from *"emergency"* to *"normal"* (e.g., if the person feels better and indicates that (s)he would not need emergency treatment any more) and the application would hence have to stop dealing with the emergency help arrangement and would have to go back to just transmitting data, then what would happen if, for example, an ambulance is traveling to the location of the person? Should the application also take care of informing the approaching medical specialist(s) that the emergency situation has been cancelled? Those examples show that *switching between application behavior variants is not trivial, and this challenge needs to be adequately addressed at design time.*

Summarizing the above, a *context-aware system* can be seen as concerning a sequence of *actions* that achieve **S** (*sensing* and *capturing*), **I** (*interpretation* and *state derivation*), **w** (*switching*), and **P** (*provisioning*), as shown in Fig. 3.6.

Fig. 3.6 A simplified view on a context-aware system (Source: [3], p. 228; ©2008, Springer, reprinted with permission)

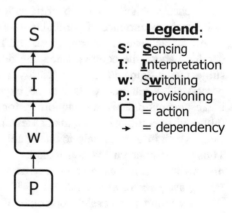

Legend:
S: **S**ensing
I: **I**nterpretation
w: **Sw**itching
P: **P**rovisioning
▢ = action
→ = dependency

With regard to **S**: the system should be able to *sense context* and *capture this context as context data.*

With regard to **I**: the system should be able to interpret the captured context data and derive from it "meaningful" higher-level context information, such that (for example) a context state change is identified; this, in turn, is supposed to trigger another application behavior variant.

With regard to **w**: the system should be able to *handle the switching between its alternative behavior variants.*

With regard to **P**: the system should be able to provide services (delivered through application behavior variants) covering all possible context states; it is to be emphasized that this counts not only for those application behavior variants that have been "prepared" at design time but also for those variants assuming run time "configuration."

This is obviously a simplified model, since each of those actions represents a potentially complex process, and the dependencies between those normally involve multiple instances of information exchange and triggering. Anyway, we are not discussing this in more detail in the current section because we find the above discussion sufficient, especially as it concerns enterprise information systems and the need to properly consider environmental issues. At the same time, we find it necessary to explicitly address the (probabilities driven) context analysis challenge because, in our view, knowing which context states are most likely to occur would be of great help to those designing an enterprise information system. Hence, this will be considered further in the next section.

3.4   Context Analysis, Context States, Occurrence Probabilities, and Context Parameters

In conducting context analysis, the designers of context-aware applications should approach the possible context states and corresponding desired application behaviors (behavior variants) [3]; in this, designers should study the context states and their occurrence probabilities, discovering as well useful context parameters whose values indicate the occurrence of particular states.

As far as **occurrence probabilities** are concerned, we note that in deciding about the context states, the designer is sometimes inevitably driven by subjective judgments that are hardly supportable by rules: How is a situation perceived? What behaviors can be expected? Further, the designer must often make pragmatic decisions—ignoring, for example, states that usually do not occur (although they might occur). In our view, besides such subjective decisions, there are steps which in general help to adequately approach the context analysis challenge. Those steps concern the consideration of **random variables**. Exploring their probabilities allows us to apply **statistical analysis**, including *hypotheses testing* and *parameters estimation* [24].

Considering just possible outcomes is sometimes not enough in approaching a phenomenon; we might need *to refer to an outcome in general*. This is possible if we have a *random variable* and we study the outcomes' *occurrence probabilities*.

Let us consider, for example, *land border security* and particularly the activities of border police officers on preventing illegal border crossings, supported by technical infrastructure and devices [11]. Further, let us focus on the case of distant monitoring, referring to the example: there is a video camera transmitting in real time and a border police officer (who is away from the camera) is considering the visual information being received; essential in this case is <u>whether the camera is transmitting or not</u> (if the camera is not transmitting, this would be alarming and there may be numerous reasons for that, such as illegal human intervention, outage, natural cause, and so on).

We can consider here the *random variable* **Y** with respect to those outcomes, namely, *camera transmitting* and *camera not transmitting*, **Y** would be a *discrete random variable* [24] since it may take on only a countable number of distinct values—two in our case. Provided the number of possible distinct values is exactly two, we have the case of **a priori probabilities** of each of the alternative outcomes (one of those probabilities can be calculated by deducting the other one from **1**).

Hence, if (for example) statistical information from the border authorities indicates that within a certain time frame, *in 80% of the time a particular camera was transmitting*, we would conclude that the *a priori* probability of the first of the mentioned possible outcomes (namely, *"camera transmitting"*) is **0.8**. The a *priori* probability of the second alternative outcome is thus **0.2**.

Hence, our *context states* represent the *"camera transmitting"* and *"camera not transmitting"* alternatives, with a *priori* probabilities **0.8** and **0.2**, respectively—Fig. 3.7:

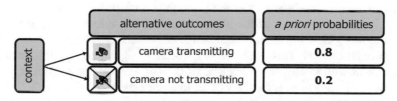

Fig. 3.7 Two context state alternatives (©2017, The Author, reprinted with permission)

It is to be noted, with regard to the current example, that even though we observe whether a camera is transmitting or not, it is not the camera that is the *end-user* of what a *context-aware application* is delivering because the *context-aware application* is not supporting the camera but the border police officer who is using the camera's output. Hence, those alternative outcomes point to two alternative situations concerning the border police officer, namely, (1) *the border police officer is counting on the camera* and (2) *the border police officer is not counting on the camera*. Depending on the situation of the border police officer, the *context-aware application* would deliver one kind of support or another.

Therefore, knowing the *occurrence probability* of each outcome helps in deciding about the *de fault* system behavior variant, about the optimal allocation of resources, about risks, and so on.

Further, in order to prescribe how to recognize each of the states (two in our case), we assume that the state at a particular moment is recognizable through observing the values of appropriate **parameters**. If we have **n** *parameters* appropriate to our scenario and if each of them has certain possible values, then each value combination would point to a particular state.

Then, by considering the *value combinations*, we can know the context state, by simply observing the values at any moment [3].

It is also necessary to analyze potential context states, such that the ones of high occurrence probability are identified. We argue that this may be done intuitively or on the basis of *statistical information*. We are hence interested in considering the latter in more detail.

With regard to this, we consider *statistics*, *data analysis*, and *probability theory*, and for this we refer to Freund [8].

Although *descriptive statistics* is an important branch of *statistics* and it continues to be widely used, statistical information usually arises from **samples** (from observations made on only part of a large set of items), and this means that its analysis requires *generalizations* which go beyond the data—this is an observed shift in emphasis from *descriptive statistics* to the methods of *statistical inference*. As for *probability theory*, it provides the basis for the methods which are used when *generalizations* are made from observed data, namely, when the methods of *statistical inference* are used.

Let us take an example featuring the delivery of support by a *context-aware application* to workers: The application supports a worker, by *informing him/her of the environmental conditions*, in general, and the concentration (in the air) of sulfur oxides, in particular, such that the worker knows if it is safe to be out or not. It is hence necessary knowing the concentration levels of sulfur oxides, which are of high occurrence probability. This would allow for better designing the application and for being able as well to establish a realistic work plan, knowing (approximately) how many working days to plan for the worker to work outside the factory.

In our example (taken from [8]), we have made *80 observations*—one *sample* per one day, hence 80 days in total; let us consider the following example results (sulfur oxides in tons):

15.8	26.4	17.3	11.2	23.9	24.8	18.7	13.9	9.0	13.2
22.7	9.8	6.2	14.7	17.5	26.1	12.8	28.6	17.6	23.7
26.8	22.7	18.0	20.5	11.0	20.9	15.5	19.4	16.7	10.7
19.1	15.2	22.9	26.6	20.4	21.4	19.2	21.6	16.9	19.0
18.5	23.0	24.6	20.1	16.2	18.0	7.7	13.5	23.5	14.5
14.4	29.6	19.4	17.0	20.8	24.3	22.5	24.6	18.4	18.1
8.3	21.9	12.3	22.3	13.3	11.8	19.3	20.0	25.7	31.8
25.9	10.5	15.9	27.5	18.1	17.9	9.4	24.1	20.1	28.5

Since the smallest value is 6.2 (put on gray background) and the largest value is 31.8 (put on gray background as well), we make a choice for the following classification assuming seven classes:

- 5.0 – 8.9: first class.
- 9.0 – 12.9: second class.
- 13.0 – 16.9: third class.
- 17.0 – 20.9 fourth class.
- 21.0 – 24.9: fifth class.
- 25.0 – 28.9: sixth class.
- 29.0 – 32.9: seventh class.

It is now necessary to establish how many items fall into each class (those are called "*class frequencies*") and what is the corresponding percentage and the cumulative percentage:

- 3 items (out of 80) into   first class   3.75%   3.75%.
- 10 items (out of 80) into   second class   12.50%   16.25%.
- 14 items (out of 80) into   third class   17.50%   33.75%.
- 25 items (out of 80) into   fourth class   31.25%   65.00%.
- 17 items (out of 80) into   fifth class   21.25%   86.25%.
- 9 items (out of 80) into   sixth class   11.25%   97.50%.
- 2 items (out of 80) into   seventh class   2.50%   100.00%.

This is graphically presented as histogram in Fig. 3.8:

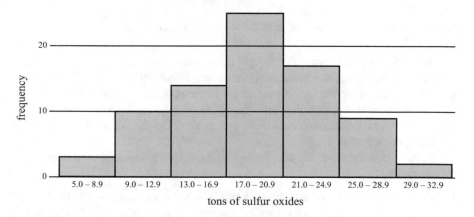

Fig. 3.8 Histogram of the distribution of the sulfur oxides emission data

As it is seen from the figure, most items (25) fall into the fourth class:

- 31.25% of all sample items show between 17.0 and 20.9 tons of sulfur oxides.
- 33.75% of all sample items show less than 17.00 tons of sulfur oxides.
- Therefore, 65.00% of all sample items show less than 21.00 tons of sulfur oxides.

Further, let us calculate the *mean* by summing up the 80 numbers (15.8 + ... + 28.5) and dividing the resulting number by 80: 1511.7/80 = 18.9. In this case, we can trust that number because each of the 80 days has equal *importance weight* in contrast to cases when this is not the case, as, for example, observations summarized in big London against observations summarized in small Delft.

In order to avoid the possibility of getting misled using the mean (as above mentioned), it is recommended to consider the *median*—see Fig. 3.9:

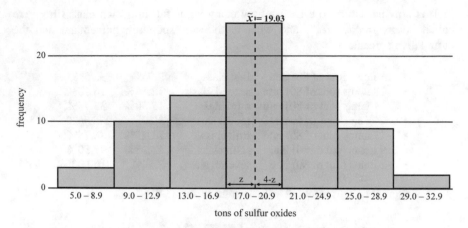

Fig. 3.9 The median of the distribution of the sulfur oxides emission data

The median should *"split"* the sample items, such that 50% of them have values smaller than the value the median points to and hence 50% of them have values greater than the value the median points to. In the considered example, we need to find this number that fulfills the following: 50% of the sample sulfur oxides values are smaller than the number and 50% are greater. On the figure, the median is displayed in dashed line.

We find the median of the distribution of the sulfur oxides emission data in the following way:

1. We note that 33.75% of the sample items have values lower than 17.00 (this can be seen from the numbers presented above); we note also that 50.00% of the sample items have values lower than the so-called *"median value"* (pointed by the *median* as shown in Fig. 3.9). The difference between the two is 50.00% − 33.75% = 16.25%. We note also that the mentioned 33.75% corresponds to first class + second class + third class, while at the same time 31.25% corresponds to the fourth class only (those are values greater than 17.0 and smaller than 20.9). Thus the median value corresponds to the fourth class (because 16.25% is smaller than 31.25%). For this reason, we state that the median value equals to 17 + z, which means that the *"distance"* between the median value and 21 (where the fifth class "begins") equals to 4 − z, because we have class intervals of 4 (9.0 − 5.0 = 4, 13.0 − 9.0 = 4, and so on).

2. We then split the fourth class into two sub-classes, namely, fourth-L and fourth-H, such that (1) the items belonging to the fourth-L sub-class have values that are greater than 17 and smaller than the median value and (2) the items belonging to the fourth-H sub-class have values that are greater than the median value and smaller than 21. Thus (a) 31.25% of all sample items belong to fourth-L sub-class + fourth-H sub-class; (b) 16.25% of all sample items belong to the fourth-L sub-class (50.00% − 33.75% = 16.25%; see above); (c) thus, 15.00% of all sample items belong to the fourth-H sub-class (31.25% − 16.25% = 15.00%);

and (d) 52.00% of the sample items belonging to the fourth class belong to the fourth-L class ((16.25/31.25) ∗ 100).

3. We assume that the values in each class are *evenly distributed* (spread evenly throughout the class); this would mean that if 52.00% of all values belonging to the fourth class belong to the fourth-L class, then 52.00% of the whole class interval (i.e., 4) corresponds to z (Fig. 3.9) which is the "sub-class interval" corresponding to the fourth-L sub-class. This would mean **$\underline{z = 52\% * 4 = 2.08}$**.

4. The way amounts have actually been grouped in the considered example is precise to the point of the nearest tenth of a ton (5.0, 8.9, 9.0, and so on), and this is to assume *refinement* to some extent—for example, considering that 5.0 includes everything from 4.95 to 5.05, the class 5.0–8.9 includes everything from 4.95 to 8.95, and so on. Such a desired *level of precision* points to the so-called "*class boundaries*"—if we assume such *level of precision* for the example, this would mean that **the lower boundary of the fourth class is 16.95**.

5. Hence, in order to find the median value, we should add the corresponding sub-class interval (2.08) to the lower boundary of the class (16.95): **16.95 + 2.08 = 19.03**, as also seen from Fig. 3.9.

Hence, half of the sample items have values that are smaller than 19.03 and the other half of the sample items have values that are greater than 19.03.

In summary, in the current example:

- The MEAN equals to 18.90.
- The MEDIAN equals to 19.03.

In the example, as explained already, both values are very close and we could *round this to* **19.00**, hence claiming that for the period in which the sample values were taken, it may be expected that **the amount of sulfur oxides (in tons) in the air would be around 19**. If this is acceptable, according to the regulations, then this would mean that it is to be planned that in most days workers would be able to work out; otherwise, it is to be planned that in most days workers are to be kept inside the factory, for example.

Let us *assume* that *19.00* points to *possibility to work out*. In this case, **the default application behavior variant would assume that the end-user is working out** and only if the situation of the end-user changes—the amount of sulfur oxides in the air goes above the norm, the application would switch to another behavior variant that assumes instructing the end-user to get inside, and so on.

Thus, in developing context-aware applications, it is helpful conducting *data analysis* as above-suggested, such that the default application behavior variant is adequately determined—with regard to this, the *data distribution* is to be considered, as well as the *mean* and/or the *median* values; still, with regard to those issues, we are not going in more detail in the current section, noting nevertheless that what *statistics* and *probability theory* offer can be even more instrumental (through other concepts and approaches as well) with regard to *context analysis*.

As mentioned at the beginning of the current chapter, in the following section, we will briefly discuss the relevance of *classification* (and *decision trees*, in particular) as a prediction "instrument" in the cases when sensing technology is inapplicable.

3.5   Context-Awareness and Classification

As discussed already in the current chapter, it is essential being able to "capture" changes in the (environmental) situation, if any, such that the system behavior is adapted accordingly. As discussed as well, sensors are often used for that purpose. For example, it is easy to establish if a person is at home or in his/her car, using sensors. Nevertheless, it is not always possible/affordable to use sensors, especially when the (environmental) situation concerns behavior patterns/attitudes of persons. Imagine that an online platform is to distinguish between "devoted users" and "hesitating users," such that it would address devoted users in one way and hesitating users in another way. Obviously, there are no sensors that would help establishing whether John Hudson (e.g., who would be a "new" person approaching the platform) is a devoted user or a hesitating user. It seems thus logical to expect that in such cases the platform would have to count on some kind of artificial intelligence to "decide" about John Hudson.

This brings us to the area of **data analytics**, for which we refer to [9]. It is hence challenging to bridge our studies (that are related to enterprise engineering and software engineering) to another discipline. Here we build upon the previous section that has already introduced relevant concepts, from the perspective of statistics. Still, we should introduce and comment several other essential concepts and we note that some label nuances may differ between data analytics and enterprise engineering (or software engineering).

Firstly, it is important to mention that all this is about ANALYZING DATA for **descriptive** and/or **predictive** purposes—in our example, we need to know whether John Hudson is / would be a devoted user or a hesitating user, such that we address him in the appropriate way. Said otherwise, we need to know which the current context state is—is it "dealing with a devoted user" or "dealing with a hesitating user." Here we have no sensors and we only count on **DATA**. How do we get data then? We get it from any data entries that may have relevance to the situation at hand. In the example, probably John Hudson has registered to use the platform, and in doing this, he has provided some information. Then, the **data entries** can be associated with **classes** or **concepts**. For example, through the abovementioned platform, a company may deal with <u>classes of items for sale</u>, such as *computers*, *books*, *souvenirs*, and so on, and <u>concepts of customers</u> may include *devoted users* and *hesitating users*. Sometimes it would be useful to describe individual *classes* and *concepts* in summarized, concise, and yet precise terms; such descriptions of a *class* or a *concept* are called *class/concept descriptions*.

Classification in the *data analytics* context is the process of finding a *model* (or *function*) that describes and distinguishes data *classes* and *concepts*. This is derived based on analyzing **training data**—data objects for which the *class* labels are known. Hence, such a model is used to **predict the class label of objects for which the class label is unknown**. An effective technique in this regard that is also claimed to be easily combinable with context-aware system models is the *decision tree* technique.

In *decision tree learning*, a new example is *classified* by submitting it to a series of tests that determine the *class* label of the example. These tests are organized in a *hierarchical structure* called a **decision tree**.

Let's consider a simple example: Alice is doubtful about whether or not to take an umbrella with her when leaving her flat. There are *three things* here, namely, (1) the **decision**: whether or not to bring the umbrella; (2) the **uncertainty**: whether it's going to rain; and (3) the **payoff** is Alice's satisfaction.

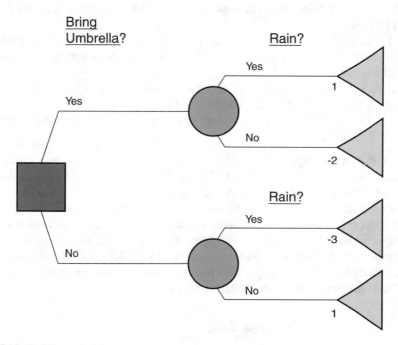

Fig. 3.10 Building a decision tree

We build a decision tree featuring the example, visualizing this in Fig. 3.10. As it is seen from the figure, the square in the left visualizes the main *decision* reflected in the question: BRING UMBRELLA? Further, the disks in the middle visualize the *uncertainty* reflected in the question: RAIN? Finally, the leaves in the right visualize Alice's *satisfaction*, "measured" accordingly.

Explaining things further, we put the main question (Bring Umbrella?) and "see" what "happens":

- If Alice would bring an umbrella with her (the YES branch), then we have two possibilities:

  - It would rain (YesYes).
  - It would not rain (YesNo).

- If Alice would not bring an umbrella with her (the NO branch), then we have two possibilities as well:

  - It would rain (NoYes).
  - It would not rain (NoNo).

Hence, we have to "measure" payoff (Alice's satisfaction) for all four possible "outcomes," and this can be, for example:

- +1 YesYes: If Alice would take an umbrella and it would rain, then her "satisfaction" is 1.
- −2 YesNo: If Alice would take an umbrella and it would not rain, then her "satisfaction" is −2 (it is lower because Alice would have carried the umbrella with her but not using it).
- −3 NoYes: If Alice would not take an umbrella and it would rain, then her "satisfaction" is −3 (because Alice would have gotten wet).
- +1 NoNo: If Alice would not take an umbrella and it would not rain, then her "satisfaction" is 1.

This is just a simple example that is helpful in introducing and explaining decision trees. On that basis, one could certainly think of more complex examples, such as the case in which we need to know whether a person is motivated to wait in line at a restaurant or not. In this, we may consider many attributes/questions: Is the person hungry? Are there persons inside the restaurant? What kind of food is served in the restaurant? This would be a complex decision tree. In the end nevertheless, such a decision tree would help us decide what CONTEXT STATE to expect—and in this example, the context states are just two: "the person is motivated to wait in line" and "the person is not motivated to wait in line."

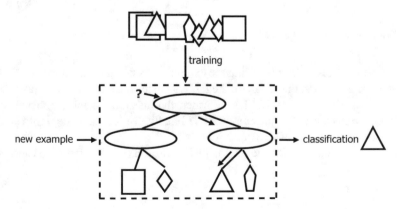

Fig. 3.11 Training a decision tree

Then the question is HOW are we TRAINING and USING the *decision tree*? Actually, we firstly use a number of "instances" to train the *decision tree* (in the above example this may be, for instance, 200 persons or 2000 persons) and we then identify "splitting attribute(s)," applying the concepts of `Entropy` and `Information Gain`. Then we use those identified "best splitting" attributes to decide about a new instance popping up; and we *classify* this new instance accordingly. We are not going in more detail here and we only visualize the overall process of training + using a decision tree—see Fig. 3.11. As it is seen on the figure, we may need to distinguish among several classes of objects—for example, among vehicles, animals, and buildings or as it is in the figure, among rectangles, diamonds, triangles, and pentagons. We should train the decision tree, by providing a set of many rectangles, diamonds, triangles, and pentagons. And we refer to considered attributes and corresponding questions. In the end we know that, for example, if a new instance "responds" in a particular way to the questions, then it is a triangle (as in the example visualized in Fig. 3.11).

Similarly, we may use a decision tree to establish in which context state we are and trigger accordingly the system behavior.

* * *

IN SUMMARY, in the current chapter, we have addressed the challenge of system behavior adaptation driven by (environmental) changes, referred to as context-awareness. We have introduced three system behavior perspectives relevant to context-awareness and we have conceptually elaborated on context-awareness. We have also considered context-aware applications. Finally, we have studied some relevant potentials of statistics and data analytics. In the following two chapters, we will present relevant social theories (Chap. 4) and computing paradigms (Chap. 5), elaborating on how the concepts and views considered in the current and the previous chapters can be rooted both enterprise-wise and technology-wise.

References

1. Google Dictionary (2018) The website of Google Dictionary. http://www.google.com
2. Shishkov B, Larsen JB, Warnier M, Janssen M (2018) Three categories of context-aware systems. In: Shishkov B (ed) Business modeling and software design. BMSD 2018. Lecture notes in business information processing, vol 319. Springer, Cham
3. Shishkov B, van Sinderen M (2008) From user context states to context-aware applications. In: Filipe J, Cordeiro J, Cardoso J (eds) Enterprise information systems. ICEIS 2007. Lecture notes in business information processing, vol 12. Springer, Berlin
4. Brun Y et al (2009) Engineering self-adaptive systems through feedback loops. In: Cheng BHC, de Lemos R, Giese H, Inverardi P, Magee J (eds) Software engineering for self-adaptive systems. Lecture notes in computer science, vol 5525. Springer, Berlin
5. Kephart JO, Chess DM (2003) The vision of autonomic computing. Computer 36(1):41–50
6. AWARENESS (2008) Freeband AWARENESS project. http://www.freeband.nl
7. Friedman B, Hendry DG, Borning A (2017) A survey of value sensitive design methods. Found Trends Hum-Comput Interact 1:76

8. Freud JE (1988) Modern elementary statistics. Prentice-Hall International Editions, Upper Saddle River, NJ
9. Han J, Kamber M, Pei J (2012) Data mining, concepts and techniques. Elsevier, Waltham
10. LandBorderSurveillance (2012) The website of the EBF LandBorderSurveillance Project. http://ec.europa.eu/dgs/homeaffairs/financing/fundings/projects
11. Shishkov B, Mitrakos D (2016) Towards context-aware border security control. In: 6th international symposium on business modeling and software design (BMSD'16). SCITEPRESS, Rhodes
12. Muehl G, Werner M, Jaeger MA, Herrmann K, Parzyjegla H (2007) On the definitions of self-managing and self-organizing systems. In: Communication in distributed systems—15. ITG/GI symposium, Bern, Switzerland, 2007, pp 1–11
13. Huebscher MC, McCann JA (2008) A survey of autonomic computing—degrees, models, and applications. ACM Comp Surv 40(3):7
14. Mahdavi-Hezavehi S, Avgeriou P, Weyns D (2016) A classification framework of uncertainty in architecture-based self-adaptive systems with multiple quality requirements. In: Mistrik I, Ali N, Kazman R, Grundy J, Schmerl B (eds) Managing trade-offs in adaptable software architectures, 1st edn. Elsevier, Amsterdam
15. Shishkov B, Janssen M (2018) Enforcing context-awareness and privacy-by-design in the specification of information systems. In: Shishkov B (ed) Business modeling and software design. BMSD 2017. Lecture notes in business information processing, vol 309. Springer, Cham
16. Shishkov B (2017) Enterprise information systems, a modeling approach. IICREST, Sofia
17. Dey AK (2001) Understanding and using context. Pers Ubiquitous Comput 5(1):4–7
18. Akkermans H, Gordijn J (2006) What is this science called requirements engineering? In: 14th IEEE international requirements engineering conference (RE'06), Minneapolis/St. Paul, MN, 2006, pp 273–278
19. Shishkov B, Mendling J (2018) Business process variability and public values. In: Shishkov B (ed) Business modeling and software design. BMSD 2018. Lecture notes in business information processing, vol 319. Springer, Cham
20. CLOSER. The international conference on cloud computing and service science. http://closer. scitevents.org
21. Shishkov B, Van Sinderen MJ (2008) On the design of context-aware applications. In: 2nd international workshop on enterprise systems and technology (I-WEST'08). SCITEPRESS, Enschede
22. Shishkov B, Van Sinderen MJ, Quartel D (2006) SOA-driven business-software alignment. In: IEEE international conference on e-business engineering (ICEBE'06), Shanghai, 2006, pp 86–94
23. Shishkov B (2005) Software specification based on re-usable business components. Delft University Press, Delft
24. Levin RI, Rubin DS (1997) Statistics for management. Prentice Hall, New York

Chapter 4
Social Theories

In this chapter, we are considering social theories. They are relevant to the **human aspects** concerning enterprise systems and EIS. As mentioned already, this is important for "grounding" our modeling views: in line with what was discussed in the previous chapters, we argue that *human* behavior, *human* decisions, *human* communication, *human* failures, and so on are all about the functioning of any enterprise system or EIS. For this reason, we need to be explicit in considering the human aspects when modeling/designing such systems. Further, we argue that just referring to a theory would be insufficiently useful because firstly, aligning in an abstract way concepts and views to a particular theory is not trivial and secondly, we cannot know in advance how appropriate a theory would be as it concerns the bottom-line goal of bringing together enterprise modeling and software specification; for this reason, we claim that effectiveness could only be achieved if concepts (and views) are bridged to theories, driven by particular **concerns** (this could adequately justify the selection of particular theories). For this reason, we firstly present several important concerns (inspired by [1]), in line with discussions carried out in the previous two chapters:

- **Intuitive Behavior**: There are human entities in any enterprise system/EIS and often their behavior is driven by interpretations, knowledge, judgments, beliefs, values, and so on—those are not always easy to objectively observe and identify. For this reason, it is claimed that intuitive human behavior is an essential concern that needs to be addressed explicitly in the analysis and design of such systems.
- The **Human Element**: In line with the above paragraph, it is to be noted that human entities differ from any other nonhuman entities, such as devices, applications, and so on, because all processes in society are human-driven—it is only humans who have rights, it is only humans who benefit from social prosperity, it is only humans who can be kept responsible, and so on. For this reason, no matter what is happening (e.g., a drone is in the air, monitoring a land border), it should be possible to "trace" this to corresponding human AUTHORITY and RESPONSIBILITY.

© Springer Nature Switzerland AG 2020
B. Shishkov, *Designing Enterprise Information Systems*, The Enterprise Engineering
Series, https://doi.org/10.1007/978-3-030-22441-7_4

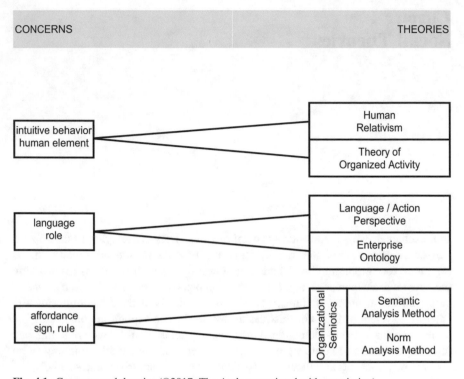

Fig. 4.1 Concerns and theories (©2017, The Author, reprinted with permission)

- **Language**: Human entities, being part of any enterprise system/EIS, communicate among each other, using language—this goes beyond what is just driven by rules, since through language, human entities give *promises*, express *disagreement*, lead *negotiations*, and so on. Such issues have impact on the functioning of such a system and need to be adequately modeled.
- **Role**: Human entities are more sophisticated in their behavior than technical entities—unlike a technical entity which follows "embedded" rules only, a person would often think, make decisions (especially in exceptional situations), and so on, and this may result in conflicts with the rules; hence, it may happen that a human entity realizes activities that are not part of his/her "job profile" (e.g., a professor faxing, with this being part of the secretary's responsibilities); for this reason, we argue that it is appropriate modeling roles, not just the (human) entities fulfilling those roles, as discussed in the previous chapters.
- **Affordance**: There are many different objects that need to be considered when modeling an enterprise system/EIS and what is important in this regard is reflecting their FEATURES and CAPABILITIES; for example, in a library, a book affords to be borrowed; thus, we consider the "affordance" concept useful as it concerns the modeling of (enterprise) systems.

- **Sign**: In an enterprise context, often something stands for something else, for the sake of properly conveying semantics to corresponding entities; for example, in case of fire within a building, if a person is not sure which direction to follow in order to leave the building and in case a green light can be seen from somewhere, the person would take this direction because it is widely accepted that "Exit" signs are colored green and illuminated; hence, the green light helps the person make the right decision how to proceed in a complex situation—this is thus a sign (we have discussed the "sign" concept in Chap. 2) and we argue that this notion should be adequately reflected in the modeling of enterprise systems/EIS.
- **Rule**: Any (enterprise) system is essentially governed by REGULATIONS and rules (NORMS), and for this reason, it is essential that we adequately reflect rules in modeling enterprise systems/EIS.

Following Shishkov [1] and considering recent studies [2], we have established that (1) **human relativism** and the **Theory of Organized Activity (TOA)** well cover the *human element* and *intuitive human behavior*; (2) the **Language-Action Perspective (LAP)** and **enterprise ontology** well cover the (language-based) *human communication* and corresponding *roles* that human entities can fulfill; (3) **organizational semiotics**, in general, and the **semantic analysis method** as well as the **norm analysis method**, in particular, well cover the concepts of *affordance*, *sign*, and *norm* (rule), as suggested by Fig. 4.1.

For this reason, in the remaining of the current chapter, we will firstly consider human relativism and TOA, secondly LAP and enterprise ontology, and thirdly organizational semiotics.

We consider those social theories as underlying with regard to our concepts, views, and way of modeling, as it concerns enterprise systems and EIS, in general, and the modeling of human aspects in this context, in particular. As mentioned before, social theories are insufficient when it also comes to ICT and software—for this we need as well computing paradigms, such that the social theories applied and the computing paradigms followed are complementary with regard to each other. Social theories are addressed in the current chapter and computing paradigms are addressed in the following chapter.

4.1 Human Relativism and TOA

In order to provide theoretical principles with respect to the necessity of properly taking into account the human element and its behavior, in [3], a new philosophical stance—**human relativism**—was proposed, together with an analysis of *human actions* seen as the kernel element of any approach following that stance. The same perspective characterizes **TOA** where *organized activity* is the key concept. Those theories will be addressed further on in the current section.

4.1.1   Human Relativism

Human relativism, as considered in [3] takes a world perspective consistent with
functionalism, social relativism, radical structuralism, and *neo-humanism,* as
presented in [4], also establishing the possibility of complementary using formal
methods and theories, for the sake of overcoming the limitations of most objectivist
stances, related mainly to cases of *unpredictable behavior* usually concerning the
human element—this including most intersubjective experiences, such as interpretation, knowledge, beliefs, intentions, values, and so on, which often remain hidden
from our senses. It is claimed that scientific methods and objectivism are unable to
deal with human behavior in general since it is impossible (from such a perspective)
to reproduce or predict things like interpretation or understanding or to regulate
mechanically human actions [3].

To tackle this from the perspective of human relativism assumes acknowledging
the *human centeredness* and the *unpredictable behavior of human entities.* Human
relativism recognizes this human centrality in all human activities, by acknowledging an objective reality as human relative. We argue that there are evidences of this
human relative view even in objectivism. The visible images transformed from
infrareds into the visible spectrum, for example, allow us to experience a different
reality where human bodies cannot be easily separated from the environment,
because there are no clear boundaries. However, this reality is in fact seen and
experienced by some animal species as science proofs. In this sense we may question
ourselves: Which is the real reality, the reality we observe with our vision or the
reality observed using, for instance, the infrared spectrum? Are they different views
of the same reality? There is no claim in human relativism that the reality we see is
the "real" reality, neither an explanation nor sense of what a *real reality* is. The
solution is more a practical one—this is the reality we have, we experience, and we
share. By assuming the human in the center, we also assume and accept his/her view
as bounded, focused, and particular.

Further, information is human-related as well—information is extracted by
humans from the reality using *perception* and *interpretation processes.* The distinction between perceptions, the process of acknowledging the external reality through
our senses, and interpretation, the meaning-making process, is a useful way to help
understanding the nature of information and its acquisition process. Only information goes through an interpretation process; the other elements of the (human) reality
are just perceived. In fact, perception filters are part of the human reality accessible to
a particular individual.

To perceive does not mean to interpret, and this separation allows us to understand what observable is. Usually, *observability* concerns what we think a human
being is able to percept or acquire through his/her senses. This excludes the
interpretation process and information as well. Usually information is not observable, but it can be extracted from observable things. Observable things can be
viewed as material or physical things from the objectivist view, for example, a
smile (which is an observable thing) may express happiness (which is not an

observable thing). At the same time nonetheless, observing a smile on the face of a person does not guarantee happiness—this is a matter of interpretation and also different persons may express themselves differently. To solve this ambiguity or meaning problem, the abovementioned *observability* concept is the first step and with regard to this, human relativism has the following assumption:

Assumption Anything that is `observable` will be more *consensual, precise,* and therefore more *appropriate* to be used by *scientific methods.*

Further, in considering the notion of "*observability,*" it is necessary to consider a related notion as well, namely, the notion of `precision`.

According to [5], to have a high degree of *precision* means to have a reduced level of ambiguity and different meanings in some term or element making it generally accepted, recognized, and shared. One way of achieving *precision*, for example, is to use physical measurements.

This leads to stating an important *human relativistic* hypothesis:

Hypothesis By adopting `observable` elements or `high precision` elements under a *human relativistic* view, it is possible to derive a scientific and theoretical well-founded approach to EIS.

Those basic *human relativistic* ideas are claimed to be aligned with social *constructivism* and *objectivism*, making a proper connection between them.

Since most enterprise systems/EIS are "challenged" by issues related to the human element, such as unpredictability (and this prevents the use of scientific and objective methods), *human relativism* identifies and highlights this point, by recognizing **human behavior** as an essential challenge with respect to those issues.

Those thoughts point to another important *human relativistic* hypothesis:

Hypothesis As it concerns *human behavior*, we may freely apply *technical approaches* if there is *no unpredictable behavior* present.

Hence, *human relativism* points a way to overcome the difficulty in dealing with unpredictable behavior, in particular *human behavior*. When approaching *human behavior*, one would realize that what is "seen" is just the *observable* part of the behavior—the *observable human actions*. One should then acknowledge the importance of the unpredictable aspects of *human behavior*, for building adequate models of enterprise systems/EIS. Still, besides just acknowledging those issues, *human relativism* proposes ways to cope with *ambiguities* resulting from unpredictable *human behavior*:

- To reduce the dependability of enterprise systems/EIS on *human behavior*.
- To better use the power of *human behavior*, through support coming from tools that are not only facilitating humans but are also stimulating them to generate feedback that in turn could help to better capture the different aspects of *human behavior*.

Thus, building upon other philosophical stances, human relativism is essentially focusing on human behavior with recognition of the fact that even though precision can be achieved, observable behavior is just a part of the complex human behavior, and in order to cope with this complexity, one could either make systems less dependent on human behavior or introduce tools that not only support humans with regard to their actions but also help the system better capture the different aspects of human behavior.

As already mentioned, in the following sub-section, we will further the discussion on *human behavior*, by addressing the *Theory of Organized Activity—TOA*.

4.1.2 TOA

The *Theory of Organized Activity* (*TOA*) proposed by Anatol Holt [6] considers a concept relevant to *human behavior*, namely, the concept of `Organized Activity`, or `OA` for short, and Anatol Holt states the following with regard to that concept:

> "*I intend the expression "organized activity" to mean a human universal. Like language, organized activity exists wherever and whenever people exist. It will be found in social groups of a dozen or in social groups of millions—in the jungle and in New York City, in every culture, and at every stage of cultural/technological history. It is manifest in every form of enterprise, whether catching big game, coping with a fire, or running a modern corporation—even acquiring and communicating by language.*"

This is how Anatol Holt positions the *OA* concept. He acknowledges that *TOA* emphasizes the following issues that concern any *OA*:

- A common communication language—expressed not only by words, but by actions and things as well, known as *units* and recognized by people sharing or involved in the same activity. Behind this idea, there is an essential and associated meta-theory called the *Theory of Units*.
- *Actions*—which directly affect, involve or act on things or materials. *Actions* are related to a *temporal dimension*.
- *Bodies*—representing things or materials, related to a *material dimension*.
- *Action Performers*—always *persons* and/or *organizational entities*.

TOA is thus mainly considering *actions*, *bodies*, and *action performers* as well as their interrelationships.

As far as *actions* are concerned, *TOA* emphasizes especially the *human actions*, acknowledging that *responsibility can only be attributed to humans*, which would mean that *computers and other tools cannot perform actions*.

As for *action performers*, *human actions* are motivated and driven by them (in the interest of the *action performers*).

Figure 4.2 [6] defines the OA kernel. The figure is presenting two dichotomies, namely, *persons* ↔ *organizational entities* and *actions* ↔ *bodies*, suggesting that (as according to Anatol Holt) any OA, no matter how complex and subtle, can be usefully represented in those terms.

Besides the *action* and *body* concepts, *TOA* also defines the concepts of *state* and *information*. A *state* in *TOA* only applies to *bodies* and is only understood within specific domains of *action*. This notion makes a *TOA state* different from the usual technical description of a *state*. Regarding *information*, in *TOA* it has the exclusive end use of making decisions, which determines the following course of *actions*: *Information* in *TOA* is carried in lumps by *bodies*, with the lumps being exclusive properties of those *bodies*. *Information* contents of a *body* depend on the context of information's use and on the particular actors performing the *actions*. The same *information* can be used differently by different actors or in different contexts.

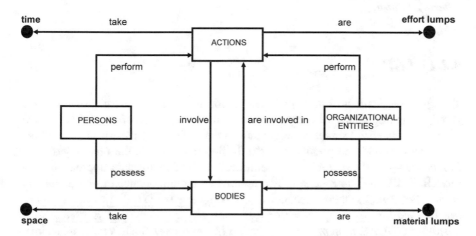

Fig. 4.2 The OA kernel (Source: [6], p. 56; ©1997, Kluwer Academic Publishers, reprinted with permission)

Anatol Holt claims that it is only TOA that:

- Relates *information* to human decision.
- Has the potential to define *measures* consistent with those of Claude Shannon.
- Makes explicit all real-world operations performed on real-world *information*.

Thus, we claim that both *human relativism* and *TOA* provide a useful perspective on enterprise systems/EIS, emphasizing on *human behavior*. In the following section, we are going to consider the (*language-driven*) *communication* among (human) entities.

4.2   LAP and Enterprise Ontology

According to *Definition 10*: "*A complete model is a model that is elaborated at least in three perspectives, namely, structural perspective, dynamic perspective, and data perspective,*" and as suggested in Chap. 2, if one would be considering an *enterprise system* or an *EIS*, one would be interested in capturing the *structure* of the system, the system's *behavior*, and the corresponding *data flows*. Nevertheless, as it is also suggested in the mentioned chapter, the *human-to-human communication* (characterizing *enterprise systems* and *EIS*) needs to be considered as well—actually, the *communicative actions* (related to *human-to-human communication*) are related to the *transaction* concept (Definition 5) and *transactions* are considered as the elementary building blocks of *enterprise systems*. For this reason, besides addressing *structural* issues, *behavioral* issues, and *data* (or *factual*) issues, we need to take as well a **communicative perspective** concerning *human-to-human communication*. This perspective is addressed in the current section and in particular *LAP* and *enterprise ontology*.

4.2.1   LAP

Taking a *communicative perspective* in approaching an *enterprise system* is motivated by the importance of grasping not only the *structural, factual*, and *behavioral (dynamic) enterprise system* aspects but also the *communicative* aspect [7], and one of the most sound and popular theories behind that issue is the *Language-Action Perspective—LAP* [8]. *LAP* is a theoretical orientation towards approaching the modeling of *business processes*, by emphasizing the importance of *interaction* and *communication*. The theory recognizes that <u>language is not only used for exchanging information, as in reports (for example), but that language is used also to perform ACTIONS, as in promises or orders (for example)</u>. Such *actions* are claimed to represent the foundation of communities and organizations and must be understood to create effective *EIS*. For this reason, it is claimed that adequately capturing the *communicative aspects*, characterizing the considered *enterprise system(s)*, would contribute to the creation of sound and complete *business process models* [1]. Further, referring to the *white-box* vs. *black-box* enterprise systems modeling, reflecting *construction* vs. *function* (Fig. 2.9), it is to be noted that applying LAP allows for revealing the *construction* and *operation* of an enterprise, not just capturing the enterprise dynamics. Such a direction corresponds to the consideration of *transactions* as enterprise modeling elements (Definition 5).

Hence, taking a **white-box perspective** and considering the notions of *actor, production*, and *coordination* (as explained in Chap. 2), *LAP* suggests that the *functional behavior* of an enterprise is brought about by the *collective working of its constructional components* [1]. The *construction* and the working of a system are most near to what a system really is, to its ontological description [9]. Acknowledging Bunge's vision, Dietz takes a *LAP* perspective in considering enterprises, claiming that an *enterprise is a discrete dynamic system in the category of social systems, having social individuals or actors, each of them having a particular authority to perform production acts (<u>P-acts</u>)* and a corresponding responsibility to do that in an appropriate and accountable way; *the structure of an enterprise consists of coordination acts (<u>C-acts</u>)*, i.e., the *actors* enter into and comply with commitments regarding the performance of *P-acts* [10]—that all points to the *generic white-box model* of an enterprise, consisting of the actors, the *P-world*, and the *C-world* [1], as presented in Fig. 4.3:

Fig. 4.3 The white-box model of an enterprise (Source: [11], p. 3)

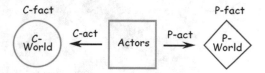

C-acts concern *human-to-human communications*. An instance of such kind of communication consists of *two human processes*:

- *A sender (role 1) expressing something (a message).*
- *A receiver (role 2) interpreting the message.*

What can be communicated between a sender and a receiver? *Elementary communicative acts*, such as **request**, **promise**, **state**, **accept**, and so on, are considered from the *LAP* perspective. This is consistent with *Definition 5* according to which "*a transaction is a finite sequence of coordination (communicative) acts between two actors concerning the same production fact.*" Hence, **production acts** and **coordination(communicative)acts** appear to be performed in particular sequences or chains that can be viewed as paths through a **generic pattern** pointing to a *transaction* [10], and also, in the enterprise context *Role 1* (see above) would correspond to **customer** while *Role 2* to **producer**.

Hence, a more elaborated (and *LAP*-driven) view on *transactions* suggests that a *transaction* is a **finite sequence of C-acts between two actor-roles**, the *customer* and the *producer*. It takes place in *three phases*: the **order phase** (*O-phase*), the **execution phase** (*E-phase*), and the **result phase** (*R-phase*). *O-phase* is a conversation that starts with a request by the *customer* and that, if successful, ends with a promise by the *producer*. *E-phase* basically consists of the performance of the *P-act* by the *producer*. *R-phase* starts with a statement by the *producer* that the requested *act* is performed and ends, if successful, with an acceptance by the *customer*. All this is reflected in the generic transaction pattern, proposed by Dietz, depicted in Fig. 4.4.

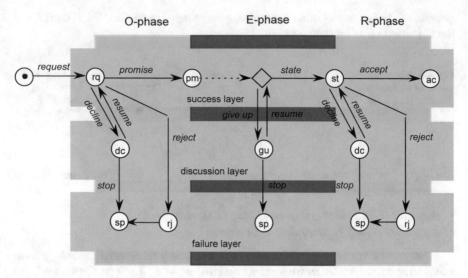

Fig. 4.4 The transaction pattern (Sources: [1], p. 36, ©2005, The Author, reprinted with permission; [11], p. 10)

As it is seen on the figure, besides the three phases, *O-phase*, *E-phase*, and *R-phase*, there are as well three layers, namely, *success layer*, *discussion layer*, and *failure layer*; further, the considered *elementary communicative acts* and their abbreviations are as follows:

– **rq**: *request*.
– **pm**: *promise*.
– **st**: *state*.
– **ac**: *accept*.
– **dc**: *decline*.
– **rj**: *reject*.

and as well two "factual" acts are considered, namely, **sp** (*stop*) and **gu** (*give up*). The generic transaction pattern needs to be further explained, and for this we will use a toy example reflecting the situation in which a customer enters a small pizza shop.

Let us firstly consider the *success layer*:
The customer (John) enters the shop and requests a pizza to be delivered to him, assuming to pay for this according to the announced prices. The person at the desk (Tim), realizing that the ingredients for the requested pizza (such as cheese, tomato paste, and so on) are available, promises to deliver a pizza to John. Then Tim goes to the kitchenette and prepares the pizza for John. Up to this point, we have two *elementary communicative acts*, namely, *request* and *promise* (as it can be seen from the figure, communicative acts are presented as *disks*), and one *production act*: the pizza preparation (as it can be seen from the figure, production act is presented as *diamond*). Further, after having prepared the pizza, Tim comes back to John, bringing the pizza to him, stating that the request was fulfilled. John takes the

pizza and pays, implicitly meaning that he is satisfied with the result and accepts what was delivered (a pizza in this case). **It is only the acceptance that makes the transaction completed**. Said otherwise, if such an acceptance is not reached (and for example John refuses to pay and goes out), then there is no transaction, no matter how many *communicative/production acts* have taken place.

Let us secondly consider the *discussion layer*:
If after John asks for a pizza, Tim, realizing that not all pizza ingredients are available, declines the request, this puts John and Tim into some kind of *negotiations*. As part of such *negotiations*, Tim may announce that even though he cannot deliver a pizza, he can deliver a sandwich instead, for example. Then, there are two possibilities—John either agrees to have a sandwich or not. If John agrees to have a sandwich, this means that John introduces a new request (instead of requesting a pizza, John is already requesting a sandwich). To this Tim promises to deliver a sandwich to John (new promise) and all goes back to the *success layer*. If nevertheless, John would decide that he would not go for a sandwich, then all goes to the *failure layer*, as shown on the figure. Considering further the *discussion layer*: if after having started the pizza/sandwich preparation, Tim unexpectedly experiences an electricity outage, this would result in his impossibility to adequately finalize the delivery—this puts John and Tim into *negotiations*. As part of such negotiations, Tim may announce that due to an electricity outage, he cannot deliver the pizza/sandwich within reasonable time but, based on information from the electricity supplier, he expects all to be back to normal within one hour, for example, and hence, he can deliver the pizza/sandwich with a 1-hour delay (for example), because he had to temporarily give up the pizza/sandwich preparation, causing in this way inconvenience to John, but this could be compensated by a lower price, for example. If John would agree, this would mean that implicitly John has made a request assuming the "new" conditions (new request) and Tim has promised to deliver according to the "new" conditions (new promise), and Tim is in the process of preparing the pizza/sandwich according to the "new" conditions (new production). Then all goes back to the success layer. If nevertheless, John has no time to wait, then all goes to the failure layer, as shown on the figure. And in the end, if the pizza/sandwich is ready and Tim delivers it to John, *stating* that what was *requested* was fulfilled, it is possible that instead of *accepting* the pizza/sandwich, John declines accepting the delivered result, for example—if John finds the way the pizza/sandwich looks inadequate. This puts John and Tim into *negotiations*. Tim may offer a lower price as compensation for the inadequate look of the pizza/sandwich, for example. If John would agree, then all goes back to the *success layer*, and this would mean that implicitly John has made a request (new request) and Tim has made a promise (new promise) as according to the "new" conditions, the pizza/sandwich was delivered (new production and new statement) and paid according to the new conditions, the result is accepted, and this means that the **transaction is completed**. If nevertheless John would not like to accept the delivered pizza/sandwich even at a new (lower) price, then all goes to the *failure layer*.

Let us finally consider the failure layer:
No matter if the transaction has reached the failure layer because John would not like to have a sandwich instead of a pizza (O-phase) or because John would not like to wait more (E-phase), or because John would not like to accept a pizza/sandwich that according to John has a look that is inadequate, even at a lower price (R-phase), as in the considered example, the **transaction is incomplete**; this means that *nothing essential has objectively happened in reality.*

Thus, by modeling an *enterprise system/EIS* in terms of *actor-roles* and *transactions*, we assume the `potential` for anything to take place among *actor-roles*, which is nevertheless not necessarily to happen.

Further, as mentioned in Chap. 2, we consider *transactions* as the *atomic enterprise modeling units*, and this does not contradict with the fact that *transactions* in turn represent a sequence of *C-acts* (as mentioned above). What matters with regard to the *business processes* is whether there is a completed *transaction* or not—the *C-acts* alone are not enough to justify a *business process*. For example, if a person would use a cash machine just to enter his/her personal identification number and would then stop, this would leave no "business trace," or if a person would just ask (within a pizza shop) what the price of a pizza is and would then leave. In those examples, we observe *C-acts* but no completed *transactions*.

Finally, our *systemics* concepts and views are claimed to be consistent with *LAP* and for this reason, we especially emphasize the `transaction` concept that is considered to have essential importance in this regard.

In the following sub-section, we consider the theory of *enterprise ontology* as proposed by Dietz [12] not only because this theory is partially based on *LAP* but also because some views of Dietz have influenced our previous work [1].

4.2.2   Enterprise Ontology

The *DEMO methodology* [13] has been developed on the basis of *LAP* and reflected in the *SDBC approach* [1]. This has inspired Dietz [12] to consider *LAP* in combination with *philosophical ontology* [9] and *organizational semiotics* [14] in proposing the **Ψ**-*theory*, underlying **Enterprise Ontology** (**EO**). The overall goal of the **Ψ**-*theory/EO* is **to extract the essence of an enterprise from its actual appearance**, such that corresponding *white-box* models could be adequately derived; this is the enterprise ontological modeling. The **organization theorem** has crucial importance with regard to the abovementioned goal and the *theorem* in turn is essentially backed by four axioms, namely, the **operation axiom**, the **transaction axiom**, the **composition axiom**, and the **distinction axiom**, as shown in Fig. 4.5:

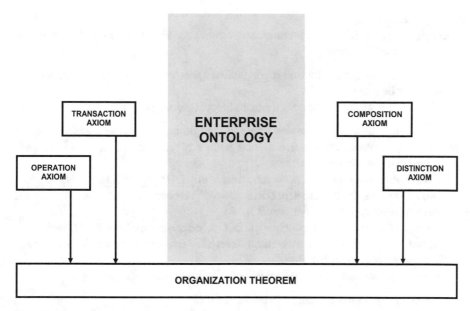

Fig. 4.5 EO—background (©2017, The Author, reprinted with permission)

Hence, in the remaining of this sub-section, we will firstly consider the *operation axiom*, secondly the *transaction axiom*, thirdly the *composition axiom*, fourthly the *distinction axiom*, and finally the *organization theorem*.

Operation Axiom

The *operation axiom* states that the **operation** of an *enterprise* (see Fig. 2.9) is constituted by ***actors*** (see Chap. 2) who perform two kinds of *acts*, namely, ***P-acts*** and ***C-acts*** (see Fig. 4.3), as according to *LAP*.

By performing **P-acts**, *actors* contribute to bringing about the *goods* and/or *services* that are delivered to the *environment* of the *enterprise* under consideration (assuming that in the current sub-section we consider *enterprise systems*—see *Definition 2*).

Further, in line with the discussion on *material things* and *immaterial things* (see Chap. 2) related to the notion of "*product*" (see *Definition 2*), we note that *P-acts* could be either *material* or *immaterial*:

- Examples of *material P-acts* are manufacturing acts, storage acts, transportation acts, and so on.
- Examples of *immaterial P-acts* are judgment acts of a court (e.g., to sentence someone), decision acts of an insurer (e.g., to grant an insurance claim), appointment acts (e.g., bringing someone to the presidency of a company), and so on.

By performing **C-acts**, *actors* enter into and comply with *commitments* towards each other regarding the performance of *P-acts*.

Transaction Axiom

Referring to the *LAP*-driven *transaction pattern* (see Fig. 4.4) and to the *operation axiom*, we establish that:

- A *C-act* is performed by one *actor* (called *"producer"*) and directed to another *actor* (called *"customer"*).
- *C-acts* are always, either directly or indirectly, about *P-acts*.

Thus, the notion of *transaction* refers to the question how *P-acts* and *C-acts* are related to each other, and the *transaction pattern* is referred to as a *generic coordination pattern* in the above context.

Hence, the *transaction axiom* recognizes *the LAP-driven transaction pattern* according to which **transactions** always involve two *actor-roles* and are aimed at achieving a particular *result*.

Further, taking the perspective of EO, a **conversation** is defined *as a sequence of C-acts between two actor-roles that are aimed at achieving a well-defined result concerning a P-act*.

Thus, a *transaction* actually consists of two *conversations*, namely:

- An *actagenic* conversation (it is about the *order*).
- A *factagenic* conversation (it is about the *result*).

If we consider the *transaction pattern* (Fig. 4.4), we see that the *actagenic conversation* points to the *order phase* and the *factagenic conversation* points to the *result phase*, while between them is the *execution* of the *P-act*, which both *conversations* are about.

What can also be seen from the pattern is that the *INITIATOR* of the *transaction* is the *customer* while the *EXECUTOR* of the *transaction* is the *producer* (e.g., it is the *customer* who would *request* a pizza and this would *initiate* the *transaction*, and also with respect to the same example, it would be the *producer* who would prepare and deliver the pizza, in this way *executing* what has been requested). Hence:

- In the *order phase*, the *initiator* and the *executor* work to reach an agreement about the intended *result* of the *transaction*, i.e., the *production fact* that the *executor* is going to create as well as the intended time of creation.
- In the *execution phase*, this *production fact* is actually brought about by the *executor*.
- In the *result phase*, the *initiator* and the *executor* work to reach an agreement about the *production fact* that has actually been produced, as well as the actual time of creation (both of which may differ from what was originally requested). Only if that agreement is reached will the *production fact* come into existence, as discussed already.

Composition Axiom

The *composition axiom* concerns the **business process** notion (see *Definition 6*), considering a *business process* to be a structure of CAUSALLY related *transaction* types. All causally related *transactions* are executed in order to fulfill a *starting transaction*—such a *starting transaction* is either *activated* from the *enterprise environment* or is *self-activated* on the basis of some kind of *self-activation condition*.

Said otherwise, something is requested to be delivered but in order for it to be delivered, the result of something else would be needed, and so on—we will illustrate this by means of a hardware example:

– A Local Area Network—LAN [15] is requested to be installed in an office.
– Before configuring the LAN, the following is needed: a server, Personal Computers (PCs), a switch, a router, printer(s), and so on.
– Before a PC is delivered, the following is needed for its assembly and configuration: a motherboard, HDD(s), a monitor, speakers, and so on.

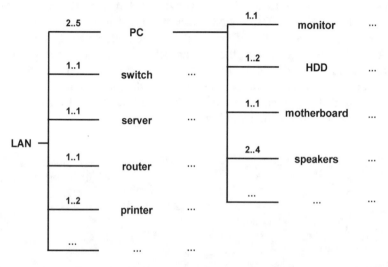

Fig. 4.6 A component structure of a LAN (©2017, The Author, reprinted with permission)

This is illustrated in Fig. 4.6 to be read from left to right, suggesting that in order to configure a LAN (in the particular case), one would need 2–5 PCs, one switch, one server, one router, 1–2 printer(s), and so on, for example, and in turn for a PC to be configured, one would need one monitor, 1–2 hard drives (HDD), one motherboard, 2–4 speakers, and so on. Hence, one should firstly get the monitors, HDDs, motherboards, speakers, and so on, such that the PCs are configured, and then the same for the switch, the server, the router, and so on, and only after all of this has been realized, the LAN would be ready to be installed—this is a good example for **causal relationships** (which was discussed in the previous paragraph). The same is with the *transactions* belonging to a *business process* in an *enterprise* context: similarly to the need to configure a LAN (as in the above example), some kind of *starting transaction* needs to be *executed*, and in order for it to be executed, it is necessary that (*before it gets executed*) other *transactions* get executed, and they may need in turn still other *transactions* to be executed, and so on. For this reason, the way we have presented such causal relationships in Fig. 4.6 is considered helpful, and we will stick to the same way of representation (one entity type depends on the entity types to the "right").

Let us consider a simple example from the enterprise domain: A student (John) visits a property agency asking ADVICE in the form of recommendation—which is the best available property for rent, matching his demands. The consultant (Steve) from the agency is capable of delivering such kind of advice to John, assuming that John would pay for the delivered consultancy. Nonetheless, in order to deliver the advice, Steve would need (before delivering the advice) to realize some kind of MATCH-MAKING "between" the demands of John and the characteristics of the available properties. And in turn, in order for Steve to realize such kind of match-making, he would have to do (before realizing the match-making) two things, namely, (1) REQUEST PROCESSING, such that the demands of John are appropriately reflected in standardized forms such that their effective use is possible and (2) DATA SEARCH, such that there is an actual list of all currently available properties. Thus, Steve should firstly do the request processing and the data search, and only on that base he would be able to realize the match-making, and it is the match-making that is needed by Steve, such that he is able to deliver the requested advice to John. This is illustrated in Fig. 4.7:

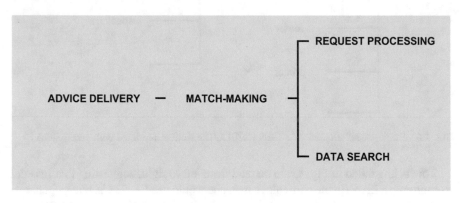

Fig. 4.7 Illustrating a causal relationship (©2017, The Author, reprinted with permission)

Thus, reading the figure from left to right suggests that ADVICE DELIVERY can be realized but under the condition that MATCH-MAKING is realized first. What the figure suggest as well is that MATCH-MAKING can be realized but under the condition that REQUEST PROCESSING and DATA SEARCH are realized first.

This represents a *business process* that is *driven by the goal of fulfilling the ADVICE DELIVERY starting transaction.*

Hence, after considering *elementary acts* (see the *operation axiom*) and *transactions* (see the *transaction axiom*), we are considering the *composition axiom* that addresses **business processes**.

Distinction Axiom

The *distinction axiom* serves to separate the distinct human abilities playing a role with regard to `communication`. In order to give a useful background (claimed to be helpful in understanding the axiom), we refer to the so-called *semiotic ladder* [14] that presents the (human-to-human) *communication* in terms of *layers*, in the following way:

- PHYSICAL WORLD: If two persons would like to communicate, they need physical conditions—this could be their closeness in terms of space, such that they can hear each other or a telecommunications channel, such as telephone connection, and so on.
- EMPIRICS: Even if the persons have physical conditions to communicate, the communication channel itself is to also be adequate—for example, if the persons are close to each other but there is too much noise, they would not be able to hear each other or if they have established a telephone connection but the quality of service is too low for them to hear each other well and without delays.
- SYNTAX: If the persons have adequate physical conditions and communication channel, this is still not enough for a full value communication to take place because they need to speak the same language or use the same communication patterns.
- SEMANTICS: If the persons are adequately exchanging information using the same language, for example, this is still not enough if they do not get the correct meaning. For instance, if John is at a garage, needing his car to be repaired urgently and he sees a queue of ten cars, and it looks obvious that the garage would not be able to serve all those cars within the day, and if John asks the receptionist whether it would be possible his car to be treated urgently, and the receptionist answers, "Yes, as long as the cars from the queue get served," this actually means "no," because it is obvious that the car of John would not be served the same day. If the receptionist had wished to mean "yes," he would have answered, for example, "There are many cars in the queue but we will make an exception and treat you with priority." This example shows that the syntactic "Yes, as long as the cars from the queue get served" has the meaning of "no." Hence, getting correctly the semantics is necessary in order to communicate of full value.
- PRAGMATICS: Even if the persons are adequately handling the communication both physically and also empirically, syntactically, and semantically, they also need to adequately handle the context in which they are communicating—for example, if John's colleague says to John "I am freezing" and John is close to the widely open window during winter time, it is not enough that John gets the right meaning of what his colleague has said; what goes beyond the meaning is that John should realize that by saying this, his colleague is trying to convince John to close the window, and John is expected to "participate" in this negotiation (about whether to close the window or not); hence, the idea of John's colleague is not to discuss the way he/she is feeling but to convince John to close the window.

- SOCIAL WORLD: Even if pragmatics, semantics, and so on are all handled adequately, there are societal norms of behavior that need to be respected. In the above example, it is expected that John would close the window even if John is not feeling cold because it is societally adequate to respect (when possible) the needs of the persons around. In this case, the colleague of John is not feeling good, and John may like to help because closing the window would not immediately hurt John's comfort—still, this would help another person feel better and this is to be considered good behavior from a societal point of view.

In order to align the above semiotic perspective to communication, we consider the corresponding views of Habermas [16] who has identified three spheres of human existence that play a role with respect to communication, namely, (1) objective world: those are the things that are outside the subject and to a large extend exist on their own; (2) subjective world: unique for every distinct subject; and (3) social world: what the subjects build and maintain in interaction. Then:

- With regard to (1), the (human-to-human) communication is aligning the concept of TRUTH ⇒ Here we have the class of acts for which the dominant validity claim is the claim to truth, for example, *assertions*. (John asks Betty what time it is, for instance, and then Betty would assert the current time.)
  This is labelled as **constativa**.
- With regard to (3), the (human-to-human) communication is aligning the concept of JUSTICE. ⇒ Here we have the class of acts for which the dominant validity claim is the claim to justice, for example, *requests* and *promises*. (If I request a loaf from the baker, for instance, I primarily claim that I am in the social position to do so and that the baker is in the social position to be addressed with the request; I hence accept the authority and responsibility of the baker to respond to the request, and the baker accepts my authority and responsibility to make a request, as exemplified by Dietz [12]).
  This is labelled as **regulativa**.
- With regard to (2), the (human-to-human) communication is aligning the concept of SINCERITY. ⇒Here we have the class of acts for which the dominant validity claim is the claim to sincerity, for example, *praises* and *apologies*. (If I bump into somebody, for instance, my apologizing is to convey to the person information that I am sincere, otherwise, an apology would not make sense.)
  This is labelled as **expressiva**.

Next to that, "nondominant" claims are possible as well, mixing up the above issues and several examples considered by Dietz [12] are brought forward in this regard:

- If I appear to be near a head of state and I ask him/her what time it is, things about *truth* and *justice* are mixed up because it is not considered adequate that one asks the time to the head of state.

- If I ask from a baker 100 loaves at the same time, things about *justice* and *truth* are mixed up because objectively, it is impossible for him to deliver at one 100 loaves.
- If John asks Richard what time it is and after hearing the answer, he asks Betty the same question, things about *truth* and *sincerity* are mixed up because if John knows the time already, is he sincere saying to Betty that he wants to know what time it is?

In this respect, **EO is primarily about regulativa** since: (a) It is assumed that the *constativa issues are taken indirectly*. (b) The *expressiva issues are disregarded* and this is not because emotions are considered unimportant but because they fall outside the ontological view on enterprises, as according to Dietz [12].

Hence, in the pizza example from the previous sub-section, just one elementary communicative (coordination) act (e.g., "the person at the desk promises to deliver a pizza"), as we label it "C-act" for short, assumes communication conforming to the semiotic ladder (see above) and in the *regulativa* perspective, and in this we bring together the pragmatic and social considerations (as according to the semiotics ladder) claiming that the following three layers bring together the above views, taking a LAP perspective:

- **PERFORMA**: This is the actual act of evoking an attitude (e.g., the customer had the person at the desk PROMISE to deliver a pizza or another example: a conversation at a library had a person REQUEST membership, and so on). ⇒This brings together the behavioral pragmatics and the societal relevance, as according to the semiotics ladder.
- **INFORMA**: This is about conveying semantics—for example, John may well explain in a library that he would like to have them deliver a pizza to him and they may get this correctly semantically but still this would not lead to a promise from their side because the situational context and social relevance are inappropriate with regard to what John is suggesting. ⇒This corresponds to the semantics layer of the semiotics ladder.
- **FORMA**: This is about conveying information of full value and using the same language or communication pattern—for example, John may utter many sentences at a pizza desk and what John is saying may be adequately heard and syntactically understood, but still, it may not be the case that they understand that John is asking a pizza to be delivered to him. ⇒This brings together empirics and syntactics, as according to the semiotics ladder.
- Finally, the physical conditions necessary for such kind of communication are acknowledged by EO but not explicitly considered since they are claimed to fall outside the ontological view on enterprises.

This is illustrated in Fig. 4.8, summarizing the *distinction axiom*.

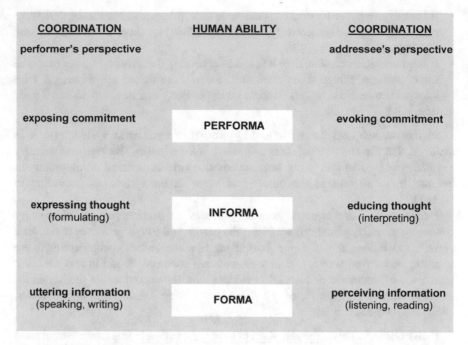

Fig. 4.8 Summary of the distinction axiom (©2017, The Author, reprinted with permission)

As it is seen on the figure: (1) The *forma ability* (bringing together *empirics* and *syntactics*) is about conveying information, as abovementioned, for example, *uttering* and *perceiving* of sentences in some language. (2) The *informa ability* (building upon the *forma* layer) is about conveying *semantics*, as abovementioned, for example, *interpreting* what was said or written, *getting the correct meaning*. (3) The *performa ability* (building upon the *forma* layer and the *informa* layer) is about *bringing in new original things*, rightfully considering the context (pragmatics) and the societal relevance, as abovementioned, for example, *engaging into commitments*.

Hence, the *distinction axiom* states that there are three distinct human abilities playing a role in the operation of actors, namely, **performa**, **informa**, and **forma**, as explained and discussed already.

We consider the performa ability as the essential human ability for doing business of any kind.

Organization Theorem

We have already introduced, explained, and discussed **four EO axioms**, namely, the **operation axiom**, the **transaction axiom**, the **composition axiom**, and the **distinction axiom**—this brought focus on the:

- *Actor-roles* as *composition elements* of *enterprise systems* as well as their potential to realize **production acts** and **coordination acts**.

- Three basic **human communicative abilities** (*performa*, *informa*, and *forma*) with regard to the performance of *production/coordination acts*.
- **Transactions** as the *atomic enterprise modeling units*.
- *Causal relationships among transactions*, justifying **business processes** as *structures of transactions*.

Fig. 4.9   Representation of the organization theorem (©2017, The Author, reprinted with permission)

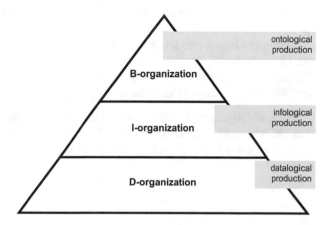

Hence, the *goal of the* `organization theorem` *is to establish, based on the mentioned axioms*, a `concise, comprehensive, coherent, and consistent enterprise notion` *corresponding to a white-box (constructional) perspective*.

The `organization theorem states that` <u>`an enterprise is a heterogeneous system`</u> `that is constituted as the layered integration of three homogeneous systems`: the `B-organization` (from BUSINESS), the `I-organization` (from INTELLECT), and the `D-organization` (from DOMUMENT), related among each other in the following way (as shown in Fig. 4.9):

- *The D-organization supports the I-organization.*
- *The I-organization supports the B-organization.*

All three *homogeneous systems*, as represented in the figure, are in the category of *social systems*, which means that they are similar as far as *coordination* is concerned: the elements are subjects that enter and comply with *commitments* to each other regarding *production acts* (in line with *LAP*). They differ only in the kind of *production*:

- The *production* in the *B-organization* is ONTOLOGICAL.
- The *production* in the *I-organization* is INFOLOGICAL.
- The *production* in the *D-organization* is DATALOGICAL.

This is the reason for considering an *enterprise* to be a *heterogeneous system* and hence the *B-organization*, the *I-organization*, and the *D-organization* represent *aspect systems* of the (total) *enterprise*.

As acknowledged by Dietz [12], an *enterprise* is more than just a well-established integration of those three aspect organizations. Firstly, human beings as *biological* beings need a particular environment to live in, as well as specific facilities to make their biological lives comfortable. Being a biological individual includes being a physical thing. Hence, *physical requirements* must be met, like the need for work space and mobility services. Moreover, a human being is an *emotional* being, a *psychological* being, and so on. While it is recognized that those additional aspects must be considered, they are *irrelevant as far as EO is concerned* since they do not directly relate to the notion of *enterprise*. Still, we consider as precondition dealing with those human aspects in a satisfactory way.

Thus, we argue that by considering LAP-EO, one could build enterprise models that are adequately rooted in corresponding real-life processes. In the following section, we are going to address *semiotics*, emphasizing on *semantics* and (business) *rules*.

4.3   Organizational Semiotics

It is considered useful applying the *Semiotics Theory* [17], regarding issues concerning the analysis and modeling of *business processes* and *enterprise systems*. Actually, a branch of *semiotics* is considered, namely, **Organizational Semiotics (OS)**, and in particular two *OS* methods: the *Semantic Analysis Method* and the *Norm Analysis Method* [14, 18, 19]. *OS* focuses on the *nature, characteristics*, and *behavior* of **signs**. The term "*organizational semiotics*" was officially coined in 1995 at an international workshop in Enschede, The Netherlands, after a long time of research on organizational studies and information systems. This section considers briefly some essential issues related to the *OS* theory.

Peirce founded *semiotics* as the "*formal doctrine of signs*" [20]. A *sign* is defined as *something that stands to someone for something else in some respect or capacity*. *OS* and the analytical methods [14, 18, 19] offer a theory to understand *enterprises*, with or without the computerized *information systems*. *Enterprises* are deemed as *systems* where *signs* are *created, transmitted*, and *consumed* for *business purposes*.

Stamper and his *school of OS* argue that in contrast to the concept of *information*, *signs offer a more rigorous and solid foundation to understand information systems*. For example, within a business context, a banknote is much more than a piece of colored paper with digits on it. It stands for the banknote holder's wealth and ability to pay, as well as the issuing bank's authority and credibility, and much more. Large quantity of underlying social relationships and behavior possibilities are attached to those business concepts; oversimplifying them into pure digits would be dangerous. On one hand, computers can only process and manipulate such digits; on the other hand, the underlying meanings and possibilities must be exposed to enable the correct processing. Adopting the concept of *sign* enables us to study the *enterprise* in a more balanced way, taking account of both *the technological issues and the human and social aspects of information resources, products, and functions*.

OS adopts a <u>subjectivist philosophical stance</u> and an <u>agent-in-action ontology</u>. This philosophical position states that, for all practical purposes, <u>nothing exists without a perceiving agent and the agent engaging in actions</u>.

Stamper adopts the concept of **affordance** from the perceptual psychologist James Gibson, who defined *the affordances of the environment* as "what it offers the animal, what it provides or furnishes, either for good or ill. . ." [21]. Based on the OS theory, since a person perceives things by recognizing what he/she can do with them or to them, a *thing* can be defined as an *invariant repertoire of behaviors, either substantive affordances or social norms that are available to the responsible person* [18]. For example, in the context of a university library, a book affords to be borrowed by a library user.

Borrowing a book is a *potential ability*, which may or may not be implemented in reality. Nevertheless, once it is implemented, *new possibilities may emerge*. For example, a borrowed book may be retained or returned to the library by the user. Under certain circumstances, the library may also call it back. This shows that *affordances have dependency relationships among them*. In *OS* such a relationship is called *ontological dependency*.

We may schematically show this relationship as following, with the **antecedents** on the left side and the **dependencies** on the right, and the solid line denotes the *ontological dependency*:

$$book - borrow - return$$

Ontological dependency does not only show the logic relationship between the concepts. What's more important is that it shows the *dependencies get their meaning from the existence of the antecedents*. Since the existence of *dependencies* would not be possible without the existence of the *antecedents*, the life cycle of the *dependencies* is always included by that of the *antecedents*. The existence of the *antecedents* thus forms a context for the *dependencies*.

For example, talking about returning a book without referring to the fact that the book was previously borrowed from the library would be off the topic.

Further, two essential *OS methods* considered (as it was mentioned already) are the **Semantic Analysis Method** and the **Norm Analysis Method**. Those methods will be briefly discussed below.

4.3.1   Semantic Analysis

The *semantic analysis method* is fundamentally based on the *Semiotic Theory* that has been discussed above. This method is a method for *elicitation and specification of user requirements*. It considers the *signs* created by members of an *enterprise*.

Semantic analysis is theoretically founded in *OS* [22] and the *semiotic* framework. The method has been applied in many fields such as *user requirements* for *enterprise systems*, *organizational analysis*, *legal documents design*, and *analysis and design of computer systems* [1, 14]. The *semantic analysis* is conducted usually in *four steps*, outlined below, and the final result is a *semantic schema*, called `ontology chart`:

- Taking into account that *semantic analysis* is about analyzing documents and conversations, the first step that is to be realized is to *gather relevant data and understand the problem*. This can be called *problem statement*.
- The second step is to *produce a list of semantic units such as verbs, nouns, adjectives, and adverbs*. Those semantic units may be used to *describe human agents and their respective patterns of behavior*.
- The third step is to *further analyze the semantic units by linking them together according to their relationship in terms of generic-to-specific positioning*.
- The fourth step should *bring together all the linked semantic units into a coherent whole*, which produces a *complete semantic model*. The model is represented graphically through an ontology chart.

4.3.2   Norm Analysis

When studying *enterprises* from the *perspective of entities' behavior*, it is necessary to specify the `norms` *based on which this behavior is realized*. Norms [23] are *the rules and patterns of behavior, either formal or informal, explicit or implicit, existing within a society, an enterprise, or even a small group of people working together to achieve a common goal.*

Norms are determined by *society* or collective groups and *serve as a standard for the members to coordinate their actions*. An individual member uses the knowledge of *norms* to guide his or her actions. If the *norms* can be identified, the *behaviors* of the individuals, hence their collective *behaviors*, are mostly predictable. From this perspective, *to specify an organization can be done by specifying the norms* [24] and this holds also for enterprises.

Four types of norms exist, namely, *evaluative norms*, *perceptual norms*, *cognitive norms*, and *behavioral norms*. Each type of norms *governs human behavior from different aspects*. In *business process modeling*, most *rules* and *regulations* fall into the category of `behavioral norms`. Those *norms* prescribe *what people must, may, and must not do*, which are equivalent to *three deontic operators*: "*is obliged*", "*is permitted*," and "*is prohibited*." Hence, the following format is considered suitable for specifying *behavioral norms*.

```
whenever <condition>
if <state>
then <agent>
is <deontic operator>
to <action>
```

It is essential to recognize that *norms* are not as rigid as logical conditions. If a person does not drink water for certain duration of time, he/she cannot survive. But an individual who breaks the working pattern of a group does not have to be punished in any way. For those actions that are *permitted*, whether the agent will take an action or not is seldom deterministic. This *elasticity* characterizes *business processes*, therefore it is of particularly value to understand the corresponding *enterprise*(*s*).

A *norm analysis* is normally carried out on the basis of the results of a *semantic analysis* (for more information on *semantic analysis*, interested readers are referred to [14]). The *semantic* model delineates the area of concern of an *enterprise*. The *patterns of behavior* specified in the *semantic* model are part of the fundamental *norms* that retain the ontologically determined relationships between agents and actions without imposing any further constraints. Nevertheless, *norm analysis* could be successfully related also to other modeling tools, as studied by Shishkov [1].

In general, a complete *norm analysis* can be performed in *four steps*:

- First step: *Responsibility analysis*.
- Second step: *Proto-norm analysis*.
- Third step: *Trigger analysis*.
- Fourth step: *Detailed norm specification*.

Responsibility analysis enables one to identify and assign responsible *entities* (or "*agents*" as according to the *OS* terminology) to each *action*. The analysis focuses on the *types of agents* and *types of actions*. In an *enterprise*, responsibilities may be determined by the organizational constitution or by common agreements in the *enterprise*.

Proto-norm analysis helps one identify relevant types of information for making *decisions concerning a certain type of behavior*. After the relevant types of information are identified, they can be used as a checklist by the responsible agent to take necessary factors into account when a decision is to be made. The objective of this analysis is to *facilitate the human decisions without overlooking any necessary factors or types of information*.

Trigger analysis is to consider the actions to be taken in relation to the absolute and relative time. The absolute time means the calendar time, while the relative time makes use of references to other events. The results of trigger analysis are *specifications of the schedule of actions*.

The *detailed norm specification* concerns the specification of *norms* in two versions, a natural language and a formal language. The purposes of that are (a) to capture the *norms* as references for human decision and (b) to perform actions in the automated system, by executing the *norms* in the formal language.

For those *norms* identified in the *business processes*, some refer to the major authorities and responsibilities of the major figures in the considered *enterprise*. Those *norms* govern some trivial, relatively less important norms or those of lower priorities, from the perspective of organizational functionalities [1]. This strongly suggests that possible *hierarchies* exist not only in the *enterprise structure* but also in the *norms*. The terms *"framing norm"* and *"contractual norm"* are used to express such kinds of *hierarchies* [19].

Hence, among the *EIS*-relevant <u>strengths</u> of *OS* are the following:

- *Semantic analysis* is powerful if it is needed to put some unstructured information in order (we argue that this is unavoidable in any software project).
- *Norm analysis* is powerful if it is necessary to specify *rules* and/or to relate a number of *rules* to each other. Hence, *semiotic norms* could be much useful in both *business process modeling* and *software specification*—both tasks include consideration of *rules*.
- *Semantic analysis* and *norm analysis* are founded on the *OS* theory; it is a well-established theory relevant to both *enterprise modeling* and *software specification*.

Nevertheless, as studied by Shishkov [1], those semiotic methods alone are not capable of soundly and completely aligning enterprise modeling and software specification; those methods need to be incorporated in an approach that would not only combine them adequately with other relevant social theories (besides OS) but would also relate them to appropriate computing paradigms.

* * *

IN SUMMARY, in the current chapter, we have presented and discussed *social theories*, including *human relativism*, the *theory of organized activity*, the *language-action perspective*, *enterprise ontology*, and *organizational semiotics*, justifying their relevance to different aspects concerning *enterprise systems* and *EIS*. In the following chapter, we will consider in turn *computing paradigms* that are currently actual and also well-combinable with the studied *social theories* and consistent with the *concepts* and *views* introduced in the previous chapters.

References

1. Shishkov B (2005) Software specification based on re-usable business components. Delft University Press, Delft
2. BMSD. In: The international symposium on business modeling and software design. http://www.is-bmsd.org
3. Cordeiro J, Filipe J, Liu K (2009) Towards a human oriented approach to information systems development. In: Proceedings of the 3rd international workshop on enterprise systems and technology (I-WEST). SCITEPRESS, Sofia, Bulgaria
4. Hirschheim R, Klein H, Lyytinen K (1995) Information systems development and data modeling—conceptual and philosophical foundations. Cambridge University Press, Cambridge
5. Cordeiro J, Filipe J, Liu K (2010) NOMIS: a human centred modelling approach for information systems. In: Proceedings of the 4th international workshop on enterprise systems and technology (I-WEST). SCITEPRESS, Athens, Greece
6. Holt A (1997) Organized activity and its support by computer. Kluwer Academic, Dordrecht
7. Searle JR (1969) Speech acts: an essay in the philosophy of language. Cambridge University Press, Cambridge

8. Winograd TA (1988) Language/action perspective on the design of cooperative work. In: Greif I (ed) Computer supported cooperative work: a book of reading. Morgan Kaufmann, San Mateo
9. Bunge MA (1979) Treatise on basic philosophy, A world of systems, vol 4. D. Reidel Publishing Company, Dordrecht
10. Dietz JLG (1999) Understanding and modeling business processes with DEMO. In: Proceedings of the 18th international conference on conceptual modeling (ER), 15–18 Nov 1999. Springer—LNCS, Paris
11. Dietz JLG (2003) The atoms, molecules and fibers of organizations. Data Knowl Eng 47:3
12. Dietz JLG (2006) Enterprise ontology, theory and methodology. Springer, Heidelberg
13. DEMO. The EEI DEMO methodology. http://www.ee-institute.org/en/demo
14. Liu K (2000) Semiotics in information systems engineering. Cambridge University Press, Cambridge
15. CLOSER. In: The international conference on cloud computing and service science. http://closer.scitevents.org
16. Habermas J (1981) Theorie des Kommunikatives Handelns. Erster Band, SuhrkampVerlag, Frankfurt am Main
17. Cobley P, Jansz L (2001) Introducing semiotics. Icon Books, Cambridge
18. Stamper R (2000) Organizational semiotics—information without the computer? In: Liu K, Clarke RJ, Andersen PB, Stamper RK (eds) Information, organization, and technology—studies in organizational semiotics. Kluwer, Amsterdam
19. Stamper R (1996) Signs, information, norms and systems. In: Holmqvist B, Andersen PB (eds) Signs of work: semiotics and information processing in organizations. Walter de Gruyter, New York
20. Pierce CS (1998) Principles of philosophy. In: Hartshorne C, Weiss P (eds) Collected papers of Charles Sanders Peirce. Thoemmes, Bristol
21. Gibson JJ (1979) The ecological approach to visual perception. Houghton Mifflin, Boston
22. Stamper R (1997) Organizational semiotics. In: Mingers J, Stowell F (eds) Information systems: an emerging discipline? McGraw-Hill, London
23. Stamper R, Liu K, Hafkamp M, Ades Y (1997) Signs plus norms—one paradigm for organizational semiotics. In: Proceedings of the 1st international workshop on computational semiotics, Paris, France, 26–27 May 1997
24. Stamper R (1992) Language and computer in organized behavior. In: van de Riet RP, Meersman RA (eds) Linguistic instruments in knowledge engineering. Elsevier Science, Amsterdam

Chapter 5
Computing Paradigms

As a starting point with regard to what will be presented in the current chapter, we consider the distinction between *procedure-oriented programming* and *object-oriented programming* [1, 2]:

- *Procedure-oriented programming* (or *procedural programming*) uses a list of instructions to tell the computer what to do step-by-step. *Procedural programming* relies on PROCEDURES—a *procedure* contains *a series of computational steps* to be carried out. *Procedural programming* is *intuitive* in the sense that it is very similar to how a person would expect a program to work: if one wants a computer to do something, one should provide step-by-step instructions on how this is to be done. Examples of *procedural languages* include the early programming languages, such as Fortran and COBOL, and later on—Pascal and C, which have been around in the 1960s, 1970s, 1980s, and 1990s.
- *Object-oriented programming* is an approach to problem-solving where all computations are carried out using **objects**. An *object* is a *component of a program* that "knows" how to perform certain actions and how to interact with other elements of the program. *Objects* are the basic units of *object-oriented programming*. A simple example of an *object* would be a person. Logically, one would expect a person to have a name. This would be considered a *property* of the person. One would also expect a person to be able to do something, such as walking, for example. This would be considered a *method* of the person. A *method* in *object-oriented programming* is like a *procedure* in *procedural programming* (the key difference is that the *method* is part of an *object*). Hence, in *object-oriented programming*, the code is to be organized by *creating objects*, giving those objects *properties*, and so on. A key aspect of *object-oriented programming* is the use of **classes**. A *class* is a blueprint of an *object*: a *class* can be considered as a concept and an *object*—as an embodiment of that concept. For example, if a person is to be considered in a program, then one should be able to describe the person and have the person do something. A class called "person" would provide a blueprint

© Springer Nature Switzerland AG 2020 107
B. Shishkov, *Designing Enterprise Information Systems*, The Enterprise Engineering
Series, https://doi.org/10.1007/978-3-030-22441-7_5

for what a person looks like and what a person can do. Examples of object-oriented languages include C++, Java, and so on.

A key difference between the two is that in procedural programming, procedures operate on data and the "procedure" and "data" concepts are two separate concepts while in object-oriented programming the corresponding concepts ("property" and "method") are bundled into objects. This makes it possible to create complicated behavior with less code. The use of objects also makes it possible to re-use code. Once one has created an object with complex behavior, one could use it anywhere in the code.

A further move to *component-oriented programming* has been inspired by those advantages [3]: With *object-oriented programming* focusing on the relationships between *classes* that are combined into one large binary executable, *component-oriented programming* focuses on interchangeable code modules that work independently and don't require you to be familiar with their inner workings to use them.

Thus, we observe an evolution

```
from procedure-oriented programming
through object-oriented programming
to component-oriented programming.
```

That evolution in *programming* has not only been useful as a stimulus to more effectively and efficiently producing code but it has also influenced the broader process of *software engineering* comprising requirements analysis, system analysis, system design, coding/implementation, and testing, with justifying an evolution from *monolithic software engineering* through *component-based software engineering* to *service-oriented software engineering* [1, 4]:

Developing a **monolithic** *application* assumes as a result monolithic binary code. It may be that one even applies *object-oriented programming* and still the bottom line is *monolithic* development—one may factor the business logic into many fine-grained *classes*; once those *classes* are compiled, if the final *application* is viewed that way (to be *monolithic*), then the result is *monolithic* binary code: all the *classes* share the same physical deployment unit (typically an EXE), process, address space, security privileges, and so on. Hence, if multiple developers work on the same code base, they have to share source *files*. Thus, in such an *application*, a change made to one *class* can trigger a massive relinking of the entire *application* and necessitate retesting and redeployment of all other *classes*.

In contrast, a **component-based** *application* comprises a collection of interacting binary application modules—that is its *components* and the calls that bind them. The motivation for breaking down a *monolithic application* into multiple binary *components* is analogous to that for placing the code for different *classes* into different *files*. By placing the code for each *class* in an *application* into its own *file*, one would loosen the coupling between the *classes* and the developers responsible for them. If one would make a change to one *class*, although one would have to relink the entire *application*, one would only need to recompile the source *file* for that *class*. Further, because a *component-based application* is a collection of binary building blocks, one can treat its *components* like LEGO bricks—simply "adding" and "removing" them. If one would need to modify a *component* implementation, changes are contained to that *component* only. No existing *client* of the *component* requires recompilation or redeployment. *Components* can even be updated while a *client application* is running, as long as the *components* are not currently being used. Improvements, enhancements, and fixes made to a *component* would immediately be available to all *applications* that use that *component*, whether on the same machine or across a *network*. Finally, when one has new requirements to implement, one can provide them in new *components*, without having to touch existing *components* not affected by the new requirements. All those advantages have contributed to the increasing popularity of *component-based* applications, compared to *monolithic* applications.

The next step in those developments was marked by the appearance of **service-oriented** *software*: *component-based* software is about how one would build and implement a *system*—taking the whole *system* and dividing it into smaller better manageable *components*, and so on, while *service orientation* is about how different *systems* communicate with each other, based on defined various standards for message formats, transport security, and so on. Hence, that is about allowing users to compose *services* at high level, which *services* are realized by underlying *software components*. The advantages here are twofold: (1) the technical complexity, characterizing *software components*, remains "hidden" from the user who is composing *services* at "higher level" and (2) a user can bring together *services* whose underlying *software components* may be created by different developers, running on different servers, and so on.

Thus, we observe an evolution

> **from monolithic software engineering**
> **through component-based software engineering**
> **to service-oriented software engineering.**

That *software engineering* evolution has not only been useful as a stimulus to more effectively and efficiently producing and utilizing software but it has also influenced in a broader perspective the *way of developing* and justifying an evolution from code-centric development through model-driven development to agile development [5]:

The **code-centric** development (considered in the past) would not support the analysis and design activities by means of *modeling* while the idea to use *models* for improving software development practices was gaining increasing popularity.

That has led to the emergence of **model-driven** development—it is not only about helping developers reason at "higher level" supported by *models* but is also about distinguishing between *computation-independent* and *technology-specific* issues being reflected in corresponding *model* types. This is considered to be a viable "bridge" between the "*Software World*" and the "*Real-life World*" in the sense that firstly, domain-related specifications are defined and secondly, those domain-related specifications are reflected, by means of model transformations, in corresponding platform-specific models, envisioning platforms, such as CORBA,

J2EE, .Net, and so on. Model-driven development is hence attractive for its capability of bringing together domain-specific issues and technology-specific issues, by
allowing for model transformations, as abovementioned. Nevertheless, the lack of
sufficient development flexibility and collaborativeness as well as the insufficient
capability to conveniently adapt modeling to changes has justified the need for new
development paradigms.

That has inspired the emergence of **agile** development that is based on iterative
development, where requirements and solutions evolve via collaboration between
self-organizing cross-functional teams. *Agile* processes fundamentally incorporate
iteration and the continuous feedback that it provides to successively refine and
deliver a software *system*. Hence, *agile* development is people-centric, in contrast to
model-driven development that is model-centric and also in contrast to code-centric
development.

Thus, we observe an evolution

> **from code-centric development**
> **through model-driven development**
> **to agile development.**

With regard to what was stated in the above paragraphs, it is to be noted that some
of the paradigms discussed assume *distributed* computing environments (e.g., *service-oriented* software engineering would envision the composition of *services*
realized by *components* running in different computing environments) while others
implicitly assume *mobility* (e.g., *agile* development would often envision dynamic
user feedback, possibly generated through *applications* running on *mobile* devices).
This has justified an evolution from *mainframe* infrastructures, through *client/server*
infrastructures, to *cloud* infrastructures [6, 7]:

A **mainframe** infrastructure is based on a mainframe and terminals. A mainframe can be looked upon as a "giant server" since only it serves "dumb" terminals; a
terminal has no drives, no independent operating system, and so on—it has just a
screen and a keyboard. All data of any type is contained in the mainframe. Any
information changed or added from a terminal would change the data in the
mainframe accordingly.

In contrast, a **client/server** infrastructure assumes the partitioning of tasks
or workloads between the providers of a resource or service, called *servers*, and
service requesters, called *clients*. Hence, those principles are underlying with regard
to current distributed computing environments. What such distributed computing
environments lack as capability nevertheless is enabling "outside" stakeholders to be
served, possibly through their portable devices connected to the Internet.

This has inspired the emergence of **cloud** infrastructures assuming the provision
of shared computer processing resources and data to computers and other devices on
demand. *Cloud* infrastructures have hence become underlying with regard to current
mobile computing environments.

Thus, we observe an evolution

> from mainframe infrastructures
> through client/server infrastructures
> to cloud infrastructures.

With respect to the paradigms considered above, most challenges mainly relate to functional issues. Nevertheless, there are non-functional **crosscutting concerns**, such as security, recoverability, logging, performance monitoring, and so on. In the past, this was considered as part of the requirements elicitation, then the label "*crosscutting concerns*" was dominant, and currently we speak of *aspect-oriented software development* considering *crosscutting concerns* (called "*aspects*") at all stages of the software development life cycle [8].

The computing paradigms discussed above (except for aspect-oriented software development) are presented in Fig. 5.1, reflecting their evolution over time.

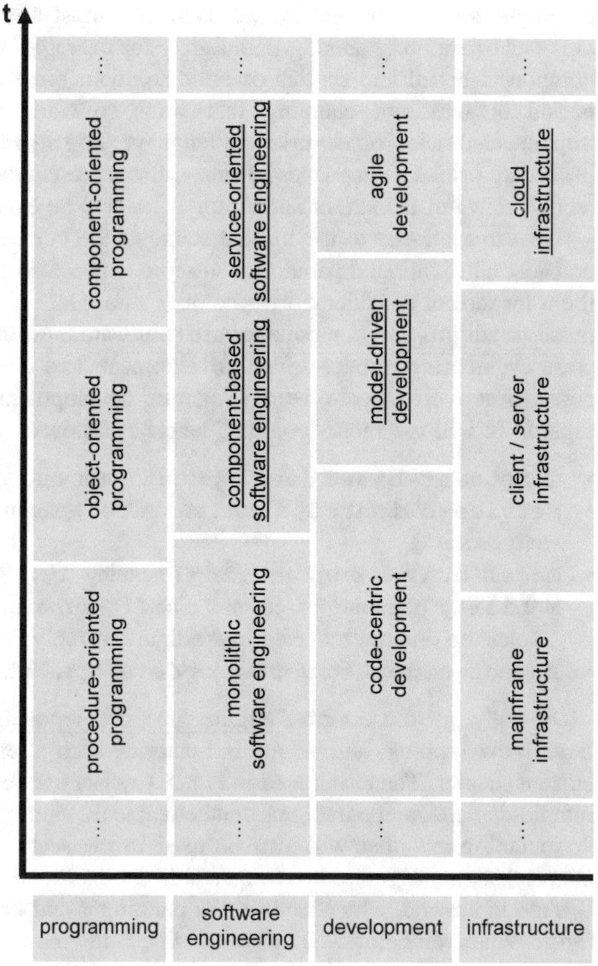

Fig. 5.1 Computing paradigms—evolution over time (©2017, The Author, reprinted with permission)

As it is seen on the figure and as discussed already, over time: programming's evolution comes through procedure orientation, object orientation, and component orientation; software engineering's evolution comes through monolithicity, component centricity, and service orientation; development's evolution comes through code centricity, model centricity, and agility; and infrastructure's evolution comes through mainframe solutions, client/server solutions, and cloud solutions. As it is seen as well on the figure, time-wise, the "evolution patterns" differ from category to category; for example, the step forward from monolithic software engineering to component-based software engineering is preceded by the step forward from procedure-oriented programming to object-oriented programming. Nonetheless, those representations in Fig. 5.1 are schematic and not numerically precise. Further, those "transitions" are claimed to be viewed differently by different members of the Software Community, and hence, there is no wide agreement on when exactly object-oriented programming has become "predominant" compared to procedure-oriented programming, when exactly service-oriented engineering has "replaced" component-based software engineering as the preferred software engineering paradigm, and so on. Finally, we claim that most often one would observe overlaps and/or mixtures among paradigms, for example, why not claiming that both component-based and service-oriented solutions were predominant in a particular period or why not claiming that some software applications have modules implemented using object-oriented languages and also modules implemented using procedure-oriented languages? Hence, that representation mainly reflects the subjective views of the author and is not claimed to be exhaustive.

Next to that, due to the limited scope of the current chapter, we are unable to consider all mentioned paradigms in more detail. Still, we have selected several of them for further consideration—the ones whose labels are underlined in the figure; those paradigms are: component-based software engineering, service-oriented software engineering, model-driven development, and cloud infrastructures. We will consider as well aspect-oriented software development, mentioned above. In this regard, we will use more "popular" labels as follows:

- **Component-based development** (meaning "*software development*").
- **Service-oriented architecture** (meaning reference to "*software engineering*").
- **Model-driven engineering** (meaning "*development*").
- **Mobility** (meaning based on a *cloud infrastructure*).
      plus the one not reflected in the figure, namely:
- **Aspect-oriented software development**.

Actually, all those terms, engineering, development, architecture, are de facto largely overlapping, and we are not entering such a terminology discussion in the current chapter. The terms used in Fig. 5.1 reflect our desire to be maximum clear in mentioning different paradigms that belong to the same category. The *corresponding* "popular" terms (that will also be used in the sections belonging to the current chapter) are supposed to be recognizable for the broad audience.

And in the end, why exactly those paradigms and not other ones reflected in the figure will be elaborated? The bottom line is the relevance to *EIS* in general and to the *enterprise-modeling-driven software generation*, in particular. **Business coMponents** have been considered in the previous chapters as a desired basis for specifying software. For this reason, in our computing paradigms consideration, we would emphasize those paradigms that are relevant to the **component-based enterprise-software alignment**. This brings us to **components** (*component-based development*) and **services** (*service-oriented architecture*) that are claimed to be useful relevant units of re-use. Further, we would emphasize on **model-driven** *engineering* because we believe that the only way to bring those two worlds (*enterprises* and *software*) together is through corresponding *models*. Finally, we would emphasize on **mobility** and **non-functional cross-cutting concerns** because we claim that they have essential importance for any current EIS and thus have to be explicitly considered and reflected in the specification of software.

For this reason, in the sections that follow we will consider *component-based development, service-oriented architecture, model-driven engineering, mobility (emphasizing on cloud computing)*, and *aspect-oriented software development*.

5.1   Component-Based Development

C̲omponent-B̲ased D̲evelopment (**CBD**) is considered to be a promising paradigm that addresses the design and development of ICT *applications* and is founded on the principles of *object orientation* [1]—*object orientation* (characterized by the fundamental concepts of *encapsulation, classification, inheritance,* and *polymorphism*) that was briefly discussed already is widely recognized as a special approach to the construction of models of complex *systems*, in which a *system* consists of a large number of *objects*. Those principles are reflected in the *component* concept. Hence, **components** are essential with regard to *CBD*—if re-usable *components* are identified, they can be used many times for designing different *applications*. Next to that, *CBD* seems beneficial for the *application* design itself. By basing *application* development on encapsulated, individually definable, re-usable, replaceable, interoperable, and testable (*software*) *components*, developers can build *applications* which possess durable configuration and a high degree of flexibility and maintainability. The process of *application* development would also be improved because building new *applications* would include using already developed *components*. This reduces development time and improves reliability. The performance and maintenance of developed *applications* would be enhanced because changes could occur in the implementation of any *component* without affecting the entire *application*. All this makes *CBD* reliable and effective.

All this further justifies the claim that *business coMponents* can be useful as basis for specifying *component-based applications* (see Chap. 2). By basing the design of *applications* on *software components* derived in turn from *business coMponents*, the *application* support to *business processes* can be improved considerably [1].

Hence, CBD has strengths reaching beyond the *application* development itself—the *component-based application development* can as well usefully support the *enterprise-modeling*-driven generation of *software*.

The idea of constructing modular software *systems* dates back to 1968, as according to Stojanovic [4], and referring to two complexity-avoidance approaches of that time is important, they are *"buy before build"* and *"re-use before buy"*. This way of thinking is considered to be an essential bottom line with regard to current *CBD* and this was even before the ideas of *object-orientation* (see above) have appeared. Anyway, during the 1990s, *CBD* has established itself as a natural extension and an evolution of *object orientation*. *Components* have firstly been introduced at the implementation level for fastly building graphical interfaces using *visual basic eXtension* controls and then we have seen the *Component Object Model* of *Microsoft*, the *CORBA* components, and *Enterprise Java Beans components*—all of them proposed as "standard" *component-based* implementation solutions. This has contributed to a shift of emphasis from developing small, centralized, monolithic *systems* to developing complex *systems* consisting of functional units deployed over nodes of the Web, and two key concepts have emerged, namely, (1) *components as large-grain building blocks of a system* and (2) *architectures and frameworks as blueprints of the system describing its main building blocks and the way of composing them into a coherent whole* [4]. That conceptual evolution has been reflected in several widely popular *component* **definitions**:

- According to Szyperski [3], *a software component is a unit of composition with contractually specified interfaces and explicit context dependencies; a software component can be deployed independently and is subject to composition by a third party.*
- According to Lewandowski [9], *a component is defined as the smallest self-managing, independent, and useful part of a system that works in multiple environments.*
- According to Stahl et al. [5], *a component is a self-contained piece of software with clearly defined interfaces and explicitly declared context dependencies.*

We argue that those definitions further justify *Definitions 13* and *14* (see Chap. 2) and also our way of looking at a *software component* from two perspectives, namely, taking a *constructional* view and taking a *functional* view:

- CONSTRUCTIONALLY, software components are *implemented pieces of software*, which represent *parts of an ICT application* and which *collaborate among each other* driven by the *goal* of *realizing the functionality of the application*.
- FUNCTIONALLY, a software component is a *part of an ICT application*, which is *self-contained, customizable*, and *composable*, possessing a *clearly defined function and interfaces* to the other parts of the application and which also *can be deployed independently*.

It is to be noted however that even though all above definitions suggest essentially the same view on *software components*, they differ with regard to the perspective taken. What is to be taken into account in the current chapter is the explicit *EIS* focus we are following, and this assumes that (1) software is specified based on *business coMponents* (see Chap. 2) and (2) software is delivered mainly in terms of ICT *applications*.

Hence, we <u>summarize</u> what we consider essential with regard to *software components*, taking into account the above-stated perspective:

- **A software component is an implemented piece of software.**
- **A software component is a part of an ICT application.**
- **A software component is self-contained.**
- **A software component possesses a clearly defined function and goal (in context).**
- **A software component possesses clearly defined interfaces to the other parts of the ICT application.**
- **A software component can be deployed independently.**
- **A software component can work in multiple ICT applications and in multiple environments.**

Hence, establishing the way the *component* notion and the *object* notion relate to each other is important, and for that we refer to the studies of Stojanovic [4] where *components* are considered as *larger-grained objects* that are deployed and as such they would "reveal" one or more *classes* "inside." It is thus concluded that **granularity** is the main issue in distinguishing *components* and *objects*. Further, if *objects* are identifiable *instances* of *classes*, then *component instances* (representing programming language *objects*) are *instances* of *component types*. Hence, *components* have much in common with *classes*. Nevertheless, there are some significant differences:

- *Classes* represent <u>logical abstractions</u> while *components* represent <u>physical things</u>.
- *Components* represent the <u>physical packaging</u> of otherwise logical elements and are at a <u>different level of abstraction</u> than *classes*.
- *Classes* may have *attributes* and *operations* <u>accessible directly</u>, in general, and *components* have operations that are reachable <u>only through</u> *component* interfaces.

Therefore, a *component* is a <u>physical thing</u> that conforms to and realizes a set of <u>interfaces</u>. Internally, a *component* may be implemented <u>by a single class</u>, <u>by multiple classes</u>, or even <u>by traditional procedures</u> in a *procedure-oriented programming language*.

For this reason, an explicit discussion is necessary on *component* **interfaces**.

As already suggested, a *component* is an encapsulated unit with a completely hidden behavior behind an *interface*. As studied by Stojanovic [4], the *interface* provides an explicit separation between the *outside* and the *inside* of a *component*, by:

- Answering the question *WHAT*—What useful services are provided by the *component* to the *context* of its existence?

- Not answering the question *HOW*—How are those service actually realized?

We relate that to the *black-box* and *white-box* perspectives, respectively, as discussed already (see Fig. 2.9). A precisely defined *interface* allows for using the behavior (services) delivered by the *component* without knowing how that behavior is actually realized. Said otherwise, the *component* "interior" remains hidden (and not important) for the *component's environment* as long as the *component* provides services, following the constraints defined by its contractual *interface*—it is often that the *interface* reflects the only information that shows the *component's* "user" what the *component* actually does.

An *interface* is defined by Szyperski [3] as *a named collection of operations that are used to specify a service of a class or a component*, hence defining a *component interface* as *a specification of the component's access point*.

Thus, if a *component* has <u>multiple access points</u>, each of which represents a different service offered by the *component*, then the *component* would be expected to have <u>multiple</u> *interfaces*.

Further, an *interface* offers <u>no implementation of any of its operations</u>; instead, it merely <u>names a collection of operations</u> and provides their descriptions—it is hence possible to replace the implementation part without changing the *interface* [4]. Following Stojanovic further:

- A PROVIDED *interface* points to the services and operations that the *component* provides to its *environment*, in realizing its *function*.
- A REQUIRED *interface* specifies the services and operations that the *component* requires from its *environment*, in order to realize its *function*.

According to [2], any *interface* would have four *attributes*:

- **Name** (each *component interface* is to have a unique name).
- **Keys** (they are based on the search record definition of the *component*).
- **Properties** (they relate to the record fields of the *component*).
- **Methods** (a method is like a function that can perform a specific task according to corresponding requirements).

Finally, we claim the following: FIRSTLY, in order to make an interoperable *component* feasible, it is necessary to consider a corresponding **component implementation model,** and in Sect. 5.1.1, we present three popular and widely accepted *component implementation models*, namely, the *Microsoft Component Model*, the *Enterprise Java Beans Component Model*, and the *CORBA Component Model*, as according to Stojanovic [4]. SECONDLY, with an implementation technology not being sufficient by itself for adequately developing *component-based applications*, methods and approaches are needed for establishing how to reflect business requirements in the design and development of such *applications*—this we refer to as **component-based development methods,** and in Sect. 5.1.2, we present three popular and widely considered *component-based development methods*, namely, the *Rational Unified Process*, *KobrA*, and *Catalysis*, as according to Shishkov [1].

5.1.1 Component Implementation Models

In the current sub-section, we will consider firstly the *Microsoft Component Model*, secondly the *Enterprise Java Beans Component Model*, and thirdly the *CORBA Component Model*.

Microsoft Component Model

The **Component Object Model,** or **COM** for short, is a *language-independent*, *binary component standard* [10] whose core concepts include:

- A binary standard for function calling between *components*.
- The typed grouping of functions into *interfaces*.
- A base *interface* providing mechanisms for (1) other *components* to dynamically discover the *interfaces* implemented by a *component* and (2) a reference counter, allowing *components* to track their own "lifetime" and delete themselves when appropriate.
- A globally unique identifier mechanism for *components* and their *interfaces*.
- A *component* loader to set up and manage *component* interactions.

COM provides as well mechanisms for shared memory management between *components* and also error and status reporting. In *COM*, an *interface* is represented as a pointer to an *interface node,* and in turn, the *interface node* contains a pointer to a table of operation variables and those variables in turn point to the actual implementation of the operations.

Enterprise Java Beans Component Model

The **Enterprise Java Beans Component Model,** or **EJB** for short, is a *server-side component* model for the development of *applications* in the programming language *Java* [11], where a *component* is called an *enterprise bean*. Further, there are two kinds of *enterprise beans*:

- *Session enterprise beans* (those are transient *components* that exist only during a single client/server session).
- *Entity enterprise beans* (those are persistent *components* that control permanent data kept in permanent data stores, such as databases).

Moreover, an *enterprise bean* resides inside a *container* with a *container* in turn consisting of a deployment environment for *enterprise beans*. Further, the *container* provides a number of services for each *enterprise bean*, such as life-cycle management, state management, transaction management, and so on. Next to that, an *EJB* server provides a runtime environment for one or more *containers*.

Finally, the client *application* interacts with the *enterprise bean*, by using two *interface types* that are generated by the *container*, namely, (1) *home interface* (it can be used by clients to create, destroy, or find an existing *enterprise bean instance*) and (2) *object interface* (it provides access to the application methods of the *enterprise bean*).

CORBA Component Model

The **CORBA Component Model,** or **CCM** for short, is a *server-side component* model extending the CORBA core *object* model with a deployment model; *CCM* is as well providing a higher level of abstraction for CORBA and *object* services; the two major advances introduced by the *CCM* are a *component* model and a runtime *environment* model; and a *component* is an extension and specialization of a CORBA *object* [12]. As for the model of a CORBA component type:

* Any CORBA *component* is denoted by a *component* reference.
* CORBA *components* support a variety of surface features, called ports, through which clients and other elements of an *application environment* may interact with those *components*.

This is presented on Fig. 5.2, inspired by Stojanovic [4]:

Fig. 5.2 CORBA component (©2017, The Author, reprinted with permission)

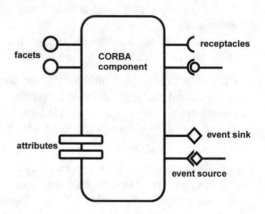

As seen from the figure, there are five different kinds of *ports*:

* *Facets*—they are *interfaces* provided by the *component* for client interactions.
* *Receptacles*—they are connection points that describe the *interfaces* used by the *component*.
* *Event sources*—they are connection points that emit events of a specified type to interested event consumers.
* *Event sinks*—they are connection points into which events of a specified type are announced.
* *Attributes*—they are named values primarily used for *component* configurations.

Further, a *component* may have multiple *facets*, *receptacles*, *event sources*, *event sinks*, and *attributes*.

Finally, there are four categories of *components*, as studied by Stojanovic [4]:

* *Service components*—they are stateless, have no identity, and support a single invocation per instance.
* *Session components*—they have a transient state, have no persistent identity, and support more than one invocations per instance.

- *Process components*—they have an explicitly declared state that is managed by the runtime environment, have an identity managed by the client, and have a behavior that may be transactional.
- *Entity components*—they are similar to process components, except for their identity which is visible to the client but managed by the runtime environment.

In summary, in the current sub-section, we have briefly presented three popular *component implementation models*; in the following sub-section, as already mentioned, we will consider three popular *component-based development methods*.

5.1.2 Component-Based Development Methods

In the current sub-section, we will consider firstly the *Rational Unified Process*, secondly *KobrA*, and thirdly *Catalysis*.

Rational Unified Process

The `Rational Unified Process,` or `RUP` for short, is not only the development process usually applied with *UML* (the *Unified Modeling Language*) but also a useful development method (process) as far as *component-based development* is concerned, which method covers the entire software development life cycle [13].

The key *RUP* concept is the definition of *activities*, called *workflows*, throughout the development life cycle, such as requirements elicitation, analysis, design, implementation, and testing. Unlike the classical *waterfall* process, those *activities* can be overlapping and performed in parallel [4]. Within each of the *activities*, there are well-defined stages of inception, elaboration, and transition. A support to *component-based development* is encouraged even though that support is just declarative and implicit, being directed towards physical packaging, as it can be seen from the RUP's defining a *component* as a *"nontrivial, nearly independent, and replaceable part of a system that fulfils a clear function in the context of a well-defined architecture and that conforms to and provides the physical realization of a set of interfaces."* Finally, one of the main advantages of *RUP* is that it provides an opportunity for iterative and incremental *system* development, which is seen as the best development practice [4].

KobrA

Our analysis featuring `KobrA` has been supported mainly by the following two sources: [14, 15]. Interested readers could find there information about all concepts related to *KobrA*, which have not been considered in the current sub-section.

The *KobrA* method is a state-of-the-art approach to *component-based* product-line engineering with *UML*. Among the key characteristics of *KobrA* are architecture-centricity, systematic *COTS component* re-use, and integrated quality assurance. The major strengths of *KobrA* are its overall consistency, the embracement of the *component* concept in all phases of the software life cycle, and the UML-based graphical specification of *components*. The main limitation is that there are no clear guidelines on how to relate the specification of software to a prior *enterprise analysis and modeling*.

A complementary workbench has been developed to support the use of the *KobrA* method in conjunction with commercial *CASE* tools. A test bed for the approach has been provided in the domain of *enterprise resource planning*.

KobrA is conceptually based on the foundation of *product-line engineering*. Said otherwise, *product-line engineering* is an inherent part of the *KobrA* method. When pursuing a *product-line* approach in *KobrA*, the overall software life cycle consists of two basic *product line engineering* activities (we would briefly introduce them, before proceeding further):

- *Framework engineering*. It applies the *komponent* (*komponent* means *component* as seen from the perspective of the method *KobrA*) modeling and implementation activities, accompanied by additional sub-activities for handling variabilities and decision models, to support a family of similar *applications* (i.e., development for re-use). A framework therefore contains a generic *komponent* tree that captures the common and variable characteristics of a *product line*.
- *Application engineering*. It uses the framework developed during framework engineering to build particular *applications*. Since one of the goals of *application* engineering is to remove the variabilities in the framework, and resolve the decisions in the decision model, *komponent* containment trees for *applications* are very similar to those for a single *system*. The only difference is that *komponents* are accompanied by a decision model instance, which captures the decisions made in resolving the decision model for a particular *komponent*.

Based on the (above outlined) brief information about *KobrA*, we will come (below) through some basic principles and issues characterizing the method.

A core principle of *KobrA* is the strict and systematic separation of concerns, so that at all times during a development project, developers are aware of what they should be attempting to do and what *concern* they are working on. A manifestation of this principle in *KobrA* is in the separation of the *product* from the *process* (contrary to methods which arbitrarily mix the description of *what* engineers should be trying to produce with the definition of *how* they should produce it). Another fundamental separation of concerns in *KobrA* is the organization of the method in terms of three orthogonal dimensions of development: one dealing with the *level of abstraction*, one dealing with the *level of genericity*, and one dealing with *composition*.

At the largest level of *granularity*, the *product-line* paradigm takes precedence in *KobrA*. This *splits the overall development cycle into two parts*: (1) one dealing with the development of a framework, a re-usable set of software artifacts whose core is embedded within all products developed by the *enterprise*, and (2) the other one concerned with the development of an application—a concrete instance of the framework, adapted and extended to meet the needs of a specific customer.

At the intermediate level of *granularity*, *KobrA* is driven by the *component* paradigm. *KobrA* frameworks and *applications* are all organized in terms of hierarchies of *components*. However, the *components* in *KobrA* represent the *logical* building blocks of a software *system* (not *physical components*, as in *CORBA*—see above).

A central goal of *KobrA* is to enable the full expressive power of the *UML* to be used in the modeling of *components*. To this end, the use of the *UML* in *KobrA* is driven by four basic principles:

* *Uniformity*. Every behavior-rich entity is treated as a *komponent*, and every *komponent* is treated uniformly, regardless of its *granularity* or location in the containment tree.
* *Encapsulation*. The description of *what* a software unit does is separated from the description of *how* it does it.
* *Locality*. All descriptive artifacts represent the properties of a *komponent* from a *local perspective* rather than a global perspective.
* *Parsimony*. Every descriptive artifact should have "*just enough*" information, no more and no less.

As for the *KobrA* life cycle, at the highest level of *granularity*, this life cycle is composed of a sequence of phases in which new versions of the central framework are developed and new applications are instantiated from it to meet the expectations of new customers.

In summary, the strict *separation of concerns* makes *KobrA* compatible with a large number of practical implementation and middleware technologies. Its embracing the *component* paradigm allows for adequately benefiting from re-use possibilities. Its being soundly founded on the principles of the *product-line engineering* provides a good theoretical foundation. Its consistency with *UML* results in a specification of software, which is fully in tune with the current software design standards.

We outline as a limitation nonetheless the way *KobrA* is addressing the very early software specification tasks and in particular the relation to the original *enterprise system* that is to be supported by the software-to-be. As mentioned before, *there are no clear guidelines how to relate the specification of software to a prior enterprise analysis and modeling*. This could be improved either by extending *KobrA* "backwards" (towards a consideration of *enterprise* modeling) or by combining it with an enterprise modeling tool.

Catalysis

Our analysis featuring **Catalysis** has been supported mainly by the following source: [16]. Interested readers could find there information about all concepts related to *Catalysis*, which have not been considered in this sub-section.

Catalysis is a method for *component-based* and *object-oriented* software development, which provides a strongly coherent set of techniques for *enterprise* analysis (characterized by unambiguity about requirements) and *system* development using *UML* as well as a coherent method for *object-oriented* analysis and design. *Catalysis* provides also well-defined consistency rules across models and powerful mechanisms for composing different views to describe complex *systems*.

Catalysis is specifically targeted as a method for *component-based* development, in which <u>families of products are assembled from kits of</u> *components*. The method also allows for <u>re-use of other artifacts of the design process</u>, such as frameworks of collaboration between *objects*.

Catalysis includes techniques to *map* between (*UML*-based) *system* design artifacts and analysis models. The gap and inconsistencies are reduced by:

- Unambiguous *interface* specification.
- Techniques to define powerful *component* "connectors" abstracting above the level of *object-oriented* messages.
- "Retrieval" techniques for relating the differing models that different *components* (especially bought-in or *legacy components*) usually have (e.g., this might include different notions of what a customer is).

Use cases [1] have a central role in *Catalysis*; they are applied at different abstraction levels. With each decomposition, the *objects* interact to fulfill the goals of the more abstract *use cases*.

The *Catalysis* method basically comes through the following *phases*:

- A <u>model of the domain</u> is produced, specifying firstly what *objects* are there and secondly the goals which are associated with the major *use cases*.
- <u>Scenarios</u> are drawn up on how (certain) *component* could help realizing the major *use cases*, breaking them down into individual steps.
- Viewing <u>a *component* as a specification</u> (that would be possible because at this stage it is to be known what a *component* is supposed to do). The *component* has some defined responsibilities and defined collaborations with the actors around it.
- <u>*Component's* responsibilities</u> are distributed among *objects* inside it and also, interactions between *components* are defined (*use cases* are used for that goal). It is possible (if necessary) defining generic interactions among *components*, so that they are made "pluggable." This is done through template models.

Thus, essential <u>*characteristics*</u> of the *Catalysis* method are:

- Usability of generic chunks of software with robust, well-defined *interfaces*. The <u>dynamic coupling of</u> *components* is just one form of re-use. Other forms include the <u>import of a generic chunk of design</u> into many other designs. In this sense, a "*component*" can include any piece of development work (code, models, rules, design patterns, and so on).
- Issues which concern the <u>*inter-component connections*</u>—"connectors" play a significant role in this task. They are specified independently of the specification featuring (relevant) *components*. Like *objects*, <u>connectors are encapsulated</u>: the specification of what one achieves is independent of its implementation.
- Software development evolving firstly through the rapid <u>assembly of end products from</u> *components* and secondly through the <u>development of high-quality</u> *components*.

In *Catalysis*, there are particular _validation mechanisms_. The validation suite is a set of *ancillary components* for two purposes: (1) some of them test a *component* once it is installed in a particular *context*, to ensure it is running properly, and (2) others are test versions of *components,* exercising the *components* they are connected to, to make sure they behave as required.

According to Shishkov [1], *Catalysis* has certain _limitations_, particularly as it concerns the proper alignment between *enterprise* modeling and software specification since:

- The method does not offer a solid mechanism for the reflection of the original business requirements in the specification of the software functionality—that is because *Catalysis* is not rooted in any way in any *social theory* that would have allowed for a better grasp of real-life aspects.
- *Catalysis* is insufficiently focused as it concerns *re-use*, considering for *re-use* not only *components* but also pieces of code, rules, and so on—this would assume thorough multi-perspective *re-use* guidelines and such guidelines are not available.
- *Catalysis* is insufficiently capable of grasping human-to-human communication, similarly to *KobrA*.

In summary, we have considered *CBD*, touching upon its main characteristics, the *component* notion, *component* implementation models, and *component-based* development methods. In the following section, we will consider *service orientation*.

5.2   Service-Oriented Architecture

S̲ervice-O̲riented A̲rchitecture (SOA) is considered to be a promising paradigm building upon *CBD*, which shifts the focus from the operation of a software *component* to the **service** the *component* is delivering to its user(s) [17].

Our analysis on *SOA* has been supported mainly by the following source: [18].

SOA was originally motivated by the need of *enterprises* to better match *information systems* to the enterprise goals, combined with the market trend towards more and more flexible cross-organizational collaborations between enterprises [19]. Vertical integration (*business-IT alignment*) and horizontal integration (*IT-supported cross-organizational collaboration*) are considered crucial for current *enterprises*, but traditional IT architectures have serious integration deficiencies. Architectures often comprise monolithic (silo) *applications* that are effective as it concerns the specific purpose they were created for but which do not allow integration without custom coded connections. Architectures with *component-based applications* provide units of business logic, which ease the definition of connections but still require that the flow of control and the transformation of data formats are bound into the business logic.

SOA is an *IT architectural style* that tries to achieve integration by way of **defining composite applications as an orchestration of services**, with *services* potentially offered by different organizations. A *service* externalizes public functions of an *application* that implements a repeatable business task. Since a composite *application* can also be offered as a *service*, integration may involve *multiple levels of composition*, and a *service* can be internal to an organization or cross-organizational.

Those issues will be addressed in the remaining of this section, by (1) surveying (in Sect. 5.2.1) the concepts and architectural elements of *SOA* and (2) briefly discussing (in Sect. 5.2.2) *web services* that constitute one of the widely adopted technologies to implement *SOA*.

5.2.1 SOA Foundations

The central concept of *SOA*, the *service* concept, has several interpretations, partly due to the fact that *SOA* addresses two distinct disciplines, namely, *enterprise engineering* and *software engineering*, and each of those two disciplines has been considering the *service* notion in its own perspective:

- In an *enterprise context*, a *service* involves the exchange of some action or performance for value between a client and a provider [17]. Examples are transportation *services*, health *services*, education *services*, outsourcing *services*, and helpdesk *services*.
- In an *IT context*, a *service* refers to the external behavior of an IT *system*, as can be observed and experienced by the users of that *system* [20]. Examples are data communication *services* and application *services*.

For convenience, we will use the terms *business service* and *IT service* to distinguish between the *enterprise* view and the IT view on *services*.

SOA holds the promise to bring business and IT together, by repeated aggregation of *IT services* into composite *applications* supporting *business services* that in turn are aggregated into *business processes* [21]. Figure 5.3 shows **the basic architectural pattern that underlies SOA**. In this pattern, three roles are distinguished: *service provider*, *service broker*, and *service requestor* [22]. A *service provider* offers one or more *services*, which may be implemented using arbitrary technologies and involving *backend systems* protected by a firewall. Each *service* has well-defined *interfaces* referred to in a *service* description. *Service* descriptions may be published with a *service broker*, thus opening the possibility for *service requestors* to find *services* by providing required *service* properties to the *service broker*. The *service broker* searches for *service* descriptions that satisfy the required *service* properties, and the *service requestor* can select from the result of this search. Based on the location/access details in the *service* description, the *service requestor* can then bind to a *service provider* that offers the selected *service*. After a successful binding, the *service requestor* can invoke the *service*, according to the *interface* details in the *service* description.

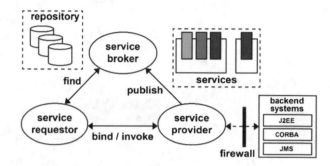

Fig. 5.3 The basic SOA pattern (Source: [18], p. 5; ©2009, SCITEPRESS, reprinted with permission)

Using this pattern, *vertical integration* is tackled by presenting a *service* as a virtual *component* that can be implemented by alternative concrete *components* using different technologies. The *service requestor* is therefore decoupled from the implementation concerns of the *service provider*. Using *SOA* for *application* design and providing a *service* wrapping for legacy *applications* thus presents a viable approach to *enterprise application integration*.

The *business-to-business integration* requires that each potential business partner defines a public view on its private process, with corresponding *services* and associated incoming and outgoing message exchanges that allow linking to external partners. The previously presented basic *SOA* pattern only shows a single *service provider* and a single *service requestor* role. In a *business-to-business* collaboration scenario, business partners may play either role for any number of supported *services*. An individual partner coordinates the *services* used and provided through its private process. Since this in general does not determine the overall coordination involving all partners, a **coordination protocol** can be defined that concerns the public view on how the partners should work together. Such a *coordination protocol* does not provide a concrete and executable process for the coordination of a service. It only defines the order in which messages should be exchanged, where messages are used to invoke a *service* or return a *service* result in accordance to a *service* provided by one of the partners. A definition at this level of abstraction is also referred to as *service* **choreography**; see Fig. 5.4 (up):

Fig. 5.4 Service choreography and service orchestration (©2017, The Author, reprinted with permission)

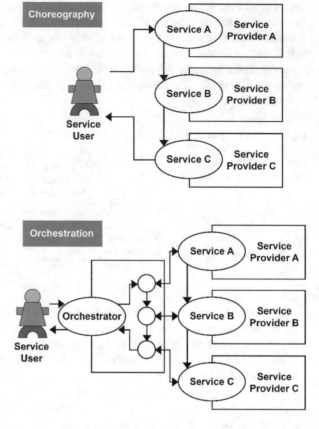

Said otherwise, the *choreography* reflects the collaboration among different *services*. *Services* participating in the *choreography* may belong to different providers; the aim is that the participating *services* collaborate to implement a *business process* [23]. In Fig. 5.4 (up), the *business process* consists (for example) of three different *services*. The *service user* triggers the *business process*, by invoking *Service A* with a request. *Service A* processes the *user* request and then invokes *Service B*. *Service B* processes the request from *Service A* and then invokes *Service C*. *Service C* processes the request from *Service B* and then sends the result to the *service user*.

It is to be noted that we use the term SERVICE REQUESTOR in Fig. 5.3 and we use the term SERVICE USER in Fig. 5.4. Those terms are not conflicting, and we use different terms because both figures mentioned above reflect a simplified view on reality. In Fig. 5.3, we recognize a *service requestor*, emphasizing on the role of formulating a request, searching for candidate *services*, making a selection, and binding to a corresponding *service provider*. We abstract from the fact that the same entity requesting the *service* is then the *service user*. In Fig. 5.4, we abstract from the request formulation, *service* discovery, and so on, emphasizing on the role of using the selected *service(s)*.

It is to be noted also that in Chap. 2, a *business process* is defined as a "structure of (connected) *transactions* that are executed in order to fulfill a *starting transaction*" (*Definition 6*), while what we discuss above concerns a structure of (connected) *services* that are executed in order to fulfill a *"starting" service*. How would then the *transaction* and *service* concepts relate to each other and how would the *business process* and *choreography* concepts relate to each other? Answering those questions is considered challenging because of the following reasons:

- The notion of *transaction* is not only grounded in *enterprise engineering* but is also reflected in a pattern (Fig. 4.4), while the notion of *service* addresses two distinct disciplines—*enterprise engineering* and *software engineering*, as mentioned above, leading to different interpretations.
- Within a *business process* as in line with *Definition 6*, a *starting transaction* is triggered and possibly, in order for it to be executed, it is necessary that another *transaction* is triggered, and this is done by the *executor* (*producer*) of the *starting transaction*—it is the *executor* who *initiates* the second *transaction*, and the *executor* of the second *transaction* (in turn) might need to *initiate* a third *transaction*, and so on. Then, each result is delivered to the corresponding *transaction initiator* which means that the result of the second *transaction* would be delivered to the *executor* of the *starting transaction* who in turn would deliver the final result to the *customer (user)*. In contrast, the collaboration among *services*, as presented above, is not that elaborate as the collaboration among *transactions* since we go as far as establishing that the *starting service invokes* another *service* which in turn *invokes* yet another *service*, and so on. Further, when we consider a collaboration among *transactions* part of a *business process*, it is the *starting transaction* that delivers the result to the *customer*, while in the *service choreography*, it is the last *service* being *invoked* that delivers the result to the *customer*, as illustrated above.

For this reason, we allow ourselves to use the term *business process* in the *service choreography* context only under the condition that we make it explicit that even though similarities can be found, a *"choreography of services"* is not the same as a *"business process of transactions."*

What we consider conceptually closer to transactions-driven *business processes* is *service* **orchestration**—see Fig. 5.4 (down)—assuming that the overall coordination (concerning the collaborative behavior of different *services*) is assigned to and executed in a centralized way by some computing node [18].

As in *service choreography*, also in *service orchestration*, the *services* (participating in the *orchestration*) may belong to different providers. The difference is nonetheless that in an *orchestration*, those *services* are coordinated from a central entity, the **orchestrator**; the *orchestrator invokes* each *service* according to a given strategy. We considered a *choreography* example featuring three *services* (see Fig. 5.4 (up)), and we now consider an *orchestration* example featuring the same three *services* (see Fig. 5.4 (down)). As it is seen from the figure, in the *orchestration* case, *services* are coordinated by another *service*, the *composite service* (called *"orchestrator"*)—this *service* defines the composition of the *services* participating in the *business process*. The *service user* triggers the *business process*, by *invoking* the *orchestrator*. Once the *orchestrator* receives the *user* request, the first action it takes is to *invoke Service A*, and *Service A* would respond in turn with a message. Then (based on this response) the *orchestrator* would *invoke Service B*, and *Service B* would respond in turn with a message. Then (based on this response) the *orchestrator* would *invoke Service C*, and *Service C* would respond in turn with a message. Then (based on this response) the *orchestrator* would deliver the result to the *service user*. It was stated above that *service orchestration* is conceptually closer to *transactions*-driven *business processes* (compared to *service choreography*) because similarly to how a customer approaches the *executor* of a *starting transaction* and in the end the *executor* of the *starting transaction* would deliver the result to the customer (no matter how many other *transactions* the *executor* of the *starting transaction* would have (directly or indirectly) triggered in order to be able to *execute* the *starting transaction*), the *service user* approaches the *orchestrator*, and in the end the *orchestrator* would deliver the result to the *service user* (no matter how many *services* the *orchestrator* would have triggered in order to be able to respond to the request of the *service user*).

In order to illustrate the patterns discussed above (the basic *SOA* pattern, Fig. 5.3, the *choreography* pattern, Fig. 5.4 (up), and the *orchestration* pattern, Fig. 5.4 (down)), we use the following simple real-life examples:

Example 1 *Jamall Caribbean Custom Tailors* (service provider) are active in the Toronto area in Canada; they have advertised their services at *http://www. yellowpages.ca*. *John* lives in Toronto; *he has ripped his trousers* (service user) and discovers *Jamall Caribbean Custom Tailors'* services in *Yellowpages*—Canada. Then *John* would contact *Jamall Caribbean Tailors*, discussing the problem and negotiating the conditions about their fixing his trousers. Once they reach an agreement, *John* would bring his ripped trousers to the nearest collection desk of *Jamall Caribbean Custom Tailors* whose rules on handling orders would be dominant and *John* would have to adapt to the conditions of their services. Those conditions concern questions, such as: For how many days this order would be handled? Are weekend days counted? What is the extra pay for a priority order? What are the compensations for damage on the clothing? and so on. Those conditions *John* must have discussed with them during the abovementioned negotiations. This example points to the basic SOA pattern.

Example 2 *Hristo* is Bulgarian; he lives in Sofia, Bulgaria; and he has a PhD degree from Delft University of Technology in The Netherlands. Hristo is appointed as assistant professor at the Bulgarian Academy of Sciences, and for this he needs a *legalization of his PhD degree*. He applies for this at *Delft University of Technology*, by (1) submitting via e-mail a scanned copy of a filled-out and signed form and (2) transferring a corresponding fee. Then:

- SERVICE 1

  - A representative of *Delft University of Technology* (Delft) would issue a duplicate of the diploma, send it to the *DUO* Agency of the Dutch Ministry of Education (Groningen), and pay on behalf of the university a processing fee to *DUO*.

- SERVICE 2

  - A representative of *DUO* (Groningen) would match the information in the document to corresponding information in their databases, and if all is OK, the person would apply on behalf of *DUO* a sticker at the back of the document, send the document to the *courthouse in Groningen*, and then pay on behalf of *DUO* a processing fee to the *court*.

- SERVICE 3

  - A representative of the *court* (Groningen) would check the details in the document and the details of the diploma holder in the Dutch registries, and if all is OK, the person would apply an apostille on the document and send the document to *Hristo*.

This example points to service *choreography* because the coordination is realized among the services themselves: *Hristo* is triggering *Service 1* and then those who are executing *Service 1* know what to do and how to deliver it and trigger *Service 2* and then those who are executing *Service 2* know what to do and how to deliver it and trigger *Service 3* that in turn delivers the result to *Hristo*.

Example 3 *Jimmy* is the leading manager of a small company in Sofia, and *Alice* is his business assistant who is authorized to sign for Jimmy declarations and application forms, to order payments on behalf of the company, and so on. Jimmy needs a *certificate of good standing* concerning the company, and he asks *Alice* to get it for him. Then:

- SERVICE 1

  - *Alice* would visit a *solicitor*, asking him or her to prepare the *application letter*, and *Alice* would pay the *solicitor* for the service, on behalf of the company.

- SERVICE 2

  - Having the *application letter* (for reference), *Alice* would go to the bank and transfer a corresponding *fee* to the *Court*.

- SERVICE 3

  - Having the *application letter* and the *proof of payment*, *Alice* would go to the *Court*, submit those documents, and immediately collect the *certificate of good standing*, if everything is OK with regard to the company.

Then *Alice* would go back to *Jimmy*, giving him the *certificate of good standing*.

This example points to service *orchestration* because the coordination is realized through *Alice* who is just like the "*orchestrator*" in Fig. 5.4 (down): *Jimmy* is triggering *Alice* who knows what and how to do, and in what order, *Alice* would firstly sort things out with the *solicitor*, then she would do the fee payment, and finally, she would go and collect the *certificate of good standing* at the *Court*. Based on this all, *Alice* would go back to *Jimmy* and deliver the *certificate* to him.

Even though those examples illustrate the corresponding *SOA* patterns in terms of underlying internal logic, the examples are not to be considered straightforwardly because they are reflecting real-life situations while *SOA* is an *IT architectural style*, as already mentioned.

Finally, after outlining the basic *SOA* pattern and touching upon *service coordination*, it is necessary to discuss **service composition** since often the user needs cannot be satisfied by simply using one particular *service* and *composite services* are to be considered. According to Eduardo Goncalves da Silva [23], the *service composition* is initiated by the specification of a *service* request where the *service requestor/user* indicates requirements and preferences for the *composite service* to be created. Following that, candidate *services* for the *service composition* are discovered in the *service registry*. In case no *services* are discovered, the requirements for the *service* may need to be refined and/or reformulated. Following that, the discovered *services* are composed to meet the specified requirements, and this may be accompanied by further interactions with the *service registry*, in case other *services* are necessary to complement the already discovered *services*; once the specified *service* requirements can be fulfilled by the created *service composition*, the resulting *service* can be executed, such that the *service requestor/user* makes use of it. It is also possible that the *service developer* is driving the *service composition* process—in such a case, the resulting *service composition* may be published in the *service registry* so that it can be used by other *users* or *service developers* in the future.

As it concerns the **implementation** of *SOA*, we mentioned at the beginning of the current section that we will consider (in the following sub-section) *web services* that constitute one of the widely adopted technologies to *implement SOA*.

5.2.2 Web Services

Web Services (**WS**) are a collection of standards, which are widely accepted as the technology of choice for implementing *SOA* [22]. *WS* to a large extent support the concepts, patterns, and principles mentioned in the previous sub-section. An application designed and implemented according to the *WS* standards is self-contained and modular, has a description which can be published, can be found on the basis of its description, and can be located and invoked over networks.

The core **WS standards** are the following:

- **Simple Object Access Protocol** (**SOAP**): this is an *Internet* protocol for *web* (*service requestor* and *service provider*) *applications* to communicate on top of other standard *Internet* protocols, including *HTTP*. *SOAP* defines how messages are structured and processed in a platform-independent way. It comprises two message exchange patterns, viz. one-way and request-response.
- **Web Services Description Language** (**WSDL**): this is the language for specifying the *WS* interfaces. It is used to provide a description of the *service* for

the (potential) *service requestors*. Such a description includes information on which messages are related to each operation that is supported by the *service*, how those messages are related (e.g., operation input and output), and how *SOAP* messages are exchanged.

*   <u>U</u>niversal <u>D</u>escription, <u>D</u>iscovery, and <u>I</u>ntegration (**UDDI**): this standard is defined to enable the storage of information for organizing and discovering *WS*. *UDDI* consists of data structures and APIs ("API" stands for "Application Programming Interface") for publishing and querying *WS*. The *UDDI* APIs are WS themselves; they are described / can be invoked as any other *WS*.

In addition, all *WS* standards rely on the Extensible Markup Language (XML) to represent structured data. *XML* documents and schemas are defined to standardize the format and type of data communicated by *WS*. The basic *SOA* pattern (see Fig. 5.3) can be supported with *SOAP*, *WSDL*, and *UDDI*. Those standards are, nevertheless, insufficient to correlate messages exchanged between a *service requestor* and a *service provider*, to distinguish between multiple instances of the same *service*, or to coordinate the use of different *services*. Also, they do not address policies that govern the use of WS and non-functional aspects of *WS* such as reliability and security. For this purpose, several other *WS* standards have been developed. Figure 5.5 shows an overview (inspired by Van Sinderen [18]) of standards supporting different aspects of *SOA*.

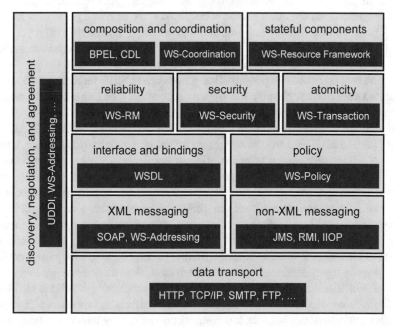

Fig. 5.5 WS and some standards supporting SOA (Source: [18], p. 9; ©2009, SCITEPRESS, reprinted with permission)

We argue that those standards have reached a certain level of technical maturity and thus represent an adequate *WS* basis with regard to the implementation of *SOA*. This in turn reflects promising, in our view, developments based on *CBD* (see the previous section), such that <u>COMPONENTS</u> are considered useful UNITS OF DEVELOPMENT while <u>SERVICES</u> are considered useful UNITS OF UTILIZATION with regard to developing (distributed) software and making it available to users. Complementing this, we will consider (in the following section) *model-driven engineering*, featuring the development process itself, no matter if this concerns *component-based development of software applications* or *composition of services* for the sake of generating software-based solutions.

5.3   Model-Driven Engineering

Any subject using a *system A* that is neither directly or indirectly interacting with a *system B*, to obtain information about the *system B*, is using *A* as a `model` for *B*, according to *Definition 9*. In reflecting that definition in real life, we establish that the human mind would often "rework" reality, simplifying things, driven by an intuitive "push" to identify similarities among *objects*, emphasizing those similarities in perceiving different *objects*. For example, both the small *Mitsubishi Colt* and the big *Cadillac Eldorado* are intuitively matched to the "*car*" *model* by a person, firstly, and the huge differences between those two *objects* go on second place. Said otherwise, upon perception, a person would firstly try to relate the observed *object (s)* to a category item already existing in his or her mind, abstracting from very many details. **Abstraction** (pointing to the capability of finding the commonality in many different observations) is hence essential with regard to how people perceive reality and reason about it—people often generalize specific features of real objects (**generalization**), classify the objects accordingly (**classification**), and aggregate objects into more complex ones (**aggregation**). Thus *abstraction* reflects the natural human behavior in real life while in science, ABSTRACTION RELATES TO MODELING, as suggested by the above definition. Hence, a *model* is a simplified and/or partial representation of reality. Models are of importance in many scientific disciplines, such as *physics* and *chemistry*, for example, where through simplified *models* of natural phenomena, one would draw conclusions about the phenomena themselves. In this, one would aim either at addressing (through *modeling*) just a selection of relevant properties, hence reducing complexity or at considering the features of an individual for the sake of *generalization*. Further, *models* can be used to describe reality, to determine the scope and details at which to study a problem, and so on. Through *modeling*, features of products can be analyzed and discussed before the corresponding products get produced. Finally, with us focusing on the development of software artifacts in this chapter, we would consider particularly **model-driven engineering**, by which we mean model-driven *software development*. According to [24], the need for *model-driven engineering* is justified taking into account the following facts:

- Software artifacts are becoming more and more complex, and therefore they need to be discussed at different *abstraction levels*, depending on the profile of the involved stakeholders, phase of development, and objectives of the work.
- Software is more and more pervasive in real life, and the expectation is that the need for new pieces of software or the evolution of existing ones will be continuously increasing.
- Software development is not a self-standing activity: it often imposes interactions with non-developers (e.g., customers, managers, business stakeholders, and so on) who need some mediation in the description of the technical aspects of development.

For this reason, it is not surprising that by applying *model-driven engineering*, software developers increase efficiency and effectiveness [24]. This nonetheless does not assume just using *models* and corresponding notations, for example, *UML*; in *model-driven engineering*, *models* do not constitute just documentation but are considered equal to code, as their implementation is automated; for example, a car order that includes customer features is straightforwardly reflected into reality, in the context of a current advanced automotive production line. Hence, the **domain** is essential for *models*. *Model-driven engineering* thus aims at finding *domain-specific abstractions* and making them accessible through formal *modeling*, this leading to automation of software production, which in turn leads to increased productivity (since both the quality and maintainability of software *systems* increase)—*models* that are *domain-specific* and *computation-independent* can be understood by *domain* experts and at the same time, those *models* are restricting accordingly the *technology-specific models* that are essential for the *construction* of the software *system* under development. To successfully apply this, three requirements must be met: (1) *Domain-specific* languages are required to allow the actual formulation of *models*. (2) Languages that can express the necessary *model-to-code transformations* are needed. (3) Compilers, generators, or transformers are required that can run the transformations to generate code executable on available platforms [5]. Said otherwise:

- It is necessary to consider computation-independent *models* that capture adequately the *domain* features, abstracting from any computation and technical details; such *models* would ideally capture the *as-is* situation, featuring a black-box view over the software *system*-to-be.
- It is necessary to consider technology-independent *models* of the software *system*-to-be, which *models* are already focused on the *system*-to-be (maybe both *functionally* and *constructionally*) but just conceptually, not imposing any technical restrictions whatsoever.
- It is necessary to consider technology-specific *models* that capture adequately all technical features of the software *system*-to-be, which *models* are straightforwardly reflect-able to corresponding code.

As studied by Shishkov [1], two *modeling* facilities are meeting those requirements, namely, the **M̲odel-D̲riven A̲rchitecture** (**MDA**) and the *O̲pen D̲istributed P̲rocessing Architecture* (*ODP*), with *MDA*'s adopting influences from *ODP*. Further, **meta-modeling** is one of the most important aspects of *model-driven engineering* since so-called "*meta-models*" are needed for describing the *abstract* syntax of *domain-specific modeling* languages, and that in turn allows *models* to be validated against the constraints defined in the *meta-model*, and that allows also for mappings between two *meta-models*; this is all necessary with regard to the desired automated code generation. Hence, *meta-models* are *models* that make statements about *modeling*. Four *meta-levels* being defined and considered widely are reflected in **MOF**—the **Meta-Object Facility** [5]. For this reason, we will consider *MDA* and *MOF* in Sects. 5.3.1 and 5.3.2, respectively.

5.3.1   Model-Driven Architecture

Model-Driven Architecture (*MDA*) is a software architecture framework consisting of a set of standards that assist in *system* creation, *system* implementation, *system* evolution, and *system* deployment [5]. The key *MDA* technologies are *UML*, *MOF* (to be considered in the following sub-section), and the *XML Meta-data Interchange –XMI* [25, 26]. *MDA* emphasizes the importance of *modeling* for the software architecture design, suggesting a three-layered approach:

- **Computation-Independent Model** (**CIM**) describing a system from the computation-independent point of view, to address structural aspects of the system.
- **Platform-Independent Model** (**PIM**) defining a system in terms of a technology-neutral virtual machine or a computational abstraction.
- **Platform-Specific Model** (**PSM**) capturing the technical platform concepts and geared towards implementation.

A taxonomy of the models that play a central role in MDA is presented in Fig. 5.6.

Fig. 5.6 Classification of models in the MDA context (©2017, The Author, reprinted with permission)

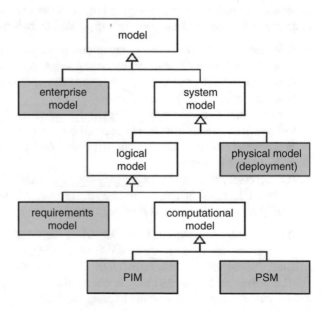

Since resolving the mismatch between (user) requirements and software application functionality is an essential software development concern [1], *MDA* needs to address it and in this regard, one would inevitably face the necessity of bridging different *abstraction levels*—a high-level *business* logic and a technology-driven application functionality. A *business function* (corresponding to a unit of *business logic*) is specific for a particular *business* and necessarily abstracts from technological solutions that can be used to support it. A *technology platform* offers a generic engineering abstraction (hence *hiding implementation details*) that is nonetheless technology-oriented. According to [17], an adequate business-application alignment can only be achieved if the **initial *enterprise model*** is (1) a valid reflection of the **relevant real-life aspects** and (2) a suitable foundation for the **generation of application *models***, preferably by using automated transformations. The alignment nevertheless cannot be accomplished only by prescribing how to define an *enterprise model*—an additional demand should be that (3) the "**architectural style**" used for organizing the application *modeling* should facilitate the alignment; it cannot be obtained solely from *top-down*, but also requires a *bottom-up* "preparation."

Hence, we consider *enterprise modeling* to be *computation-independent*, with no focus on the (partial) automation of *business processes*—this corresponds to the *CIM* layer. Further, we consider *application modeling* from a *platform-independent* perspective, with no focus on the specific technological platform(s) on which the application *components* are (to be) implemented—this corresponds to the *PIM* layer. Thus and under the condition that CIM goes "broader" than MDA suggest, reaching beyond just the software *system*-to-be:

> the enterprise-modeling-driven
> generation of software specifications
> corresponds to a CIM-to-PIM transformation.

As for the *PSM*, it is specific with regard to *J2EE*, *.NET*, or other implementation platforms. A *platform-specific model* is created from a *platform-independent model* via a *model transformation*. Thus:

> the application-modeling-driven
> implementation of software
> corresponds to a PIM-to-PSM transformation.

In Sect. 5.3.2 we consider *meta-modeling* and *MOF*, as already mentioned.

5.3.2   Meta-Object Facility

The *Meta-Object Facility* (*MOF*) provides an open and *platform-independent* meta-data management framework and associated set of meta-data services to enable the development and interoperability of *model-driven* and meta-data-driven *systems*. Examples of *systems* that use *MOF* include *modeling* and development tools, data warehouse systems, meta-data repositories, and so on [27]. The abovementioned four meta-levels are of importance with regard to *MOF* [5]— they are (1) **M0**—Instance; (2) **M1**—Model; (3) **M2**—Meta-model; and (4) **M3**—Meta-meta-model.

Between **M0** and **M1**, we have typical *classification/instantiation*, at **M1** we have the *class* level, and at **M0** we have the *instance* level; for example, a *class* is given the name "Person" and has a number of *attributes*, in the example—"surname" and "first name"; an *instance* of that *class* is created at level **M0**; in the example, "Person" is *instantiated* to the persons with "ID 12345," and we give corresponding *values* to the *attributes* "surname" and "first name," "Smith" and "Michael," respectively, in this case. Logically, a *class* can have more than one *instance*. As seen in the above example, during the *instantiation* of a *class*, *values* are assigned to its *attributes*.

As for **M2**, at this level the constructs that are used at the **M1** level are defined. The elements of the **M1** *model* are hence *instances* of the elements of the *meta-model* at the **M2** level; since in the above example we use *classes* in the **M1** model, the construct *Class* must be defined in the **M2** *meta-model*. The construct *Class* in turn is to be considered as an *instance* of the meta-meta element *MOF Classifier* (*MOF classes* are hence defined at the **M3** level). Said otherwise, the *MOF* serves to define *modeling* languages (e.g., *UML*) at the **M2** level.

Further, besides meta-relationships in which *meta-models* define the concepts needed for creating corresponding *models*, it has to be acknowledged that *models* can be located at different **abstraction levels** even though they can be located at the same *meta-level*, for example, *CIM*, *PIM*, and *PSM* (see above). As already discussed, *transformations* are used to map *models* at a *higher abstraction level* to models at a *lower abstraction level*, and as mentioned before, each *model* is inevitably an *instance* of a *meta-model*.

If we take the *PIM*-to-*PSM transformation* (where we reflect the *higher abstraction level model PIM* to lower level *PSM*), we stay at the **M1** level because no matter the *abstraction level*, both *PIM* and *PSM* represent *models*. Each of those *models* thus has a corresponding *meta-model* (at the **M2** level): the *PIM* is an *instance* of the *PIM meta-model* and the *PSM* is an *instance* of the *PSM meta-model*. In turn, both *meta-models* are *instances* of *MOF*, *MOF* being positioned at the **M3** level. This is illustrated in Fig. 5.7:

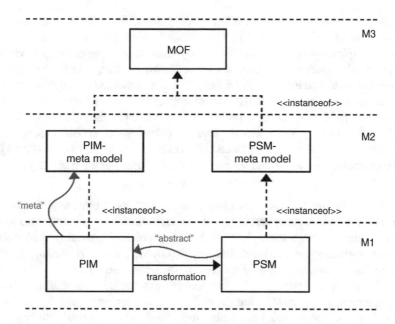

Fig. 5.7 Meta versus abstract (©2017, The Author, reprinted with permission)

In this section, we have considered the *model-driven* software development, touching upon *abstraction levels*, *meta-levels*, and corresponding *transformations*. In the following section, we will consider the impact of *mobility* on the development and utilization of software *systems*, featured mainly by *cloud computing* and corresponding infrastructures.

5.4   Cloud Computing

Consolidated *enterprise-IT* solutions have proven to enhance business efficiency when significant fractions of local computing activities are migrating away from desktop PCs and departmental servers and are being integrated and packaged on the *Web* into the *computing cloud*, according to Ivanov [28]. No matter which one of the popular "labels" we use: *grid computing*, *utility computing*, or `cloud computing`, the idea is basically the same. What is important is that instead of investing in and maintaining expensive applications and *systems*, users access and utilize dynamic computing structures to meet their fluctuating demands on IT resources efficiently and pay a fixed subscription or an actual usage fee. The immense economic demands in the last several years, in conjunction with the immediate reduction of upfront capital and operational costs when cloud-based services are employed, increase the speed and the scale of *cloud computing* adoption both *horizontally* (across industries) and *vertically* (in organizations' technology stacks). All that poses the need for organizational changes, organizations would have to re-think and re-engineer (in some cases) their traditional IT resources, advancing them with cloud architectures and implementing services based on dynamic computing delivery models. The changes and business transformations are underway on a large scale, from providers and customers to vendors and developers. The key issues are not only in economics and management, but essentially how emerging IT models impact organizational structures, capabilities, business processes, and consequential opportunities.

There are usually three cloud service models under consideration, namely, **Software as a Service (SaaS)**, **Platform as a Service (PaaS)**, and **Infrastructure as a Service (IaaS)**, that relate to the **cloud provider** [7]:

- *SaaS* moves the task of managing software and its deployment to third-party services, such as security services, caching services, networking services, and so on.
- *PaaS* functions at a lower level than *SaaS*, typically providing a platform on which software can be developed and deployed, such as streaming platforms, application development platforms, web platforms, and so on.
- *IaaS* in turn comprises highly automated and scalable computing resources, complemented by cloud storage and network capability which can be self-provisioned, metered, and available on-demand, such as e-mail building blocks, ERP building blocks ("ERP" standing for "Enterprise Resource Planning"), CRM building blocks ("CRM" standing for "Customer Relationship Management"), and so on.

The *cloud* provisioning is hence bottom-lined by a *SaaS-PaaS-IaaS* basis and reaching out to customers via the Internet, such that the customers' computers, servers, databases, mobile devises, and so on can actually benefit from corresponding *cloud services* that are in turn utilized by customers in the form of images, news, music, chat facilitations, ID management, TV, and so on, as illustrated in Fig. 5.8.

As the figure suggests, customers utilize *cloud services* at high level, in an intuitive and seamless way, such that the underlying *SaaS-PaaS-IaaS*-related technical complexity remains hidden and would only become explicit for the customer as reflections in corresponding (subscription) contracts. Thus, *cloud computing* brings together many technical, organizational, contractual, and other concerns which we will not discuss in more detail in the current chapter. Our goal was to present *cloud computing* as a natural "extension" of *service orientation* (already discussed) where the utilization of *services* is combined with the utilization of resources, empowering **mobility**—it is only through *cloud computing* that it is possible to access distant resources/systems through a (portable) mobile device.

All this reflects the move from *components* through *services* to *cloud solutions*, and we acknowledge the relevance of *model-driven engineering* (discussed already) to the challenge of developing such *component*-based, *service*-based, and/or *cloud*-based *systems*. What remains uncovered nevertheless is the adequate consideration of non-functional issues, such as *privacy*, for example, which are crosscutting and have reflection in different components, at different development phases. We will discuss this in the following section.

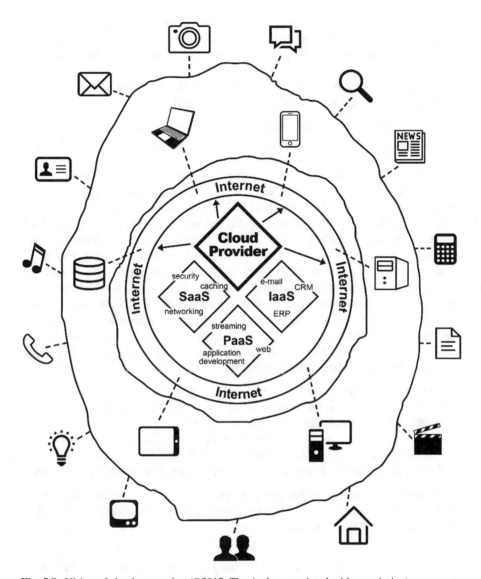

Fig. 5.8 Vision of cloud computing (©2017, The Author, reprinted with permission)

5.5   Aspect-Oriented Software Development

Privacy, transparency, traceability, and so on are labelled **values** that are to be *weaved* in the functioning of *enterprise systems* and *EIS* [29], and for this reason, they are considered as **crosscutting concerns** because:

- Weaving them in the functioning of a *system* would not assume reflections in one particular *component* only; instead multiple *components* would need to be "refactored" as well as their interrelations, and also their relations to other *components*.
- Addressing such *values* in the software development context would come through all the phases of the software development life cycle.

Further, such *values / crosscutting concerns* have a *non-functional* essence because they do not have any particular purpose or function; instead they represent something like "desired system qualities."

Finally, even though the *values / crosscutting concerns* are *non-functional*, we should find *functional* solutions for them, because we argue that a *system* could only *functionally* achieve effects with impact on its *environment*.

This all (as above stated) concerns broadly *enterprise systems* touching upon both human issues and technical issues. Narrowing this further to software *systems* nevertheless brings us to such *crosscutting concerns* that are particularly touching upon software development issues, such as security, distribution, recoverability, logging, performance monitoring, and so on [8]. This is featuring the notion of **aspect-oriented software development** whose foundations concern separation of concerns, filter technologies, improving modularity, integration of new features, and so on [30]. We are not going in more detail in this direction.

What we would only like to emphasize is that addressing such *non-functional* concerns is to be *functional* which means that:

- We should "translate" those concerns into system requirements.
- System development should not go in any unusual way; it should just ensure that all requirements are properly reflected in the design and implementation.
- Introducing metrics and/or performance indicators would be necessary for establishing how well the desired *values* have been reflected in the performance of the *system*, and if it is necessary, the requirements may have to be refactored.

Aspect orientation is thus necessary for properly *weaving* desired *values* in the functioning of the *system*-to-be. It is featuring *non-functional* issues that nevertheless have to be resolved *functionally*.

* * *

IN SUMMARY, in Chaps. 2 and 3 we have considered some essential *concepts* and *views*; in Chap. 4 we have presented and discussed *social theories*, including *human relativism*, the *theory of organized activity*, the *language-action perspective*, *enterprise ontology*, and *organizational semiotics*, justifying their relevance to different aspects concerning *enterprise systems* and *EIS*; and in this chapter we have considered *computing paradigms* that are currently actual and also well-combinable with the addressed *social theories* and *concepts*. In the following chapter, we will introduce the *SDBC approach*, bringing all those issues together.

References

1. Shishkov B (2005) Software specification based on re-usable business components. Delft University Press, Delft
2. Wikipedia, The free encyclopedia. http://en.wikipedia.org
3. Szyperski C (1998) Component software, beyond object-oriented programming. Addison-Wesley, Harlow, England
4. Stojanovic Z (2005) A method for component-based and service-oriented software systems engineering. Delft University Press, Delft
5. Stahl T, Völter M, Bettin J, Haase A, Helsen S (2006) Model-driven software development—technology, engineering, management. Wiley, Heidelberg
6. AWARENESS (2008) Freeband AWARENESS project. http://www.freeband.nl/project.cfm?id=494&language=en
7. CLOSER, The international conference on cloud computing and service science. http://closer.scitevents.org
8. BMSD, The international symposium on business modeling and software design. http://www.is-bmsd.org
9. Lewandowski SM (1998) Frameworks for component-based client/server computing. J ACM Comput Surv 30(1):3–27
10. Williams S,Kindel C (1994) The component object model: a technical overview. Microsoft Corporation White Paper, Microsoft
11. EJB, The ORACLE enterprise JavaBeans technology. http://www.oracle.com/technetwork/java/javaee/ejb/index.html
12. CCM, The OMG CORBA component model. https://www.omg.org/spec/CCM/About-CCM
13. Kruchten P (2003) The rational unified process: an introduction. Addison-Wesley, Reading, MA
14. Atkinson C, Bayer J, Bunse C, Kamsties E, Laitenberger O, Laqua R, Muthig D, Paech B, Wust Z, Zettel J (2001) Component-based product line engineering with UML. Addison-Wesley, Reading, MA
15. Atkinson C,Muthig D (2002) Enhancing component reusability through product line technology. In: Proceedings of the 7th international conference on software reuse, Austin, TX, USA, 15–19 Apr 2002
16. D'Souza DF, Wills AC (1998) Objects, components, and frameworks with UML, The catalysis approach. Addison-Wesley, Reading, MA
17. Shishkov B, Van Sinderen M, Quartel D (2006) SOA-driven business-software alignment. In: Proceedings of the ICEBE'06 IEEE international conference on e-Business Engineering, IEEE
18. Van Sinderen MJ (2009) From service-oriented architecture to service-oriented enterprise. In: Proceedings of the 3rd international workshop on enterprise systems and technology (I-WEST), 29–30 July 2009. SCITEPRESS, Sofia, Bulgaria
19. OASIS (2006) Reference model for service oriented architecture 1.0. OASIS Standard. http://docs.oasis-open.org/soa-rm/v1.0 (12Oct 2006)
20. Van Sinderen MJ,Pires LF (1998) Protocols versus objects: can models for telecommunications and distributed processing coexist? In: Proceedings of the 6th IEEE workshop on future trends of distributed computing systems (FTDCS), IEEE
21. Unger T, Mietzner R, Leymann F (2009) Customer-defined service level agreements for composite applications. J Enterp Inform Syst 3(3):369–391
22. Papazoglou M (2008) Web services: principles and technology. Prentice Hall, Upper Saddle River, NJ
23. Goncalves da Silva EM (2011) User-centric service composition, towards personalised service composition and delivery. University of Twente, Enschede
24. Brambilla M, Cabot J, Wimmer M (2012) Model-driven software engineering in practice. Morgan & Claypool, San Rafael, CA
25. XML, The W3C extensible markup language. http://www.w3.org/XML

26. XMI, The OMG XML meta-data interchange. http://www.omg.org/spec/XMI
27. MOF (n.d.) The OMG meta-object facility. http://www.omg.org/mof
28. Ivanov I (2012) Cloud computing in education: the intersection of challenges and opportunities. In: Filipe J, Cordeiro J (eds) Web information systems and technologies 2011. LNBIP, vol 101. Springer, Heidelberg, pp 3–16
29. Ahmed MA, Janssen M, Van Den Hoven J (2012) Value sensitive transfer (VST) of systems among countries: towards a framework. J Electr Gov Res 8(1):26–42
30. Filman R, Elrad T, Clarke S, Aksit M (2004) Aspect-oriented software development. Addison-Wesley, Reading, MA

Chapter 6
The SDBC Approach

We make a clear distinction between issues that concern the **enterprise-engineering** aspects of *Enterprise Information Systems (EIS)* and issues that concern the **software-engineering** aspects of such systems—see *Chap. 1*. At the same time, we need to bring together **enterprise modeling** (driven by **social theories**—see *Chap. 4*) and **software specification** (driven by **computing paradigms**—see *Chap. 5*) for the sake of bridging the **enterprise-software gap** (as discussed in *Chap. 1*). We have put *conceptual foundations* for this in *Chap. 2* (by considering **systemics**) and we have explicitly addressed the **environmental and user perspectives** with regard to EIS (see *Chap. 3*). What is nevertheless missing so far is the **operationalization perspective**—we need an *approach* and *methodological guidelines* on **what** to do and **how** to do it in order to actually realize an **enterprise-modeling-driven software generation**; this is a challenge because most current approaches and methods are either rooted in *social theories* or based on *computing paradigms*—this claim has been justified in the previous chapters of the current book. For this reason, we consider previous works of the Author [1] who has been studying and addressing the mentioned challenge for *more than 15 years* already, reflecting *innovative ideas* in his **SDBC APPROACH**—"*SDBC*" stands for "$\underline{S}oftware\ \underline{D}erived\ from\ \underline{B}usiness\ \underline{C}omponents$." Hence, the reasons for considering and developing further this approach are the following:

- Its strengths in aligning enterprise modeling and software specification.
- Its component-orientation and support for re-use.
- Its previous use for specifying context-aware and privacy-sensitive systems [2, 3].

The remaining of the current chapter is hence organized as follows: In Sect. 6.1, we will briefly introduce *SDBC* and outline its main *concepts* which are not only in line with the **meta-model**, presented in *Chap. 1* (see Fig. 1.6), but are also consistent with the **definitions** presented in *Chap. 2*. In Sect. 6.2, we provide

© Springer Nature Switzerland AG 2020   143
B. Shishkov, *Designing Enterprise Information Systems*, The Enterprise Engineering
Series, https://doi.org/10.1007/978-3-030-22441-7_6

further *foundational* and *conceptual elaborations*. In <u>Sect.</u> 6.3, we present the *SDBC* `process outline`. Finally, in <u>Sect.</u> 6.4, we present the *SDBC* `notations`.

6.1   Outline and Concepts

SDBC is an *approach* (consistent with *MDA*—see the previous chapter) that is focused on the *derivation of software specification models on the basis of corresponding (re-usable) enterprise models*. SDBC is based on <u>three key ideas</u>: (1) The software system-to-be is considered in its enterprise context, which means that the *software specification models* are to stem from corresponding *enterprise models*; this means in turn that a deep understanding is needed as it concerns real-life (enterprise-level) *processes*, corresponding *roles*, *behavior* patterns, and so on. (2) By bringing together two disciplines (*enterprise engineering* and *software engineering*), SDBC pushes for applying *social theories* in addressing enterprise-engineering-related tasks and for applying *computing paradigms* in addressing software-engineering-related tasks, and also for integrating the two, by means of sound methodological guidelines. (3) Acknowledging the value of *re-use* in current software development, SDBC pushes for the identification of re-usable (generic) *enterprise engineering building blocks* whose *models* could be reflected accordingly in corresponding *software specification models*. We refer to [1, 2] for information on SDBC and we are reflecting the SDBC outline in Fig. 6.1.

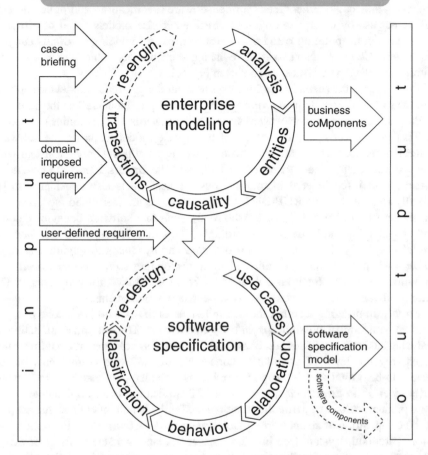

Fig. 6.1 SDBC—a general outline (Source: [4], p. 48; ©2017, SCITEPRESS, reprinted with permission)

As the figure suggests, there are two SDBC modeling milestones, namely, **enterprise modeling** (*first milestone*) and **software specification** (*second milestone*). The first milestone has as input a case briefing (the initial (textual) information based on which the software development is to start) and the so-called domain-imposed requirements (those are the domain regulations to which the software system-to-be should conform). Based on such an input, an analysis should follow, aiming at structuring the information, identifying missing information, and so on. This is to be followed by the identification (supported by corresponding social theories) of enterprise modeling entities and their interrelations. Then, the causalities concerning those interrelations need to be modeled, such that we know what is required in order for something else to happen [5]. On that basis, the dynamics (the entities' behavior) is to be considered, featured by *transactions*

[1, 2]. This all leads to the creation of *enterprise models* that are elaborated in terms of *composition*, *structure*, and *dynamics* (all this pointing also to corresponding *data* aspects)—they could either "feed" further software specifications and/or be "stored" for further use by enterprise engineers. Such enterprise models could possibly be reflected in corresponding **business coMponents** (models of *business compo-nents*—see *Chap. 2*). Next to that, revisiting such models could possibly inspire enterprise redesign activities, as shown in Fig. 6.1.

Furthermore, the second milestone uses as input the enterprise model (see above) and the so-called user-defined requirements (those requirements reflect the demands of the (future) users of the software system-to-be towards its functioning).

That input "feeds" the derivation of a use case model featuring the software system-to-be. Such a software specification starting point is not only consistent with the **Rational Unified Process (RUP)** and the **Unified Modeling Language (UML)** (considered in the previous chapter) but is also considered to be broadly accepted beyond RUP-UML [2]. The *use cases* are then elaborated, inspired by studies of Cockburn [6] and Shishkov [2], such that software behavior models and classification can be derived accordingly. The output is a *software specification model* adequately elaborated in terms of *statics* and *dynamics*. Applying *decompo-sition*, such a model can be reflected in corresponding *software components*, as shown in the figure. Such an output could be an inspiration for proposing in the future software redesigns, possibly addressing new requirements.

Further, in bringing together the first milestone of SDBC and the second one, we need to be aware of possible *granularity mismatches*. The enterprise modeling is featuring business processes and corresponding business coMponents, but this is not necessarily the level of granularity concerning the software components of the system-to-be. Often an ICT **application** is considered as matching the granu-larity level of a *business component*—an ICT application is an implemented soft-ware product realizing a particular functionality for the benefit of entities that are part of the composition of an enterprise (sub-)system and/or a (corresponding) enterprise information (sub-)system (see Fig. 2.5). Hence the label **software specifica-tion model**, as presented in Fig. 6.1, corresponds to a particular ICT application being specified. **Software components** in turn are viewed as *implemented pieces of software*, which represent parts of an ICT application and which collabo-rate among each other driven by the goal of realizing the functionality of the application (functionally, a software component is a part of an ICT application, which is self-contained, customizable, and composable, possessing a clearly defined function and interfaces to the other parts of the application and which can also be deployed independently—see Chap. 2). As according to Definition 15, a **software coMponent** is a conceptual specification model of a software component; the second SDBC milestone is hence about the identification of software coMponents and corresponding software components.

We now bring together the essential SDBC features (presented above), the conceptual meta-model (see Fig. 1.6), and the relevant definitions presented in Chap. 2, and we put forward (from an SDBC perspective) the following key concepts [7]:

Basic Concepts (General)

SYSTEM:	A collection of elements possibly interacting with each other, driven by the purpose of delivering a service to another entity or group of entities.
SUB-SYSTEM:	A system part identified based on a functional decomposition with regard to the system (hence, a system can optimize itself, by optimizing corresponding sub-systems).
ENVIRONMENT:	Anything not belonging to a system belongs to the system environment.
	Part of the environment concerns those environmental entities that are assumed to have some interaction with the system.
ENTITIES:	Composition elements with regard to a system/environment.
	– Human vs artificial entities
	– Passive (a passive entity is an entity that only performs actions when another entity interacts with it) vs autonomous (an autonomous entity is an entity that performs actions on its own initiative) entities
	– Sensing (capturing context data in support of the system's service delivery) vs actuator (causing changes in the environment on behalf of the system) entities
ROLE:	The state of carrying out certain objectives.
	– The entity-role combination is labelled "actor-role."
ACTOR:	An (autonomous) entity that can enact a role.
USER:	An actor that is serviced by the system.
ACTION:	Something done by an entity.
	– A sequence of actions, occurring between two entities that are collaborating in support of a service delivery, is labelled "interaction."
OBJECTIVE:	The motive behind a service delivery.
REGULATIONS:	Reflection of the existing norms that have impact on a service delivery, prescribing what is allowed in some situations, forbidden in others, and so on.
VALUES:	Reflection of the public perception towards what is important regarding the service delivered by the systems.[a]

[a]We address values that are shared among environmental human entities

Further, we address the desired adaptation of the system's functioning with regard to internal/environmental changes (see Chap. 3) and this inspires the consideration of three more concepts as follows:

Basic Concepts (Featuring System Adaptation Dimensions)

SELF-MANAGING BEHAVIOR: Context-driven enforcement of system-internal optimizations
USER-DRIVEN BEHAVIOR: Context-driven service adaptation based on the user situation
VALUE SENSITIVITY: Service adaptation inspired by public values, delivered through the operationalization of such values

In the following section, we elaborate further the issues presented above.

6.2   Elaboration

As abovementioned, the initial ideas behind *SDBC* have been proposed by the author in 2005 [1], and since then the approach has been maturing slowly. We argue that no sound methodology driven by the above focus has emerged, which is also widely recognized. This "vacuum" is claimed to continue "causing" numerous software project failures. Hence, we are inspired to work further on the *SDBC* project. Nevertheless, this has never been and is not a matter of any kind of commercialization whatsoever. Neither it is related to branding or product positioning. *SDBC* remains fundamentally driven by a scientific and research inspiration, and for this reason, it is not aligned with particular commercialized development tools. Hence, *SDBC* is positioned as an <u>open modeling platform</u> that may accommodate different tools, as far as the overall principles of the approach are met, and what stays essential about *SDBC* is to address the challenge of bringing together *social theories* (in an

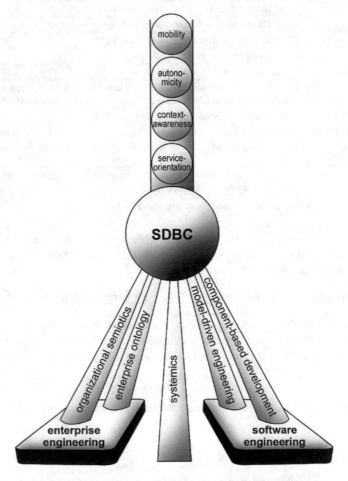

Fig. 6.2 The SDBC foundations (©2017, The Author, reprinted with permission)

enterprise engineering context) and *computing paradigms* (in a *software engineering* context), aiming at the *enterprise-modeling*-driven specification of software.

As it concerns the modeling itself, *SDBC* assumes four modeling perspectives, namely, *Structural perspective* (it reflects entities and their relationships), *Dynamic perspective* (it reflects not only the overall business processes but also the corresponding states of entities, evolving accordingly), *Data perspective* (it reflects the information flows across entities and within business processes), and *Language-action perspective* (it reflects real-life human communication and expression of promises, commitments, etc.). They are considered relevant as it concerns the goal of soundly building an exhaustive enterprise model.

In this, *SDBC* is grounded, as Fig. 6.2 shows, in the principles of *systemics* (see *Chap. 2*) and also based on:

- *Enterprise engineering* and in particular *enterprise ontology* and *organizational semiotics* (see *Chap. 4*).
- *Software engineering* and in particular *model-driven engineering* and *component-based development* (see *Chap. 5*).

As also suggested by the figure, *software specification models* derived by applying *SDBC*, can be further updated to accommodate features pointing to (1) *service-orientation* (and *mobility* utilization related to this), as studied in [8]; (2) *context-awareness* (see *Chap. 3*), as studied in [9]; and (3) *autonomic system behavior*, as studied in [10].

Further, in addition to the concepts presented in the previous section, we introduce/elaborate also the following main *SDBC* concepts:

- *Component* vs *CoMponent*: while a *component* represents a part of the whole, a *coMponent* is featuring a *model* of a *component*, adequately elaborated in all four perspectives (see above), and we could thus have *business components* (enterprise sub-systems) and *software components* (pieces of implemented software) as well as *business coMponents* and *software coMponents*, respectively. Refer to *Definition 8*, *Definition 11*, *Definition 13*, *Definition 14*, and *Definition 15*.
- *General* vs *Generic*: those concepts are both about *re-use*; still *general* is about re-using an abstract core (e.g., a general reservation engine), while *generic* is about parameterizing something that is multi-specific (e.g., a car system to be adjusted to automatic or gear regime).
- *Software Specification Model*—this is a *technology-independent functionality model* of the software *system-to-be*.

To summarize the elaborated *SDBC* outline, we use Fig. 6.3. As seen from the figure, we consider an *enterprise system* from which a *business component(s)* is to be identified and then reflected in a relevant *model*—a *business coMponent*. Another way for arriving at a *business coMponent* is by applying *re-use*: either extending a *general business coMponent* or parameterizing a *generic* one. Then, the *business coMponent* should be complemented with the `domain-imposed require-ments`, in order to add elicitation on the particular context in which its corresponding *business component* exists within the *enterprise system*. Then, a **mapping** towards a *software specification model* should take place and the

user-defined requirements are to be considered, since the derived software *model* should reflect not only the original business features but also the particular *requirements* towards the software *system*-to-be. The *software specification model* in turn needs a precise elaboration so that it provides sufficient elicitation in terms of *structure*, *dynamics*, *data*, and *language-action-related aspects*. It needs also to be decomposed into a number of *software coMponents* reflecting functionality pieces. Those *coMponents* then are to undergo *realization* and *implementation*, being reflected in this way in a set of *software components*. Some *software components* could also be purchased. The *software components* are implemented using *software component* technologies, such as *.NET* or *EJB* (see the previous chapter), for instance. Finally, the (resulting) *component-based ICT application* would support

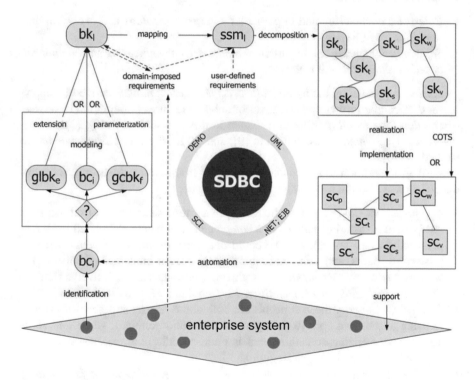

Abbreviations:

  bc – Business Component   ssm – Software specification model
  bk – Business CoMponent   sc – Software Component
  glbk – General Business CoMponent   sk – Software CoMponent
  gcbk – Generic Business CoMponent

Fig. 6.3 SDBC—an elaborated outline (Source: [1], p. 173; ©2005, The Author, reprinted with permission)

informationally the target *enterprise system*, by automating anything that concerns the considered *business component* (identified from the mentioned *system*).

In order to bring forward further elaboration with regard to the *SDBC* approach, it is necessary to consider the <u>*SDBC* design trajectory</u>: As suggested by Fig. 6.4a [1], one should firstly consider the *initial descriptive information* (provided by the future user(s) of the software *system*-to-be) which is a usual input in any software project, as it is well known. Then a *description of the approached business reality* is derived. However, it might be necessary to conduct *redesign* (imagine that the original business reality consists of a local service provider and users; with introducing mobility, we could rely on a number of service providers based in different locations; thus, before specifying the software, we would need to describe the "future" (desired) business reality accordingly). Then, we should *delimit* a relevant part of the business reality dependent on our particular software goal (what exactly are we

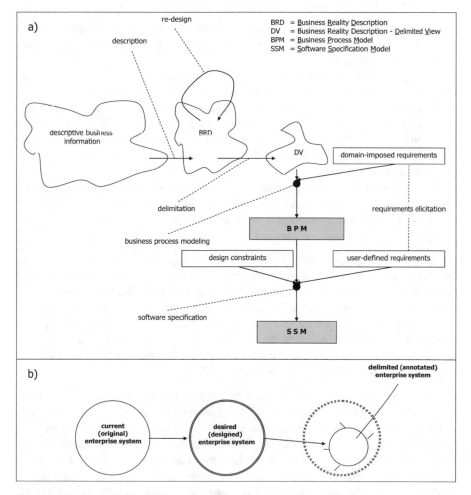

Fig. 6.4 SDBC—design trajectory (Source: [1], p. 64; ©2005, The Author, reprinted with permission)

going to automate, according to the requirements of the users). Figure 6.4b [1] summarizes those issues.

Hence, having the description of the delimited part of the original (or eventually redesigned) business reality, we could proceed towards the business process <u>model-ing</u> task (Fig. 6.4a). As seen from the figure, another related input is the *domain-imposed requirements* (already mentioned) characterizing the original *enterprise system*.

We build a *business process model* that in turn is to be mapped towards a *software specification model*. However, as it is depicted on the figure, besides the *business process modeling input*, the *SDBC design trajectory* envisions two other necessary inputs:

- The *user-defined requirements* (already mentioned)—the requirements which the future user(s) of the software *system*-to-be have stated concerning its functionality.
- *Design constraints*—the design limitations which should be followed as a result of software/hardware/netware (and other) project restrictions.

Thus, five basic tasks could be identified, namely, <u>description</u> (plus eventually re-design), <u>delimitation</u>, <u>business process modeling</u>, <u>software specification,</u> as well as <u>requirements elicitation</u>.

The figure shows as well that the *requirements elicitation* task would span not only over the *software specification* but also over the *business process modeling*.

Concerning the items depicted on Fig. 6.4a, from left to right and from top to bottom, they become smaller (in area) and more regular (in shape). This is to indicate that each following state relates to a smaller part of the original business reality (e.g., in the delimitation, we exclude issues from the original *model*) and is becoming more and more structured.

We will now bring forward further insight on four of the abovementioned tasks, since they require elaboration—those are (1) delimitation, (2) business process modeling, (3) software specification, and (4) requirements elicitation.

(1) <u>Delimitation</u>

As seen from Fig. 6.4a, before the *software specification* and even before the *business process modeling* activities take place, it is necessary to conduct a sound *business process* study that thoroughly reflects the considered business reality, achieving in this way a precise *delimitation*. We consider this necessary because, as it is well known, an adequate modeling should be conducted based on a proper description and understanding of the addressed reality as well as on a precise focus on the part of the reality to be considered in the modeling process [11]. In *SDBC*, we respond to this through "description + filtration":

- It is necessary to thoroughly describe the *enterprise system* being approached (the business reality under consideration, which might be (eventually) redesigned) and the suggested starting point in this regard is the consideration of the <u>original documentation</u> of the studied *system*; however, it should be taken into account that such information is often insufficient and/or full of errors. Thus, it should be additionally analyzed and/or refined. The decision how detailed the description should be depends on the selected granularity level that in turn should correspond to the characteristics of the software system-to-be.

- Then <u>filtration</u> needs to be applied, featuring only those issues from the description, which are relevant to the software *system*-to-be. They are to be, however, soundly rooted in the broader context of the approached business reality, such that in the end the specified software is well integrated in its *enterprise* environment.

In order to illustrate the above, we consider an example featuring a restaurant: to make a DESCRIPTION with regard to a restaurant means to cover a number of issues, such as location, opening hours, food details, price details, reservation procedures, service peculiarities, reputation, and so on. There would be much information collected along those lines which information would nevertheless remain unfocused. If we would be introducing some technology within the restaurant, for example, an electronic reservation system, then we would have to apply FILTRATION with regard to the description, such that we extract only those description elements that are relevant to the reservation procedures.

However, *description* and *filtration* are not to be always realized as two separate tasks since it is possible that they overlap. Returning back to the example, it might be obvious from the beginning that describing the porter (concierge) of the restaurant is of no use since the "functionality" of the porter is irrelevant as it concerns the restaurant (electronic) reservations; regardless of other circumstances, the porter is just supposed to stay by the restaurant's entrance during opening hours.

It might be concluded that *filtration* concerns the <u>alignment</u> between *business process modeling* and *software specification* since it focuses the business study on particular part(s) of the studied business reality, which are to be automated through (software) technology [11].

(2) Business Process Modeling

Inspired by *Definition 8*, *Definition 10*, and *Definition 11*, we establish the need to conduct *business process modeling* with providing elaboration in three perspectives, namely, (1) *structural perspective*, (2) *dynamic perspective*, and (3) *data perspective*. Further, inspired by the notion of *transaction* (see *Definition 5* and Fig. 4.4) and LAP (see Chap. 4), we add another perspective, namely, the *communication perspective*. All this is illustrated in Fig. 6.5:

Fig. 6.5 SDBC—business process modeling perspectives (Source: [1], p. 67; ©2005, The Author, reprinted with permission)

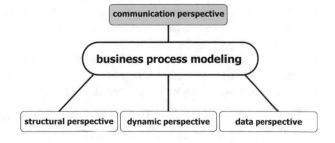

As it was explained already at the beginning of the current section, the *structural perspective* is about the entities and their interrelations; the *dynamic perspective* is about the flow(s) of events; the *data perspective* is about the factual issues; and the *communication perspective* is about the communicative acts exchanged during the business operation.

(3) Software Specification

Actually, *SDBC* is to deliver a *software specification model* that is derived based on a corresponding *enterprise model* that features in turn (among other things) *business processes* to which four perspectives are applied, as discussed above. Hence we need to reflect multi-perspective *enterprise models* (featuring business processes) in corresponding *software specifications*. Further, if possible, such an alignment *between business process modeling* and *software specification* is to be *component-based*. Said otherwise, the *software specification model* is to be derived based on (re-usable) *business coMponents*.

(4) Requirements Elicitation

Requirements relate directly to the *specification of software* [12]. They are descriptions of how the *system*-to-be should behave, application domain information, constraints on the *system*'s operation, or specifications of a *system* property or attribute [13]. Thus, a proper consideration of the original business requirements in the specification of a software's functionality is of significant importance; this concerns the process of aligning *enterprise modeling* and *software specification*. Our consideration of the *requirements* issue, as illustrated in Fig. 6.3, is in concert with the *SDBC design trajectory* (Fig. 6.4).

Building a *business process model* should concern the discovery of a part of the system *requirements*, namely, those *requirements* that characterize particularly the *enterprise system* under consideration, as discussed already. They are often called *domain-imposed requirements*, as mentioned before. It is to be noted in this regard that not only the *domain-imposed requirements* could affect the initial *business process model* by causing some updates in it but also that the *business process model* affects the *requirements* elicitation, by stimulating the discovery (or specification) of additional *requirements*.

As stated already, besides the *domain-imposed requirements*, one should identify also the so-called *user-defined requirements* that are determined by the users of the *system*-to-be and are not directly related to the *business process model*.

In summary, during the *business process modeling*, the *domain-imposed requirements* are to be discovered and considered in the mapping towards *software specifications*; next to that, the *user-defined requirements* are to complement the *business process model* in providing the input for the derivation of the *software specification model*.

Further, *transactions* (see *Definition 5* and Fig. 4.4) are considered as the fundamental *enterprise modeling* building blocks in the *SDBC* context. Still, there is a particular *SDBC* interpretation of the *transaction* concept.

SDBC interprets the *transaction* concept as centered around a particular *production fact* (see *Definition 5*). The reason is that the actual output of any *enterprise* *system* represents a set of *production facts* related to each other. They actually bring about the useful value of the business operations to the outside world and the issues connected with their creation are to be properly modeled in terms of *structure*, *dynamics*, and *data*.

However, the already justified necessity of considering also the corresponding *communicative* aspects is important. Although they are indirectly related to the *production facts*, they are to be positioned around them. As already stated, *SDBC* addresses this through its interpretation of the *transaction* concept, as depicted in Fig. 6.6; as seen from the figure, the *transaction* concept (as featured by *Definition 5* and reflected in Fig. 4.4) has been adopted, with a particular stress on the *transaction's* output—the *production fact*. The *order phase* is looked upon as an input for the *production act*, while the *result phase* is considered to be the *production act's* output. The dashed line shows that a *transaction* could be successful (which means that a *production fact* has been successfully created) only if the *initiator* (the one who is initiating the *transaction*, as presented in Fig. 6.6) has accepted the *production act* of the other party (called *executor*). As for the (*coordination*) *communicative acts*, grasped by the *SDBC transaction*, they are also depicted in the figure. The *initiator* expresses a *request* attitude towards a <u>proposition</u> (any *transaction* should concern a *proposition*—e.g., a shoe to be repaired by a particular date and at a particular price, and so on). Such a *request* might trigger either *promise* or *decline*— the *executor* might either *promise* to produce the requested product (or service) or express a *decline* attitude towards the *proposition*. Such a decline attitude actually triggers a discussion (<u>negotiation</u>), for example, "I cannot repair the shoe today, is tomorrow fine?". The discussion might lead to a <u>compromise</u> (this means that the *executor* is going to express a *promise* attitude towards an updated version of the *proposition*) or might lead to the *transaction's* <u>cancellation</u> (this means that no *production fact* will be created). If the *executor* has expressed a *promise* attitude regarding a *proposition*, then she/he must bring about the <u>realization</u> of the *production act*. Then the *result phase* follows, which starts with a *statement* expression from the *executor* about the requested *proposition* that in his/her opinion has been successfully realized. The *initiator* could either accept this (expressing an *accept* attitude) or reject it (expressing a *decline* attitude). Expressing a *decline* attitude leads to a discussion which might lead to a *compromise* (this means that finally the *initiator* is going to express an *accept* towards the realized *production act*, resulting from *negotiations* that have taken place, leading to a *compromise*) or might lead to the *transaction's cancellation* (this means that no *production fact* will be created). Once the realized *production act* is *accepted* the corresponding *production fact* is considered to have appeared in the (business) reality.

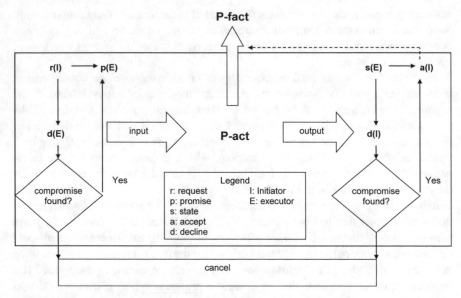

Fig. 6.6 The SDBC interpretation of the transaction concept (Source: [1], p. 70; ©2005, The Author, reprinted with permission)

Further, the **component-based enterprise-software alignment** is considered crucial with regard to *SDBC* and justified by the indisputable advantages of component-based development (see Chap. 5); those advantages include (among other things) the "power" of *re-use*. The *component-based alignment* between *business process modeling* and *software specification* is illustrated in Fig. 6.7.

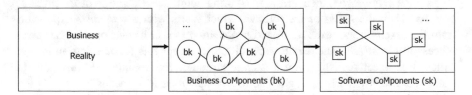

Fig. 6.7 From business coMponents to software specification (Source: [1], p. 72; ©2005, The Author, reprinted with permission)

As depicted in the figure, the target business reality is to be reflected in a set of identified *business coMponents* (see *Definition 11*). Based on them, a *component-based software model* is to be specified, in terms of *software coMponents* (see *Definition 15*). As discussed in the previous section, the *business coMponents* and *software coMponents* are not to be necessarily mapped one-to-one (the former is a purely *enterprise engineering* concern while the latter should have the perspective of the *software system-to-be*).

Still, that kind of alignment allows for (1) <u>ease of modifications</u> (both at *enterprise* level and at *software* level) that are "localized" in particular *business/software coMponents*; (2) <u>traceability</u>—one could easily "trace" between *enterprise* level and *software* level, being capable of analyzing, for example, what would be the impact in the *enterprise* from a newly introduced *software*-level feature (and vice versa); and (3) *business coMponents* and/or *software coMponents* could be conveniently re-used.

As for **re-use**, *three re-use levels* are essential for *SDBC*, namely:

- Re-use of *software coMponents* (lowest level).
- Re-use of *business coMponents*.
- Re-use of *business processes* (highest level).

Re-using *software coMponents* is an option within the *SDBC* approach. Actually, we also acknowledge the power of re-using *software components* as according to the principles of *component-based development* (see the previous chapter). Still, dealing with *re-use* at such a level goes beyond our direct scope in the current chapter because *SDBC* focuses on the derivation of SOFTWARE SPECIFICATIONS. Hence, dealing with *software coMponents* (see *Definition 15*) is well within that focus. At the same time, a methodological *re-use* of *software coMponents* could be a good basis for corresponding reflections towards the *software components* level. As for the *re-use* itself (of *software coMponents*), we will discuss it only after explaining how *software coMponents* are to be identified within *SDBC*. This is illustrated in Fig. 6.8.

As it is seen from the figure, a *business coMponent* is to be methodologically reflected in the *specification of software*. Further, as the figure suggests, such a "business process modeling input" alone is insufficient for specifying a piece of *software*. One is to consider as well what do the (future) users of the system-to-be require, as discussed already. Said otherwise, it is necessary addressing the *user-defined requirements*.

One is to consider as well some technical (and technological) issues possibly leading to design restrictions (since *software systems* are about offering technological solutions to some "problems" in the corresponding *enterprise systems*).

Based on all that input, a *business coMponent* could find its reflection in a *specification model* featuring the software system-to-be. The model could be presented, for instance, in *use case* notations [14]. However, for the purpose of *re-use*, we might find it useful to identify (by applying decomposition) some *software coMponents*. Hence, we arrive at the identification of a *software coMponent(s)*. The figure is also featuring two "situations,", namely, Situation "a" (right up) and Situation "b" (right bottom). We would more often face Situation "a" because (as suggested already in the book) a business component would usually be mapped towards an ICT application that in turn would be decomposed in terms of software component/coMponents (hence, we usually have different granularity levels as it concerns business coMponents and software coMponents). Nevertheless, Situation "b" is also possible—if a *business coMponent* is reflected in a *software specification model* and it is not wise to apply decomposition (e.g., because the model is *re-usable* as it is); in such cases we directly arrive at the identification of a *software coMponent*, on the basis of the *business coMponent*. Hence, we may either reflect a *business coMponent* in a number of *software coMponents* or we may reflect a *business coMponent* in just one *software coMponent*.

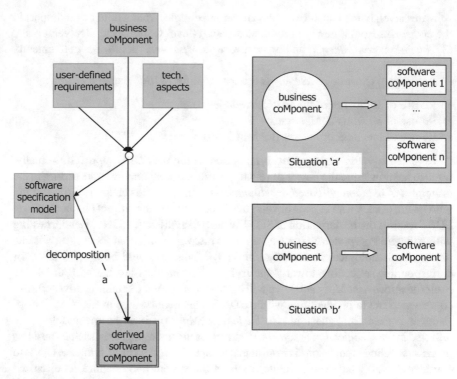

Fig. 6.8 Deriving a software coMponent (Source: [1], p. 74; ©2005, The Author, reprinted with permission)

Thus, re-use at the level of *software coMponents* is about re-using *modeling patterns* representing *software specifications*.

Re-using *business coMponents* points to the enterprise modeling level where we identify ENTERPRISE ENGINEERING BUILDING BLOCKS. As it concerns re-use, we are hence interested in re-usable (enterprise engineering) building blocks that in turn can be either GENERAL or GENERIC—see Fig. 6.9a.

To illustrate this:

- An analogy for <u>general</u> is a lorry platform—it can be "<u>extended</u>" in one way if the lorry would be transporting flowers and in another way if the lorry would be transporting cars, for example.
- An analogy for <u>generic</u> is a universal plug adaptor—it can be "<u>adjusted</u>" in one way if used in Japan and in another way if used in the UK, for example.

Hence, with regard to the *re-usability* of *business coMponents*, if *general* or *generic business coMponents* are identified, they could be *re-used* in the *specification* of different software artifacts; this could be realized either by *extending* a *general business coMponent* or by *parameterizing* a *generic business coMponent*, as illustrated in Fig. 6.9b.

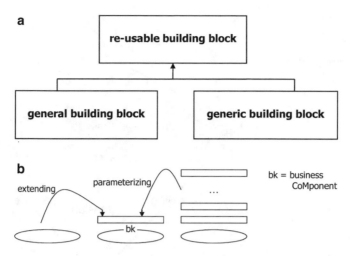

Fig. 6.9 (**a**) Re-usable building blocks (Source: [1], p. 75; ©2005, The Author, reprinted with permission). (**b**) Re-using general/generic business coMponents (Source: [1], p. 76; ©2005, The Author, reprinted with permission)

General business coMponents are *models* that reflect <u>core issues</u> and can be *extended* in a number of ways. For instance, a general brokerage model could be further developed—in one way for building an e-trade system and in another for building a hotel reservation system, to give just two examples. Hence, the particular extension of a *general business coMponent* is motivated by the purpose of use. Further, a *generic business coMponent* should contain in itself more than one optional "functionalities." Through *parameterization*, such a *coMponent* can be adjusted depending on the desired purpose of use.

In summary, within *SDBC*, it is possible to derive a *business coMponent* in *three ways*: either in the trivial way (by building a *model* corresponding to a *business process*—see *Definition 8*), or by *extending a general business coMponent*, or by *parameterizing* (adjusting) *a generic business coMponent* (Fig. 6.10):

Fig. 6.10 Deriving a
business coMponent
(Source: [1], p. 80; ©2005,
The Author, reprinted with
permission)

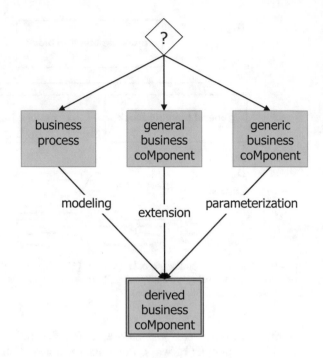

Re-using a *business process* within *SDBC* is a matter of making a general *business process description* that is sufficiently abstract, such that *re-use* is possible. For example, an <arrangement of a service> IN GENERAL may be specified as coming through <registration> + <payment> + <reduction approval> + . . ., for example. Then, this abstract description can be extended in different ways:

– One example could be a HOTEL RESERVATION ARRANGEMENT that in
  particular comes through: NO REGISTRATION + PAYMENT OF A DEPOSIT
  and PAYMENT OF ADMINISTRATIVE COSTS + EARLY BOOKING
  REDUCTION APPROVAL +. . .;
– Another example could be an AUTO INSURANCE ARRANGEMENT that in
  particular comes through: REGISTRATION IN AN INSURANCE COMPANY
  + INSURANCE PAYMENT and PAYMENT OF ADMINISTRATIVE COSTS
  + NO-CLAIM REDUCTION APPROVAL +. . .;
– and so on.

Hence, a *general business process* could be reflected in different *specific business processes*, by adding some particular content to the general business description.

We have now introduced the SDBC approach, and in the remaining of the current chapter, we will firstly outline the SDBC design process (in Sect. 6.3) and then the main SDBC notations (in Sect. 6.4).

6.3   The SDBC Design Process

Based on the essential *SDBC* features introduced already in the current chapter, this section outlines the SDBC design process. Two graphical techniques have been developed especially for that purpose: the ACTIVITY MODEL and the INPUT/OUTPUT MODEL. The development of such techniques was considered necessary because neither of the popular ones (*activity diagram, flow charts, Petri Net, IDEFo,* and so on [1]) proved to be sufficiently effective for thoroughly representing the *SDBC* steps, by providing information on both the dynamics featuring the activities to be realized and the inputs and outputs of each of them. It is particularly useful that the *activity model* and the *input/output model* are not only fully consistent with each other but they also provide views in those two essential directions (respectively). Hence, the dynamic perspective and the "input-output" perspective are soundly matched between the two models [1]. The *activity model* itself (Fig. 6.11) is sophisticated in terms of dynamics (it is featuring parallel processes, two types of synchronization, and so on) of the activities to be realized in applying *SDBC*; the *input/output model* in turn (Fig. 6.12) represents the inputs and outputs of each activity. The corresponding legend is as follows:

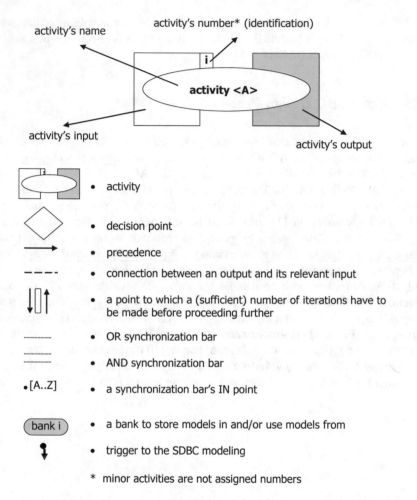

- activity

- decision point

- precedence

- connection between an output and its relevant input

- a point to which a (sufficient) number of iterations have to be made before proceeding further

- OR synchronization bar

- AND synchronization bar

- a synchronization bar's IN point

- a bank to store models in and/or use models from

- trigger to the SDBC modeling

* minor activities are not assigned numbers

Next to that: bp/bc stand for business process/coMponent

ATTENTION: Representing *business coMponents* in different figures in the current book, we use either the label "**bk**" or "**bc**." No matter if a *business coMponent* is labelled "**bk**" or "**bc**," we mean the same. The difference in labeling is only due to "convenience" with regard to the particular figures, such that all used notations are easy to follow.

We will firstly consider the *SDBC activity model*, depicted in Fig. 6.11. There are nine activities on the figure and also four minor activities (they are not assigned a number; their names are backgrounded in grey).

There are three decision points and a point to which a sufficient number of iterations have to be made before proceeding further. There are two OR synchronization bars: the first one is associated with the IN points "A" and "B" (the AB bar), and the second one is associated with the IN points "E," "F," and "G" (the EFG bar). There is an AND synchronization bar; it is associated with the IN points "C" and "D" (the CD bar). There is a <u>trigger</u> to the application of *SDBC*, pointing to *Activity 1* ("information structuring"). The last activity from the model is *Activity 9* ("integration"). *Activity 1* and *Activity 9* are thus assigned "<u>start</u>" and "<u>end</u>" labels, respectively.

The trigger is pointing to <u>Activity 1</u>. It is about the *information structuring*, concerning a focused structured description of the target business reality; this includes thus a *delimitation* step (see above in the chapter). Then we arrive at the first <u>decision point</u> ("*conduct business process generalization?*"). There a decision is to be made on whether the mentioned structured business reality description should be used for the specification (modeling) of a *particular business process* (e.g., hotel reservation match-making), as reflected in <u>Activity 2</u> ("*identification of a business process*"), or the description is to be used for achieving a *generalized view* (e.g., match-making), as reflected in <u>Activity 3</u> ("*generalization of a business process*"). The decision is to be made in the process of studying the particular domain. For example, it might be known that an issue is unique for a company and thus, there is no sense to develop a generalized *model* of it. As seen from Fig. 6.11, such a *business process generalization* (*Activity 3*) could be realized not only based on a structured description of the studied *enterprise system* but also based on the specification of a particular *business process* (this should be done if a *generalization* of such a specification will be also needed further by the modeler—see the second <u>decision point</u> ("*generalize?*")). That is why both before and after *Activity 2*, it is allowed for reaching the "<u>AB" synchronization bar</u> which leads to *Activity 3*.

As also seen from Fig. 6.11, a *model* of a particular *business process* (realized within *Activity 2*) might be used as well for building a *generic business coMponent* (<u>Activity 5</u>), as it is according to the third <u>decision point</u> ("*model a generic business coMponent?*"), in particular if the process flows towards the "<u>CD" synchronization bar</u>. Otherwise, the process would flow towards the <u>minor activity "MODELING"</u>, from where we arrive at <u>Activity 6</u> ("*constructing a business coMponent*"), through the <u>"EFG" synchronization bar</u>. This reflects the situation in which no re-use is realized—we just specify a *business process* (*Definition 6*) and reflect it into a *business coMponent* (*Definition 11*).The *re-use* facilities of *SDBC* hence relate to Activities 3, 4, and 5.

As for *Activity 3*, after it, there follows the fourth <u>decision point</u> ("*model a general business coMponent?*"). There a decision is to be made on whether a *general business coMponent* is going to be modeled; a *general model* of a business process is considered sufficient for building a *general business coMponent*. If *yes*, <u>Activity 4</u> ("*modeling a general business coMponent*") is reached, leading afterwards to the <u>minor activity "EXTENSION"</u>, from where we arrive at *Activity 6* ("*constructing a Business CoMponent*"), through the "*EFG*" *synchronization bar*. Otherwise the "*CD*" *synchronization bar* is reached. It leads to *Activity 5* ("*modeling of a generic Business coMponent*").

As seen from the figure, for *modeling* such a *coMponent*, the required input is a specification of <u>at least two</u> (seen from the "**2**" at IN point "D") models of particular *business processes* AND a *general business process specification (model)*. The reason is that the *generic model* would require not only a *general specification*

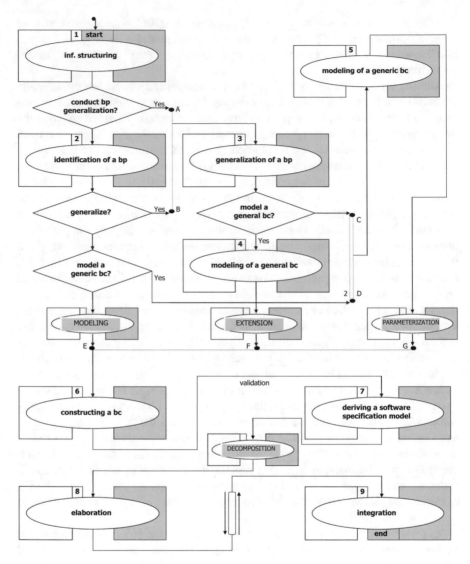

Fig. 6.11 SDBC—activity model (Source: [1], p. 83; ©2005, The Author, reprinted with permission)

which captures "core issues" (derived from a *generalized business process model*) but also at least two particular *business process specifications* to be related to (at least two) corresponding selection options (options to be selected by *parameterizing* the *model*); actually, the rationale behind using *generic modeling patterns* (that capture, as discussed already, several possible design outputs based on grasped core issues) is that the modeler would be able to easily adjust the *generic pattern*, arriving at either of the underlined optional design outputs offered by the *pattern*. After *Activity 5*, the process flows towards the minor activity "PARAMETERIZATION", from where we arrive at Activity 6 ("*constructing a business coMponent*"), through the *"EFG" synchronization bar*.

Thus, the *"EFG" synchronization bar* reflects the three ways of deriving (within *SDBC*) a *business coMponent*: either <u>without</u> realizing *re-use* (by reflecting a *business process model* in a *business coMponent*), or by <u>extending</u> a *general business coMponent*, or by <u>parameterizing</u> a *generic business coMponent* (see Fig. 6.10).

A constructed *business coMponent* is then to be reflected in a *software specification model*; hence, we arrive at <u>Activity 7</u> (*"deriving a software specification model"*). A sound mapping is to be accomplished allowing for a precise reflection between the two. Both the *business coMponent* and the resulting *software specification model* should undergo at least structural and dynamic <u>validation</u> [1]. This is indicated by the label "validation," positioned along the line between *Activity 6* and *Activity 7*.

Regarding the *software specification model*, as mentioned before, depending on the *granularity* of the source *business coMponent*, the model could or could not refer to a particular *software coMponent* (Fig. 6.8). The question concerning software *granularity* is to be addressed particularly from the perspective of the *software* system-to-be. Usually, a derived *software specification model* is to be reflected in more than one *software coMponents*. So, progressing from *Activity 7* to <u>Activity 8</u> (*"elaboration"*) comes through the <u>minor activity "DECOMPOSITION"</u> (indication for the need to *decompose* the *software specification model* into more than one *software coMponents*). However, in the cases in which no *decomposition* would be necessary, the *software specification model* is considered itself being a *software coMponent*.

Once identified, a *software coMponent* needs to be specified in more detail—further elicitation should be provided concerning the *coMponent's* entities and interactions. So, once identified and specified, a *software coMponent* should undergo *elaboration* (*Activity 8*).

And in the end, after a sufficient (see below) number of *software coMponents* have been identified, specified, and elaborated, they should be *integrated* (<u>Activity 9</u>) in the process of specifying the functionality of the software *system*-to-be. Hence, there is a "special" relation between *Activity 8* and *Activity 9*; an indication for this is the symbol positioned on the line between those activities, showing that <u>many</u> *software coMponents* would be necessary that would represent together a sufficient input for specifying a complete model of the software *system*-to-be. However, establishing what is a sufficient "basis" for integration is a delicate issue because of the following: (1) Often some members of the development team would be still tuning the overall application architecture while other team members would be considering in parallel particular *software coMponents*; for this reason, it may be not known at a particular moment which is the "full set" of *software coMponents* to be considered for integration. This may lead to situations when "clusters" of *coMponents* are integrated but this does not reflect all application components. (2) It may be that "draft" application versions are built and if this would be the case, the integration would inevitably be partial in the sense that it does not "cover" all application *coMponents*. This decision is often subjective and/or intuitive; anyway, we adopt in *SDBC* the relevant general guidelines provided in [15], related to the *component-based product-line engineering* [16].

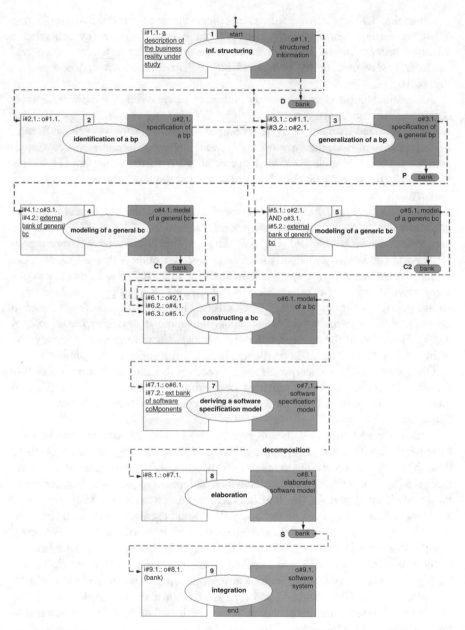

Fig. 6.12 SDBC—input/output model (Source: [1], p. 86; ©2005, The Author, reprinted with permission)

So, after considering the *SDBC activity model*, we proceed to the *SDBC input/output model*. It is depicted in Fig. 6.12. As seen from the figure, the <u>starting input</u> for applying *SDBC* is any (informal, unstructured) *description of the enterprise system* to be considered (<u>Input 1.1</u>), including *domain-imposed requirements* possibly representing *norms* [17]. The description might be *textual* or it might be a *graphical model*, a conversation or any other form. The first activity's output (Output 1.1) should be a *structured description of the studied system*. This description should thoroughly reflect the considered business reality; next to that, the description must be precisely *delimited*, as mentioned before. As seen from the figure, such a structured and delimited description might be stored in a bank (**D bank**) from where to be usable also in other relevant modeling tasks.

Such a description could be used as an input for either *Activity 2* (Input 2.1) or *Activity 3* (Input 3.1) (either for identifying a *business process* or for building a *generalized business process model*). Building a *generalized business process model* could be done as well based on an identified *business process* (Input 3.2). An indication for this is the line between *Activity 2* and *Activity 3*.

A *generalized business process model* could be stored in a bank (**P bank**) for multiple uses. It could also be used as an input for constructing (*Activity 4*) a *general business coMponent* (Input 4.1). As seen from the figure, *general business coMponents* could also be taken from an external bank (**C1 bank**) (Input 4.2). A constructed *general business coMponent* could be either stored in a bank—*C1 bank* (for use in other project(s))—or used as an input for the construction (*Activity 6*) of a *business coMponent* (Input 6.2). As seen from Fig. 6.11, this comes through *extending* the *general business coMponent*.

Regarding the modeling of a *generic business coMponent*, it should be based on a *generalized business process* model AND at least two (Fig. 6.11) models of particular *business processes*; this concerns Input 5.1, Fig. 6.12. *Generic business coMponents* could also be taken from an external bank (**C2 bank**). As seen from Fig. 6.12, a constructed *generic business coMponent* could be either stored in a bank (*C2 bank*) (for use in other project(s)) or used as an input for the construction (*Activity 6*) of a *business coMponent* (Input 6.3). As seen from Fig. 6.11, this comes through *parameterizing* the *generic business coMponent*. And finally, as seen from Fig. 6.12, the third possible input (Input 6.1) for the construction of a *business coMponent* is a *business process model* (Output 2.1).

Deriving a *software specification model* (from which *software coMponents* could be identified, by applying decomposition, as already mentioned) is based either on a *business coMponent* constructed in the above proposed way (Input 7.1) or on import of *software coMponents* from an external bank (Input 7.2).

Each of the derived *software coMponents* should be *elaborated* (*Activity 8*; Input 8.1) in terms of structural, dynamic, and data aspects (in order to bring sufficient elicitation for the further software design activities, as already mentioned) and stored in a bank (**S bank**). From there, *software coMponents* will be taken (Input 9.1) and integrated for the purpose of *specifying the software system-to-be*.

A *specification model* of a software *system* represents the final output (Output 9.1) of the *SDBC* approach. Hence, the *end point* is reached and this is indicated by labeling *Activity 9* with "end," as stated already.

In summary, we have outlined the *SDBC* design process, by means of the *SDBC activity model* and the *SDBC input/output model*, developed exclusively for that purpose. In the following section, we will present the notations to be used for the *SDBC modeling* itself.

6.4   The SDBC Notations

SDBC is an approach that has its *underlying theoretical roots* and also its *process outline* elaborating on *what* and *how* to do in implementing the approach—all those have already been introduced.

Hence, it should be possible to apply *any* (graphical) *notations* in realizing *SDBC* modeling as far as they conform to the approach's *underlying concepts*. Still, we are proposing particular graphical *notations* for the *SDBC* modeling, making sure (based on previous research [1]) that those *notations* are well aligned with *SDBC's underlying concepts* and *supportive theories*. For this reason, we recommend using those *notations* although we do not claim that they are exclusive with regard to the implementation of *SDBC*.

Since *SDBC* has two "grounding points," namely, *enterprise engineering* and *software engineering* (see Fig. 6.2), we will firstly present in this section several most important *enterprise-modeling*-related *notations* (Fig. 6.13) and then we will present several most important *software-specification*-related *notations* (Fig. 6.14).

Those notations will be considered in the following chapter, when the SDBC approach will be demonstrated by means of a case study and illustrative examples.

With regards to the *enterprise modeling notations*, as it is seen from Fig. 6.13:

- The RR ("RR" standing for "Roles and Relations") model (or chart) that is depicted up-left in the figure reflects a RELATION between TWO roles (meaning role types), assuming that any MORE COMPLEX relation can be decomposed in a number of relations that are "between" two roles. In the chart, the labels featuring the two roles that concern a relation are "put" in named boxes. Further, the label featuring the relation itself is "put" in between. Finally, the label that features the role pointing to the realization of the relation is underlined. Let us consider, for example, the roles "expert" and "customer" as well as the relation "realize expertise". Hence, we should underline the word "expert" because it is the expert who realizes the expertise. And in the end, each role-to-role relation is given a unique code—see the right side of the RR model visualization.

- The SCI ("SCI" standing for "Structuring the Customer Information") model (or chart) that is depicted up-right in the figure assumes an instantiation with regard to the addressed enterprise and elaboration with regard to its structure. In the chart, there is a big rectangle with rounded corners—this is where the labels featuring the modeled enterprise are "put." They are positioned as follows: (1) The name of the enterprise is put in a smaller rectangle with rounded corners and (2) The labels corresponding to the relevant organizational units of the enterprise are put in small rectangles. Further, there are named boxes outside the big rectangle with rounded corners. Here, we put labels featuring roles (not instantiated). Each of those roles concerns a collaboration with the enterprise. Finally, the unit-role lines indicate where in particular (in which particular organizational units) are those collaborations focused. For example, the ABO supermarket in Sofia has a number of departments including Finance department, Sales department, Marketing department, and so on, while at the same time, there are a number of related ABO-external role types, such as customer, supplier, insurer, and so on.

NOTATIONS
- enterprise modeling -

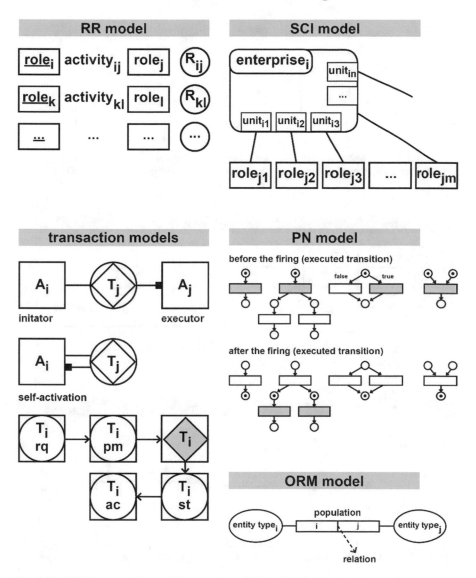

Fig. 6.13 SDBC—enterprise modeling notations (©2017, The Author, reprinted with permission)

NOTATIONS
- software specification -

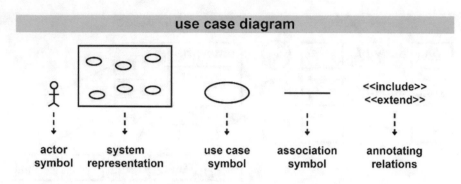

use case diagram

| actor symbol | system representation | use case symbol | association symbol | annotating relations |

UML class diagram

| class representation | aggregation | | generalization |

UML activity diagram

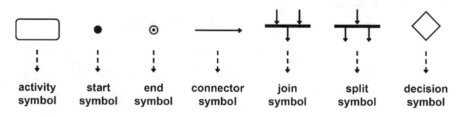

| activity symbol | start symbol | end symbol | connector symbol | join symbol | split symbol | decision symbol |

Fig. 6.14 SDBC—software specification notations (©2017, The Author, reprinted with permission)

- In the end, those relations (see above) are to be reflected in corresponding *transactions* (see *Definition* 5). They are modeled using notations as presented in Fig 6.13—see the middle-left part of the figure: we have labels featuring the *initiator* and the *executor* put in boxes while the *transaction* itself is modeled as a disk+diamond, conforming to *enterprise ontology* [18]; the small black box in the chart is to indicate who the *executor* is.

  Further, modeling self-activation is also possible, assuming that the initiator and the executor are the same "entity." Finally, "zooming in" with regard to a *transaction* is possible, such that all corresponding coordination (communicative) acts are revealed (modeled as a disk+box) as well as the corresponding production act (modeled as a diamond+box), with "rq," "pm," "st," and "ac" meaning "request," "promise," "state," and "accept," respectively.

- With *transactions* making up corresponding *business processes* (see *Definition* 6) which in turn are to be also modeled in terms of overall *behavior*, we need appropriate notations and we have opted for the Petri Net (PN) notations [1]. Those notations are depicted in Fig. 6.13—see the middle right part of the figure. We argue that those notations are intuitive; also they are considered widely popular. For this reason, we will not introduce them in the current chapter. What we would like to make explicit nevertheless is the wide applicability of the PN notations, allowing for modeling sequential behavior, parallel behavior, decision points, and so on, as the figure suggests.

- Finally, as it concerns the modeling of data (we call it factual modeling), we have opted for ORM (the Object Role Modeling). This notation has been studied in [1]. A corresponding visualization is presented in Fig 6.13—see the bottom right part of the figure. Actually, using ORM notations, one could model two types of entities/roles and a relation between them. In fact, this is similar to the RR notations. What is specific about ORM nevertheless is that it is about POPULATING the model in terms of data corresponding to instantiations. For instance, if we have the types "professor" and "department," and the relation "works for," populating the model would mean instantiating as follows, for example: Professor John Smith works for the Computer Science department, Professor Ben Starkey works for the Physics department, Professor George Ashley works for the Chemistry department, and so on.

With regard to the *software specification notations*, as it is seen from Fig. 6.14, they are based on *UML*. That is because *Unified Modeling Language* is claimed to be a de facto standard notation as it concerns the specification of software [1, 14]. In particular:

- The *use case* diagram is appropriate for modeling the functionality of the software system-to-be at high level. The system is represented as a number of *use cases* (ovals) in a rectangular area, surrounded by the primary *actor* (the *system*'s customer) and possibly by *stakeholders* with related interests. There may be relations among *use cases* or between an *actor* and a *use case*—those are represented by lines (association symbol), as it is shown on Fig. 6.14 (up). Finally, there are two *stereotypes* considered, namely, "include" and "extend."

Explaining this further is left beyond the scope of the current chapter; it is expected that most readers are familiar with UML.

- The *UML class diagram* is featuring *classification* and is capable of modeling *classes* (specifying *attributes* and *operations* accordingly), *aggregation*, *generalization*, and so on, as shown on Fig. 6.14 (in the middle of the figure). Explaining this further is left beyond the scope of the current chapter; it is expected that most readers are familiar with UML.
- The *UML activity* diagram is capable of modeling overall system behaviors, having explicit notations that allow to model *sequential behavior, parallel behavior*, and *decision/join/split* patterns, as shown on Fig. 6.14 (down). Explaining this further is left beyond the scope of the current chapter; it is expected that most readers are familiar with UML.

And in the end, it is to be noted that neither the enterprise modeling notations addressed above (see Fig. 6.13) nor the software specification notations addressed above (see Fig. 6.14) reflect exhaustive lists of notations since this is not considered necessary. The notations we have presented are possible notations of choice when applying SDBC and are expected to "cover" some typical modeling situations.

* * *

IN SUMMARY, in this chapter, we have presented the SDBC approach, elaborating its foundations, design process outline, and recommended notations. In this way, we have shared our ideas on how enterprise engineering and software engineering can be brought together, driven by the goal of specifying software. In the following chapter, we will demonstrate this, by means of a case study and illustrative examples.

References

1. Shishkov B (2005) Software specification based on re-usable business components. Delft University Press, Delft
2. Shishkov B (2017) Enterprise information systems, a modeling approach. IICREST Press, Sofia
3. Shishkov B, Janssen M (2018) Enforcing context-awareness and privacy-by-design in the specification of information systems. In: Shishkov B (ed) Business modeling and software design, BMSD 2017. Lecture notes in business information processing, vol 309. Springer, Cham
4. Shishkov B, Janssen M, Yin Y (2017) Towards context-aware and privacy-sensitive systems. In: 7th International symposium on business modeling and software design, BMSD 2017, SCITEPRESS
5. Shishkov B, Van Sinderen M, Quartel D (2006) SOA-driven business-software alignment. In: Proceedings of the ICEBE'06 IEEE international conference on e-business engineering. IEEE
6. Cockburn A (2000) Writing effective use cases. Addison-Wesley, Boston, MA
7. Shishkov B, Larsen JB, Warnier M, Janssen M (2018) Three categories of context-aware systems. In: Shishkov B (ed) Business modeling and software design, BMSD 2018. Lecture notes in business information processing, vol 319. Springer, Cham
8. Shishkov B, Van Sinderen M, Tekinerdogan B (2007) Model-driven specification of software services. In: Proceedings of the ICEBE'07 IEEE international conference on e-business engineering. IEEE

9. Shishkov B (2010) Methodological support for the design of enterprise information systems with SDBC: towards distributed, service-oriented and context-aware solutions. In: Proceedings of the 4th international workshop on enterprise systems and technology, SCITEPRESS, Athens, Greece, July 2010

10. Shishkov B, Warnier M, Van Sinderen M (2010) On the application of autonomic and context-aware computing to support home energy management. In: Proceedings of the 12th international conference on enterprise information systems (ICEIS), SCITEPRESS, Funchal, Madeira, Portugal, 8–12 June 2010

11. Shishkov B, Dietz JLG (2004) Design of software applications using generic business components. In: Proceedings of the 37th Hawaii international conference on system sciences (HICSS), IEEE, Big Island, Hawaii, USA, 5–8 January 2004

12. Wieringa RJ (1995) Requirements engineering, framework for understanding. Wiley, New York

13. Kotonya G, Sommerville I (1998) Requirements engineering. Wiley, New York

14. UML. The unified modeling language. http://www.uml.org

15. Atkinson C, Muthig D (2002) Enhancing component reusability through product line technology. In: Proceedings of the 7th international conference on software reuse, Austin, TX, USA, 15–19 April 2002

16. Atkinson C, Bayer J, Bunse C, Kamsties E, Laitenberger O, Laqua R, Muthig D, Paech B, Wust Z, Zettel J (2001) Component-based product line engineering with UML. Addison-Wesley, Boston, MA

17. Liu K (2000) Semiotics in information systems engineering. Cambridge University Press, Cambridge

18. Dietz JLG (2006) Enterprise ontology, theory and methodology. Springer, Heidelberg

Chapter 7
Case Study and Examples

The **case study** research strategy contributes (in general) to capturing some practical perspectives of the investigated problems. It is helpful for considering the knowledge of practitioners in exploring the research area. According to Yin [1], a *case study* is an empirical inquiry that investigates a contemporary phenomenon within its real-life context, especially when the boundaries between phenomenon and context are not clearly evident. The *case study* as a research strategy comprises an all-encompassing method—with the logic of design incorporating specific approaches to data collection and data analysis. Although in the past, *case studies* had been considered only as an exploratory tool [2], they have proved to be more than just an exploratory strategy. Some of the best and most famous *case studies* have been both descriptive and explanatory [1].

Usually, *case studies* are the preferred strategy when HOW or WHY questions are being posed, when the investigator has little control over events, and when the focus is on a contemporary phenomenon within some real-life context [1].

In order to realize successfully this strategy, it is essential to design properly the particular *case study*, to collect precisely consistent evidence and to analyze it.

In the current research, the *case study* strategy is applied following a specific goal, namely, to **validate the applicability of a proposed approach**.

Hence, firstly in the current chapter, the applicability of *SDBC* will be "demonstrated" by means of a test case study carried out at a **large Dutch insurance company** (since it was not considered appropriate mentioning its name, the company is referred to as "*Icomp*" coming from "Insurance company"). The goal of the *case study* is not only to provide practical evidence about the strengths of *SDBC* but also to **validate** some of the essential ideas and concepts suggested within the current book. Following the *Icomp* case, we will present (further in the current chapter) small illustrative examples for the sake of briefly illustrating issues that are not "covered" by the *Icomp* case.

This chapter is structured as follows: Sect. 7.1 presents the case study background, bringing elicitation on the case's focus, problem, and goals as well as on the selection of the target organization (where the case study has been carried out).

© Springer Nature Switzerland AG 2020   175
B. Shishkov, *Designing Enterprise Information Systems*, The Enterprise Engineering Series, https://doi.org/10.1007/978-3-030-22441-7_7

Section 7.2 outlines the collected information, to be used as an input for the application of *SDBC*. This information has been kindly delivered to us by representatives of the target organization. The particular application of the *SDBC* approach is reflected in Sect. 7.3. And in the end, Sect. 7.4 and Sect. 7.5 present (as addition) illustrative examples, as abovementioned.

7.1   Background

The preparation of the *case study* has been driven by its goal and also by the consideration of several other relevant aspects. Among them are the selection of a target organization, the *case study* focus, and the problem definition. Those issues will be briefly discussed below:

Goal of the *Case Study*
From the perspective of the needs of the current research, the main goal of the *case study* has been defined as follows: validation of the conceptual framework of the *SDBC* approach and also of its application guidelines, by applying them in a real-life case. Taking into consideration the essential elements presented as part of those guidelines, the *case study* should focus on the following aspects:

* *Enterprise* analysis and *modeling*, comprising the consideration of the initial (case) information, the structuring of corresponding elements, and the identification of relevant *business process modeling units* and their adequate reflection in *business coMponents* (soundly elicited in terms of *structure*, *dynamics*, *data*, and *communicative issues*).
* Derivation of a *software specification model*, comprising the reflection of a *business coMponent(s)* into a corresponding *software specification model*, to be further decomposed in terms of *software coMponents*.

Selection of an Organization to Be Explored
In order to adequately validate *SDBC*, a suitable organization had to be found, and it also had to get involved in the *case study*, such that relevant information is provided accordingly. The choice of an organization was based on the following criteria:

* Size of the organization. The bigger an organization, the greater the complexity of its *business processes*; this in turn concerns the sophistication of the support provided by corresponding *information systems* to those *business processes*. For instance, small organizations working in an ad hoc manner are rarely facilitated by sophisticated *information systems* and technologies. Thus, focusing (in this research) on the support to *business processes*, provided by *ICT applications* which are comparatively (more than average) complex, we have had the requirement for a large organization (with more than 2000 employees).
* The business domain. As it is well known, organizations belonging to some business domains are more dependable on a proper ICT application support than organizations belonging to other business domains. We have targeted business domains related to the financial sector because financial companies are

currently among those greatly depending on *information systems* and technologies.

Hence, as stated before, the *case study* considered in the current chapter has been carried out in a *financial* (in particular *insurance*) company, namely, the company *Icomp*. *Icomp* delivers financial products (and financial services) to end customers.

Focus of the *Case Study*
Considering the company *Icomp*, the *case study* has focused in particular on a part of the company's business, namely, the distribution of financial products. This choice has been made not only because such a focus has a direct relation to the core of the business of *Icomp* (this will be seen from the information provided further on in the current chapter) but also because the mentioned part of the business of the company strongly requires appropriate *business process modeling* and is dependent on *information systems* and technologies. Therefore, relevant improvements (and innovative ideas) in those directions could be useful for *Icomp* and beyond.

Problem Definition
Considering the available actual information featuring *Icomp* (this information is reflected in the following section), we have defined two problems to be addressed in the current *case study*:

- The *environment* of *Icomp* demands a sounder and more flexible way in which the company specifies and modifies its financial-products-related *Business Processes*, grasping adequately all essential aspects.
- A better clarity would be appreciated about the impact of eventual reorganization within the company's financial-products-related business activities. This is driven by the necessity of introducing relevant technologies in support of the mentioned activities.

Goal in Context
Considering the main goal of this *case study* (see above) and in relation to the defined problems (addressed already), we have made the following elaboration of the general case study goals, in the light also of benefits that the case study could bring to *Icomp*:

- Provide insight into the way in which the financial-products-related *business processes* of the company could be modeled so that there is a possibility for flexible modifiability (possibly counting on re-use), soundness, and completeness (regarding the essential aspects of a business reality).
  - This might include the *modeling* of essential issues characterizing the company and its *environment*.
- Provide insight into the way in which a *software specification model* could be soundly derived based on an *enterprise model (featuring business processes)*.
  - This might include a proposal featuring the introduction of an *ICT application* and a demonstration how its specification can be realized.

The following section will provide information about *Icomp*.

7.2   Icomp

As stated before, this *case study* has been carried out at the company *Icomp*. We will briefly introduce it in the current section, considering one particular view on *Icomp*, namely, the <u>financial products distribution</u> part of the company's business (in line with what has been mentioned already). From now on, by *"Icomp"* we will mean just those things (concerning the company) that are associated with this particular view.

Such a perspective on *Icomp* has been taken (as already explained) because of its direct relation to the core of the company's business: the distribution of financial products to end customers through <u>brokers</u>. As discussed already, the distribution of such products is where *Icomp* would possibly need an application support.

Distributing financial products through *brokers* means that there are a number of (insurance) financial companies, a number of brokers, and a number of end customers concerning this distribution mechanism. *Broker$_j$* distributes products of a number of companies (including *Icomp*, if it has an agreement with *Icomp*) to a number of end customers. *End_customer$_k$* might be advised by a number of *brokers* about the products of a number of financial companies. Hence, *Icomp* uses a number of *brokers* through which it distributes its (financial) products to a number of *end customers*. Thus, we could relate *Icomp* basically to two actor-role types, namely, "BROKER" and "END_CUSTOMER", as shown in Fig. 7.1. For example, as it concerns the terms we use: (1) In the financial context, "broker" would be a role type featuring a finance-related match-making capability in general; (2) "contracting broker" or "advising broker" would be particularly broker-related roles (a contracting broker would be capable of contracting on behalf of the parties while an advising broker would just connect the parties); and (3) "Company ABC" would be an instance of "contracting broker," if offering finance-related match-making with a contracting "capability." This is just to illustrate our considering the terms "instance," "role," and "role type." Now back to the case study: The BROKER role could be fulfilled by any of the intermediary (brokerage) companies registered with *Icomp*. The END_CUSTOMER role could be fulfilled by any human or organization interested in the financial products distributed by *Icomp*.

Fig. 7.1 Brokers, facilitating the relations of Icomp with end customers (Source: [2], p. 128; ©2005, The Author, reprinted with permission)

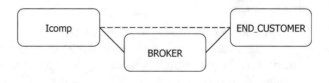

Thus, on the figure, the line between *Icomp* and END_CUSTOMER is dashed, indicating that the relation to *end customers* is indirect; it comes through *brokers*.

A *broker* collaborating with *Icomp* distributes its financial products on the basis of an agreement. It specifies which products the *broker* could sell to *end customers* and what commission it would get from *Icomp*. The following information elaborates further on the *Icomp-broker* relation:

- An agreement can be started/changed/ended between *Icomp* and a *broker*.

- A *broker* might receive support from *Icomp*. For example, if a *broker* has been successful in selling products (of *Icomp*) to representatives of a particular customer segment, it might be useful that *Icomp* provides to the *broker* a specialized training concerning this particular segment.
- The commission paid by *Icomp* to a *broker* is featured as follows:
  - For each new agreement, a *broker* gets a "starting commission."
  - For each month in which an *end customer* keeps his/her insurance (particularly advised by a *broker*), the *broker* gets "monthly commission."
- A *broker* must pay a premium to *Icomp* for an agreement initiated.

With respect to the financial products distribution, *Icomp* has relations not only with intermediary (brokerage) companies but also with *reinsurance companies, product development companies, investigation companies*, and other (less important) ones.

It is possible that in some cases a *reinsurance company takes* over insurance risk from *Icomp*.

In complicated situations, *Icomp* relies on *investigation companies* for the provision of expert support, for instance, realization of an expertise.

For keeping its product portfolio actual, *Icomp* receives support from *product development companies* delivering new financial (including insurance) products.

As for *Icomp* itself, it is essential to consider its being divided into five departments, namely, <u>Account Management</u>, <u>Acceptance</u>, <u>Claims</u>, <u>Finance</u>, and <u>Marketing</u>.

The *Account Management department* manages the *Icomp-broker* relations. It proposes agreement(s) to a *broker*, and once an agreement is signed, the department controls its execution, by making sure that the *broker's* results are in accordance to what is in the agreement.

The *Acceptance department* handles requests of end customers for financial product(s), for example, a request for a property insurance.

The *Claims department* deals with claims of end customers and the (eventual) investigation (by experts) of those claims.

The *Financial department* deals with payments, including the premium payments received by *Icomp* from *end customers*, the payments of *Icomp* to *end customers* for claims, the commission payments that *brokers* receive from *Icomp*, the payments of *Icomp* to product development companies and so on.

The *Marketing department* is responsible for the products strategy of *Icomp*, dealing with product development and also with advertising and public relations.

The following section focuses on the application of the *SDBC* approach and is essentially reflecting the content of Chap. 7 of [2]; further, the source of all the figures used in the section is the mentioned chapter (for this reason, the sources of used figures are not explicitly mentioned for each figure, only in the following section).

7.3 Applying SDBC

Based on the *case study* background on one hand and on the information about *Icomp* on the other hand (addressed consecutively in the previous sections), this section is to elaborate on how *SDBC* could be applied within the context of the *Icomp* case:

The section is divided into three sub-sections as follows:

- Section 7.3.1 will focus on the considered (within the *case study*) information and the identification (based on it) of several relevant *business coMponents*.
- Section 7.3.2 is to consider the specification and elaboration of a particular *business coMponent*.
- Section 7.3.3 will demonstrate the derivation of a *software specification model*, based on the specified *business coMponent*.

Since the steps to follow in applying the *SDBC* approach have been introduced, explained, and discussed in the previous chapter, we will now just follow those of them relevant to the tasks within the current case, without explaining in much detail the steps.

7.3.1 From the Case Information to Business CoMponents

As mentioned before, in this sub-section, we will show how *business coMponents* could be identified based on the case information (see Sect. 7.2). We provide below a *roadmap* (fully consistent with the *SDBC* outline—see Chap. 6) which gives in advance information about the modeling activities (steps) to take place within the current sub-section, in order to achieve the goal (as defined already):

Step 1 : Building of a <u>generalization hierarchy</u> for the explored domain.
Step 2 : Identification of relevant <u>actor-roles</u>.
Step 3 : Identification of the corresponding (potential) <u>inter-role actions</u> (relations).
Step 4 : Elaboration of those relations in terms of <u>semiotic norms</u>.
Step 5 : <u>Decomposition</u> of *Icomp* + a related positioning of corresponding relations.
Step 6 : Construction of a <u>SCI chart</u>.
Step 7 : Derivation of *business coMponents*.

Those seven steps will be addressed within the current sub-section.

Building of a Generalization Hierarchy for the Explored Domain
Structuring and positioning semantically the case information is in line with Activity 1 (from the *SDBC* Input/Output Model (see Chap. 6)).

As a starting point concerning the case information (see Sect. 7.2), we select the entities (natural/legal persons) who collaborate with the target company (*Icomp*). They are (in alphabetical order) *intermediary companies, investigation companies, product development companies,* and *reinsurance companies. Investigation companies* are actually a sub-type of *consultancy companies* (according to the interviewed specialists from *Icomp*). The rest of the mentioned ones are sub-types of *financial companies*. Being an insurance company itself, *Icomp* is a financial company too.

This information is sufficient for identifying a **generalization hierarchy** (organizational business objects model) for the explored domain. The hierarchy is charted in accordance with the guidelines proposed in [2], with the aim of bringing order in the original input information. The organizational business object *model* regarding *Icomp* is shown in Fig. 7.2a.

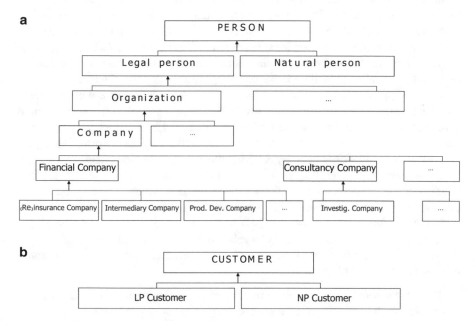

Fig. 7.2 (**a**) The organizational business object model concerning the case study. (**b**) The business object model regarding the customers of Icomp

Hence, as seen from the figure, *Icomp* collaborates with:

– Three types of financial companies, namely, (1) reinsurance companie(s), (2) intermediary companie(s), and (3) product development companie(s).
– Investigation companies which are types of consultancy companies.

The position of *Icomp* within this model is also clear—*Icomp* is an insurance company.

Besides these types of companies, *Icomp* collaborates also, of course, with its customers. According to the considered case information, a customer of *Icomp* might be any person, legal or natural. This is illustrated on Fig. 7.2b where "LP" stands for *legal person* and "NP" stands for *natural person*.

In the rest of this section, any customer, no matter to which of the two customer sub-types (Fig. 7.2b) it belongs, would be called "*customer*." The reason is that *Icomp* does not distinguish between its customers in any way. It is to be stated also that besides the term "*customer*," the materials concerning *Icomp*, including the descriptions presented in the previous section, contain also the terms "*client*" and "*end customer*". Actually, those two are synonyms of "*customer*". Hence, they will be left out for the rest of the current section and only the term "*customer*" will be used.

Identification of Relevant Actor-Roles

Following the *roadmap*, the next step is to produce an `actor-role model` based on the *business object models*. As studied and motivated already, if the actor-role concept is applied, then it would be easier to model complex *systems*; examples were mentioned already in support of this claim: for instance, if a manager sends a fax, then she/he plays the role "Secretary." Hence, in such a case, if we do not model an actor-role, we should either model the individual natural/legal persons (which is too much complicated in such situations) or oversimplify those issues (which might lead to limitations in the *enterprise model* being created). Further on in the current section, the term "*role*" will be used, meaning "*actor-role*" (see Chap. 2).

Thus, we proceed towards the identification of *roles*; this is in tune with the *SDBC* application guidelines, presented already in the current book. We start with an initial consideration of the roles which are typical for each of the identified company types (see Fig. 7.2a). In particular, the starting point is to find a suitable word ("label") for each of those *roles*; this is done by studying the case information (*customers* should be considered, too). The next step is to find out (based on the case information) whether any company could fulfill not only the role(s) typical for its type but also other roles; this was not observed considering the *Icomp* case.

However, formulating a word (label) does not give full information about the meaning of the *role*. Therefore, the <u>word</u> should be extended with some <u>elaboration</u>. By *role* elaboration is meant a description about what characterizes the particular role. We do this as follows:

- The typical *role* type for a reinsurance company is formulated as REINSURER: one fulfils REINSURER if taking over risk from an existing insurance. A reinsurance company is not expected to take other *roles*.
- The typical *role* type for an intermediary company is formulated as BROKER: one fulfills BROKER if matching *customers* to relevant financial companies, in particular insurance companies (in the current case), by (1) giving financial consultations to *customers* about those companies and (2) directing *customers* to particular companies if there is a match between *customer* requirements and company product(s)—such a direction is realized, by advising for a product of a particular company. An intermediary company is not expected to take other *roles*.
- The typical *role* type for a product development company is formulated as SUPPLIER: one fulfills SUPPLIER if delivering financial products to insurance companies. A product development company is not expected to take other roles.
- The typical *role* type for an investigation company is formulated as EXPERT: one fulfils EXPERT if delivering expertise (in the form of expert reports and/or investigations) for the benefit of insurance companies. An investigation company is not expected to take other *roles*.
- In is necessary also to formulate the *role* type CUSTOMER: one fulfills CUSTOMER if purchasing financial products (including insurance products) and providing specialized information upon request.

- *Icomp*, as the target company in this case study, fulfills the role type INSURER; one fulfills INSURER if selling financial products (including insurance products).

We stress upon the fact that we have identified *role* types (rather than particular roles). We have already discussed this in the previous section, considering an example featuring the role type "broker" and the roles "contracting broker" and "advising broker." Let us consider another example, featuring receptionists: (1) A receptionist at the Mitsubishi Dealership in Hoofddorp (NL) is supposed to meet visitors, help customers, mediate between customers and mechanics, make appointments, and so on; (2) A receptionist at the EWI Faculty of TU Delft (NL) is supposed to meet visitors, manage the campus cards of employees, assist during coffee breaks in the building (if any), check for "late workers" in the building before closing time, and so on. Both roles are "receptionist" but what is meant by this at Mitsubishi—Hoofddorp and TU Delft are different. For this reason, it makes sense considering "receptionist" as a role type (this is actually the role "receptionist" in general) and possibly modeling as different roles the "Hoofddorp features" and the "Delft features," as in the above example. Anyway, this is a matter of modeling choices that are often done intuitively by the designer. As for the current case study, considering REINSURER, for example, this is a role type; we may have "regulatory reinsurer" (just fulfilling what the state is supposed to "guarantee" to customers), "corporate reinsurer" (working for profit), and so on, as particular roles. Anyway, we are not going to discuss this further and it is not to be expected that in the current case study we will always be explicit in distinguishing between roles and role types. It is possible that we consider a reinsurance company that is just an "instance" of REINSURER, meaning that we are not interested whether the business of this company is "regulatory" or "corporate," for example.

Further, those identified *role* types are expected to somehow relate to *initiators/ executors* of particular *transactions*. This, as a part of the modeling output reflected in the current section, would facilitate the identification of *business coMponents*.

Figure 7.3 shows the identified *role* types and also their elaborations. The role type labels are depicted in rectangles outlined by double line. Attached to them are rectangles outlined with single line. The elaborations are depicted in them.

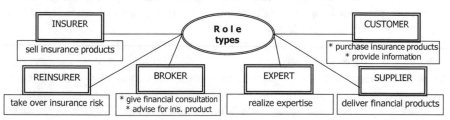

Fig. 7.3 Basic role types within the Icomp case

As seen from the figure, there are six *role* types: INSURER corresponds to insurance companies (such is the company under study (*Icomp*)). CUSTOMER corresponds to the customers of insurance companies. The other *roles types* are straightforwardly derived from the hierarchy model (see Fig. 7.2a): REINSURER (Fig. 7.3) is the *role* type typical for a reinsurance company (Fig. 7.2a), BROKER (Fig. 7.3) is the *role* type typical for an intermediary company (Fig. 7.2a), and so on. As for the *role elaborations* which are also depicted on Fig. 7.3, they have been formulated based on the case study information and interviews with employees of *Icomp*.

Identification of Inter-role Relations

Based on the identified major *role* types, the (potential) actions (relations) among them are studied. We will call those relations *inter-role relations* from now on, or "*relations*" for short. Studying the *relations* would be useful with regard to a consideration of the structure and dynamics of the explored *enterprise system*. As a first step in identifying the existence of relations, the interviewed *Icomp* employees were asked to answer whether or not a *relation* exists between each two of the *role* types. Table 7.1 contains the collected data. As seen from the table, only the grey rows correspond to an existing relation. For example, from the third row (from top to bottom), it is seen that there exists a relation between INSURER and EXPERT.

Table 7.1 Identified inter-role relations

INSURER	REINSURER	Yes, a relation exists
INSURER	BROKER	Yes, a relation exists
INSURER	EXPERT	Yes, a relation exists
INSURER	SUPPLIER	Yes, a relation exists
INSURER	CUSTOMER	Yes, a relation exists
REINSURER	BROKER	No, a relation does not exist
REINSURER	EXPERT	No, a relation does not exist
REINSURER	SUPPLIER	No, a relation does not exist
REINSURER	CUSTOMER	No, a relation does not exist
BROKER	EXPERT	No, a relation does not exist
BROKER	SUPPLIER	No, a relation does not exist
BROKER	CUSTOMER	Yes, a relation exists
EXPERT	SUPPLIER	No, a relation does not exist
EXPERT	CUSTOMER	Yes, a relation exists
SUPPLIER	CUSTOMER	No, a relation does not exist

We now have to briefly describe each identified relation. In achieving this, we will firstly consider in more detail the particular *role types* and secondly address aspects that concern their relations.

The first sub-task could be realized through binary relationships—a *binary relationship* does concern two entities and is usually described by noun-verb-noun; the nouns correspond to the entities and the verb describes the relation among them. If we take, for example, the role type COMPOSER, related to the expression "writing songs," then we could form a binary relationship. It would be between COMPOSER and SONG (between the *role* type and something related to its *output*). The verb "write" describes how those two relate.

Thus, looking at Fig. 7.3, we could analogously form binary relationships since, as it could be seen, a *role* type name plus a *role* elaboration could be considered as a *noun-verb-noun* expression. Thus we have:

INSURER	–	sell	–	(insurance) products
REINSURER	–	take over	–	(insurance) risk
BROKER	–	give	–	(financial) consultation
BROKER	–	advise for	–	(insurance) products
EXPERT	–	realize	–	expertise
SUPPLIER	–	deliver	–	(financial) products
CUSTOMER	–	purchase	–	(insurance) products
CUSTOMER	–	provide	–	(specialized) information

Further, we extend (based on Table 7.1) each of the above eight expressions with one more noun corresponding to a *role type* which relates to the *role type* represented within the particular expression. This is done as follows: For a particular *role type*, we can see the "candidate-matches" from the table. Thus, we have to choose one of them. The criterion is how it matches the context of the expression. For example, starting from INSURER, we see from Table 7.1 that it relates to REINSURER, BROKER, EXPERT, SUPPLIER, and CUSTOMER. Therefore, we ask the question: To whom does INSURER sell insurance products? The answer (according to the case information) is: "to CUSTOMER." Therefore, we extend the first expression with CUSTOMER:

INSURER	–	sell	–	(ins.) products	–	CUSTOMER

If we go further, we see from Table 7.1 that REINSURER relates only to INSURER; we ask the question: From whom does REINSURER take over risk? The answer is "from INSURER." Therefore, we extend the second expression with INSURER:

REINSURER	–	take over	–	(ins.) risk	–	INSURER

We continue analogously:

BROKER	–	give	–	fin. consultation	–	CUSTOMER
BROKER	–	advise for	–	financial products	–	INSURER
EXPERT	–	realize	–	expertise	–	INSURER
SUPPLIER	–	deliver	–	financial products	–	INSURER
CUSTOMER	–	purchase	–	ins. products	–	INSURER
CUSTOMER	–	provide	–	spec. information	–	EXPERT

We now need to consider the above expressions and check them against redundancy since there is a risk to describe twice one and the same thing, like in the following two expressions:

INSURER	–	sell	–	insurance products	–	CUSTOMER
CUSTOMER	–	purchase	–	insurance products	–	INSURER

Considering the case information, we have concluded that the information in the above two expressions is about one and the same thing, namely, the INSURER's selling of insurance products to CUSTOMER. Therefore, we randomly choose one of the above two expressions and leave out the other one. Let's select the first one.

Further, we will use the above expressions as an input for building the so-called Icomp RR chart (see Chap. 6) in order to facilitate the description of relations (we remind that "RR" stands for "Roles and Relations"). In order to build the chart, we need to consider the above expressions, putting the role type names in boxes. The names of those of the role types that relate to the realization of a particular activity (e.g., the activity: "sell insurance products") are underlined. Next to that, the name of the role type corresponding to the target (within the case study) organization should disappear. On its place we put the particular name of the organization (*Icomp*). Hence, we should replace the type role (INSURER) with the instance role ("*Icomp*"). This is because we are not interested in any company which could fulfill INSURER but in this *role* as performed in particular by the company *Icomp*.

Between each two boxes (concerning *role types* and featuring a particular relation), we should put together all the text (from the corresponding expressions above): this is between the names of the *role types*. For example, we take the text "realize expertise" from the line:

| EXPERT | – | *realize* | – | *expertise* | – | *INSURER* |

The RR chart is depicted on Fig. 7.4. As seen from the figure, each line contains two *role type* names (the name of the target company is in some places instead a *role type* name) and in between is the description of the relation. All those are derived straightforwardly from the previously constructed expressions. As it could be seen, we have also given a unique code to each relation (**R1** to **R7**). Onwards, we will refer to each of the modeled relations using those codes.

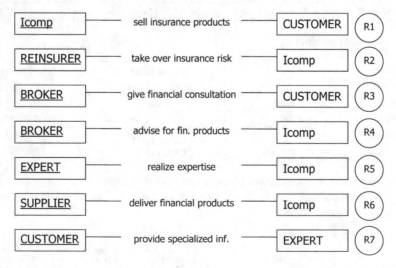

Fig. 7.4 RR model for the Icomp case

Norm Elaboration

Following the *roadmap*: an important step to take place on that basis is adding further precision to the descriptions of the relations, by applying *organizational semiotics*, and in particular *norm analysis* (see Chap. 4). The construction of *norms* has been considered in the mentioned chapter. Hence, no explanations will be made here about how the *norms* are constructed on the basis of the information featuring corresponding relations. A *norm* will be attached to each relation (see Fig. 7.4), being given a name containing "**N**" (from the word *norm*) and the code of the relation. The seven constructed *norms* are:

NR1

> **Whenever** BROKER has advised CUSTOMER in favor of a Icomp's product and CUSTOMER fits within Icomp's policy.
>
> **If** CUSTOMER decides to purchase this product.
>
> **Then** Icomp.
>
> **Is obliged to** insure CUSTOMER according to the concrete product details and based on a payment from CUSTOMER, made accordingly.

NR2

> **Whenever** there is a long run relation between Icomp and REINSURER.
>
> **If** an insurance to be realized by Icomp would include a unacceptably high risk for Icomp and the insured objects fit within REINSURER's policy.
>
> **Then** (if asked) REINSURER.
>
> **Is obliged to** take over risk(s) from Icomp regarding the particular insurance.

NR3

> **Whenever** CUSTOMER has a request for consultation to BROKER.
>
> **If** an insurance company having got an agreement with BROKER has an appropriate product with regard to the CUSTOMER's particular request.
>
> **Then** BROKER.
>
> **Is obliged to** consult CUSTOMER about this product.

NR4

> **Whenever** there is an agreement between Icomp and BROKER.
>
> **If** a product of Icomp is a best match with regard to a CUSTOMER's request.
>
> **Then** BROKER.
>
> **Is obliged to** do advice for CUSTOMER in favour of Icomp's product(s).

NR5

> **Whenever** there is a non-standard situation regarding a stated claim.
>
> **If** Icomp asks EXPERT for an expert evaluation (expertise).
>
> **Then** EXPERT.
>
> **Is obliged to** realize an expertise with regard to the stated claim.

NR6

> **Whenever** there is an agreement between Icomp and SUPPLIER about delivery of insurance products.
>
> **If** CUSTOMER wants to have a product whose production and delivery falls in the mentioned agreement as a responsibility of SUPPLIER, and Icomp has ordered this financial (in particular insurance) product to be developed.
>
> **Then** SUPPLIER.
>
> **Is obliged to** deliver the financial product.

NR7

> **Whenever** EXPERT is involved in an expert evaluation (expertise).
>
> **If** EXPERT asks CUSTOMER for specialized information.
>
> **Then** CUSTOMER.
>
> **Is obliged to** cooperate by providing the required information.

Positioning of the Relations

So far, we have realized an identification and a thorough elaboration of the essential *relations* concerning the *Icomp* case.

Our focus towards *Icomp* as the company under study requires adding more precision about the way *Icomp* handles the mentioned relations internally. Said otherwise, it is of interest to know which of the <u>departments</u> (organizational units) within the company are involved in each of the relations. Such information would be of significant importance for specifying an ICT application which, for example, might operate across some (or all) of the mentioned departments.

Therefore the next step should be to position the relations with regard to the *Icomp* organizational units. Those units have been defined based on the information featuring *Icomp* (see Sect. 7.2).

We consider Fig. 7.4 and leave out of consideration the relations **R3** and **R7** because they do not relate directly to *Icomp*. We take then the remaining relations (which all do concern *Icomp*) and conduct interviews in order to clarify for each particular relation the corresponding *Icomp* department(s) involved. Of course, it appears that often a relation concerns more than one department. For example, the relation between *Icomp* and BROKER comes firstly through the *Account Management department* (considering the agreement and also the *Icomp*-BROKER collaboration in general) and secondly through the *Financial Department* (as long as payments are concerned).

Figure 7.5 contains the results. The names of the *Icomp* departments are put in rectangles. Each relation (in circle) having connection with a department is linked to it.

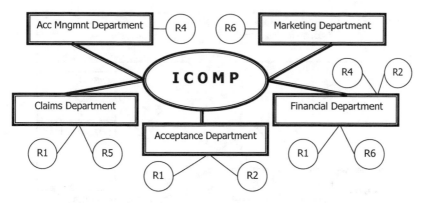

Fig. 7.5 Relations and organizational units concerning the Icomp case

We have purposefully simplified slightly the way we look at the organizational structure of *Icomp* because this would make our further modeling activities easier to understand. However, the modeling complexity would be sufficient for adequately demonstrating the strengths of the *SDBC* approach.

SCI Chart
Based on the modeling results which have been achieved so far, we will (according to the *roadmap*) apply the <u>SCI chart</u> (see Chap. 6) for summarizing the initial case information ("*SCI*" stands for "*Structuring Customers' Information*"). The modeling outputs depicted in Figs. 7.3, 7.4, and 7.5 should be a sufficient basis for constructing the chart; it is presented in Fig. 7.6 where the following abbreviations are used:

am	stands for "Account management department."
md	stands for "Marketing department."
fd	stands for "Financial department."
ad	stands for "Acceptance department."
cd	stands for "Claims department."

On the figure, the target organization (*Icomp*) is represented within the rectangle with rounded corners. Inside are depicted labels featuring the five departments (source: Fig. 7.5); within an attached rectangle is an elaboration concerning *Icomp*. In rectangles around the rounded cornered rectangle are labels featuring the five considered *role types* plus their elaborations (source: Fig. 7.3). On the basis of Figs. 7.4 and 7.5, the *role types* are linked (where appropriate) to corresponding departments within *Icomp*. Also, where appropriate, the *role types* are linked to each other. This is done using lines and each line is given a number.
    In this way, through the *SCI* chart, we have achieved a <u>compact, complete, and focused view on the target organization</u> (and additional relevant information).

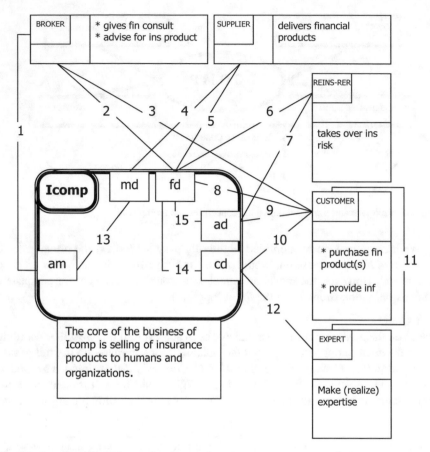

Fig. 7.6 Icomp—SCI chart

Derivation of Business coMponents

According to the guidelines for application of *SDBC* [2], a *SCI* chart could facilitate
the <u>identification of *business coMponents*</u>, particularly using the notations
concerning *transactions* (see Chap. 6).

We consider the lines from the *SCI* chart—each line originates one or more
business process patterns. In those patterns, we consider the organizational units
within *Icomp* as *roles*. Hence, the set of *business process patterns*, derived from the
Icomp SCI chart is:

1	*am*	**start**	*AGREEMENT*	*BROKER*
1	*am*	*end*	*AGREEMENT*	*BROKER*
1	*am*	*manage*	*AGREEMENT*	
2	*fd*	*pay*	*COMMISSION*	*BROKER*
3	*BROKER*	*advise*	*(for a) PRODUCT*	*CUSTOMER*
4	*SUPPLIER*	*deliver*	*new PRODUCT*	*md*
5	*fd*	*pay*	*PREMIUM*	*SUPPLIER*
6	*fd*	*pay*	*reinsurance PREMIUM*	*REINSURER*
7	*REINSURER*	*start*	*REINSURANCE*	*ad*
7	*REINSURER*	*end*	*REINSURANCE*	*ad*
8	*CUSTOMER*	*pay*	*PREMIUM*	*fd*
8	*fd*	*pay*	*CLAIM*	*CUSTOMER*
9	*ad*	*start*	*CUSTOMER AGREEMENT*	*CUSTOMER*
9	*ad*	*end*	*CUSTOMER AGREEMENT*	*CUSTOMER*
9	*CUSTOMER*	*give*	*HEALTH INFORMATION*	*ad*
10	*CUSTOMER*	*declare*	*DAMAGE*	*cd*
10	*cd*	*state*	*COMPENSATION*	*CUSTOMER*
11	*CUSTOMER*	*give*	*HELATH STATEMENT*	*EXPERT*
12	*EXPERT*	*give*	*EVALUATION*	*cd*
13	*md*	*provide*	*new PRODUCT*	*am*
14	*cd*	*order*	*CLAIM PAYMENT*	*fd*
15	*ad*	*order*	*PREMIUM PAYMENT*	*fd*

This output represents the starting point for the identification of *business coMponents*. Essential for this is the discovery of *transactions*. It is claimed (and motivated) that the above output could facilitate the mentioned discovery. Next to that, this output's being focused adds value to the overall consistency of the set of *transactions* and *business coMponents* (being identified).

We will take, for illustrative purpose, several of the above *business process patterns*. Through the identification of *transactions*, we will reflect those patterns in coordination-structure models (which represent the actor-roles, transactions, and the system boundary), identifying in this way *business coMponents*. We will consider, in particular, the patterns whose featuring lines are in bold in the above list, starting with the following one:

1		*am*	*start*	*AGREEMENT*	*BROKER*

Firstly, we are clear what the system under study is. It is *Icomp* (the *Account Management department* is one of its departments)—this is reflected in one of the *roles* in the above expression. Secondly, we are clear which the *roles* under consideration are; in this case they are "am" and "BROKER." Hence, we could model this as presented in Fig. 7.7:

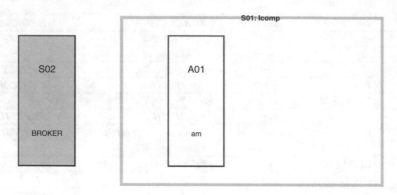

Fig. 7.7 Representation of a pattern

What we know also from the pattern is the essence of the *inter-role relation*: "start agreement." However, reflecting it directly in one *transaction* would not provide a complete view since we need to analyze this information and identify the starting transaction (see *Definition 6*). To achieve this, one would (usually) answer the helpful question: What is the cause? We have done this, discovering that a broker could have an agreement started only based on an application (submitted). Therefore, the *starting transaction* would be:

T2 application   F2 application <A> has been submitted

We then ask: What happens next? It is that **am** receives an application from a **broker** and, before being able to start an agreement with the **broker, am** needs an approval by a *controller* within *Icomp* (we have not considered it so far because of it not having a significant importance). Thus, we identify an additional *role* type, namely, CONTROLLER. As for the corresponding *transaction*, it would be:

T3 approval   F3 approval concerning application <A> has been done

Based on this approval is the starting of an agreement, by **am**:

T1 agreement   F1 agreement based on application <A> has started.

Hence, taking the information from Fig. 7.7 and also the identified three *transactions* (see above) plus the new *role* type (*controller*), we are able to build the relevant **business coMponent**. This is depicted in Fig. 7.8 (see the notations presented in Chap. 6):

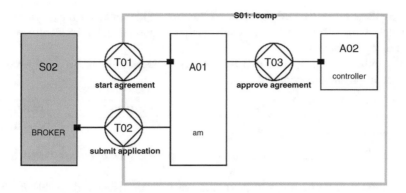

Fig. 7.8 An identified business coMponent—structural view

Considering the above modeling output and in line with the principles of *LAP* and *enterprise ontology* (see Chap. 4), we construct (see Fig. 7.9) a model that elaborates on the communicative aspects concerning those three *transactions*:

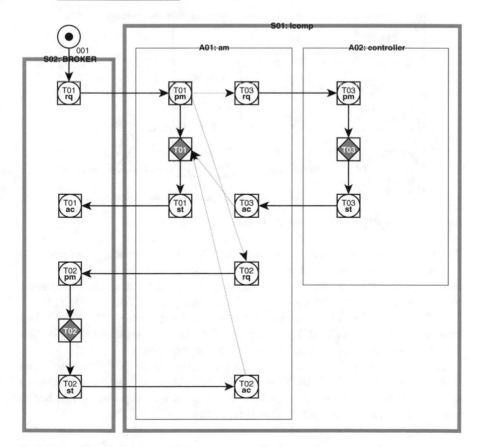

Fig. 7.9 An identified business coMponent—communicative view

We will be more detailed about the elaboration of identified *business coMponents* in the following sub-section. In this sub-section we just consider the identification of *business coMponents*.

We continue with the rest two *business process patterns* to be considered and reflected in *business coMponents*:

5	*fd*	*pay*	*PREMIUM*	*SUPPLIER*
8	*fd*	*pay*	*CLAIM*	*CUSTOMER*

Proceeding analogously, we will identify *business coMponents* based on the *patterns*.

Since both *patterns* concern payment, we propose using a re-usable *business coMponent*, in particular a *general business coMponent*. It is to be extended afterwards. We are not going to explain those issues since they have been considered in Chap. 6.

A general payment *business coMponent* specified in the same notations is depicted in Fig. 7.10.

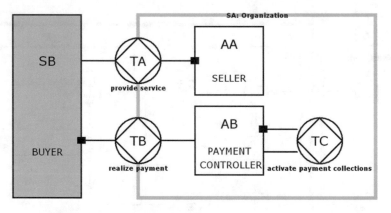

Fig. 7.10 A general payment business coMponent

As seen from the figure, in the general case, we have an organization providing a service to a customer and claiming therefore payment in return. Usually, the entity delivering the service is not the entity handling the payment: there are two internal *role* types depicted on the figure, therefore, namely, SELLER and PAYMENT CONTROLLER. SELLER delivers a service to the customer ("BUYER") and informs about this PAYMENT CONTROLLER who as a result of self-activation (on a periodic basis) would handle the payment accordingly.

Taking the first of the two considered *patterns*, we extend straightforwardly the model shown in Fig. 7.10. BUYER in this case would be *Icomp* (its *Marketing department* (**md**) buys a financial product and its *Financial department* (**fd**) has to pay to a corresponding supplier). This is represented on Fig. 7.11:

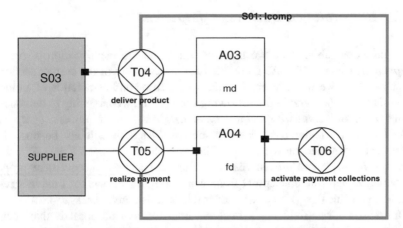

Fig. 7.11 A possible extension of the general payment business coMponent

As for the second *pattern*, we again reflect straightforwardly the information: this time the payment should be directed to a customer. However, before the payment could be initiated (as studied from the case information) it is necessary that an expert (external to *Icomp*) investigates the case. Considering this accordingly, we derive a *business coMponent*, as represented in Fig. 7.12:

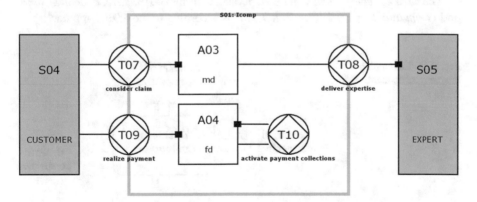

Fig. 7.12 Another possible extension of the general payment business coMponent

Hence, we have demonstrated the identification of *business coMponents*. In the following sub-section, we will consider the elaboration of a particular (identified) *business coMponent*.

7.3.2   *Elaborating a Business CoMponent*

In the previous sub-section, we have demonstrated the identification of *business coMponents*, using *SDBC*. As mentioned at the beginning of the current section, in this sub-section, we will demonstrate the specification and elaboration of an identified *business coMponent*; in the following sub-section, we are going to demonstrate the derivation of a *software specification model*, based on the *business coMponent*.

As for the particular *coMponent* to be considered, it will not be one of the coMponents identified on the basis of the *SCI* chart (see Sect. 7.3.1). It will be, instead, a *business coMponent* resulting from a <u>business improvement proposal</u> concerning *Icomp* (the conceptual framework of *SDBC* allows for **business re-design**, as a possible design step, whenever this is considered necessary).

Our reason for introducing a business improvement proposal is that such an improvement is expected to create an adequate foundation for realizing a useful software support to *Icomp* while simply automating any currently existing *business processes* within the company would bring less value to it.

Therefore, we will address the following:

- The problem concerning the need for improvement.
- A relevant business improvement proposal.
- A resulting *business coMponent*, to be adequately specified and elaborated.

The *business coMponent* will be <u>elaborated</u> in terms of *structure, dynamics, data,* and *communicative issues* (see Fig. 7.13), as according to the *SDBC* approach.

Fig. 7.13   Elaborating a
business coMponent

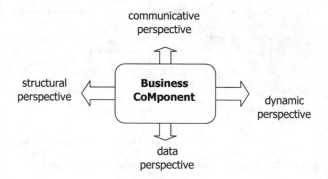

Problem Statement

Regarding some relatively simple cases in which an advice is straightforwardly deliverable (based on relevant information and rules), using human brokers is too expensive. It would be more appropriate if human brokers are used just in cases in which their particular expertise is to be applied.

The Financial Mediator: A Proposal

Reflecting the above problem, we have made a business improvement proposal according to which a new business unit is to be introduced, namely, a **Financial Mediator** (**FM**).

---

*The **FM** facilitates Dutch insurance companies. In order to use **FM**, a company should subscribe (for free). **FM** brings about the following useful deliverables:*

- *Advice (to customers or insurance brokers) on what of the offered (by the registered companies) products best satisfies a particular customer demand.*
- *Delivery (to customers) of products of insurance companies.*

*Any customer could request (for free) **FM** to do for him/her either advice or delivery of a product. The customer should firstly specify his/her request (choosing from a list): (s)he should make it clear whether the request is about a health insurance, auto insurance, and so on, specify the particular demand (e.g., to insure a car against theft with the highest possible coverage (which includes car accessories, tires, and so on)), and so on. Based on this, a request processing unit within **FM** generates a standardized specification regarding the customer's request, which is delivered to a match-making unit within **FM**. This unit is to further realize a match allowing the **FM** to do the advice. The match is driven by a particular criterion chosen by the customer (e.g., a preference for the cheapest or the most reliable product available). In order to deliver such a criterion-driven match, the match-making unit uses a data-bank of relevant rules and procedures. Besides the output given by the request processing unit, the match-making unit needs as well an output from a data search and processing unit. It searches through the information that concerns registered companies, applying procedures to it. This allows for a precise identification of candidate-matches, relevant to the particular customer's request. Thus, given this output plus the (mentioned) standardized specification of the customer's request, the match-making unit would be able to realize a match, applying the mentioned rules and procedures.*

*As for the subscription of (insurance) companies, any (Dutch) company could subscribe for free. This is facilitated by a subscription processing unit within **FM**. This unit could realize a subscription only after another unit within **FM** (a company profile builder) creates a profile of the particular company, making its data available through a data-bank (to be usable also by the data search and processing unit). Usually, **FM** creates "standard profiles"; however, several special companies could have "golden profiles" (with more benefits).*

*Allowance: a customer's using **FM** (either for advice, or contract, or product delivery) is to be limited to no more than five times per month. As*

(continued)

for (insurance) companies' allowance, a company is allowed to subscribe to
FM only if it is licensed according to the Dutch financial laws.

As for a product delivery: once a customer has chosen a product, she/he
might request that FM facilitates the actual product delivery. The customer
requests an offer (FM is to be authorized to generate offers, based on
information from the particular company, kept in its profile). Once FM (its
offer generating unit) has produced an offer, it should have it firstly approved
by the respective (insurance) company, before delivering it to the customer.
From the moment of the delivery, the particular insurance (or other financial
product) is in effect—between the customer and the corresponding (insurance)
company.

A company should pay a commission to FM for each realized (through
FM) insurance (or other product).

Financial Mediator (FM): The Business CoMponent

On the basis of the above proposal, we identify a relevant *business coMponent*,
namely, the **FM** *business coMponent*.

Since we have already demonstrated the *SDBC business coMponent* identification
mechanism, we will not demonstrate the identification itself again (it has been done
analogously, as in the previous sub-section). The current sub-section aims instead
(as stated already) at demonstrating the specification and elaboration of a *business
coMponent*.

Hence, we go directly to the identified *transactions* (the *transactions* listed below).
The first six of them relate to the **FM**'s delivering advices. The rest (backgrounded
grey) relate to the **FM**'s contracting concerning financial (insurance) products.

T1	*Deliver advice*	F1	advice <A> is delivered
T2	*Perform match-making*	F2	match of advice A is made
T3	*Generate customer's information specification*	F3	customer's information concerning advice A is processed
T4	*Generate candidate-matches*	F4	data search and processing is done concerning advice A
T5	*Realize subscription*	F5	Subscription <S> is realized
T6	*Create profile*	F6	profile is created concerning subscription S
T7	*Offer contract*	F7	contract <C> is offered
T8	*Approve contract*	F8	contract C is approved
T9	*Deliver financial product*	F9	the product specified in contract <C> is delivered
T10	*Submit agreement*	F10	agreement concerning contract C is submitted
T11	*Accept contract*	F11	contract C is accepted
T12	*Activate payment collections*	F12	payment activation <A> is realized
T13	*Realize payment*	F13	Commission for product(s) specified in contract <C> is paid

As seen from the above list, **FM** could deliver an advice. This requires that a match-making is performed, based on a standardized specification of the customer's information and on generated candidate-matches. As for the consideration of (insurance) companies, **FM** could offer them subscription. It is completed only after a particular company profile has been created by **FM**.

It is seen also that once a customer has chosen a particular financial (insurance) product, it could be facilitated by **FM** for the product's delivery. **FM** offers a contract based on which the customer would acquire the product. The contract, however, would need to be approved by the particular company, before being offered to the customer. After it has been offered, the customer should accept it and from this moment on, she/he has rights and obligations concerning the product. For each product delivery, a payment of commission should take place, from the particular financial (insurance) company to **FM**. A payment controller is activated periodically in collecting all payments due for the particular period.

Further, we will reflect those *transactions* in models, offering elaboration in two aspects, namely, structural and communicative. We will then elaborate further those models with semiotic *norms* (see the previous sub-section).

Afterwards we will derive, based on those models, Petri Net and ORM models, offering elicitation in terms of dynamics and data, respectively. We will attach to the Petri Net models some further refined norms.

Hence we will address further the structural, communicative, dynamic, and data aspect of the considered business reality. This four-aspect business view (Fig. 7.13) is in tune with the *SDBC* foundations (see Chap. 6).

Financial Mediator: Structural and Communicative Aspects
For the sake of clarity, in modeling the above *transactions*, we will firstly consider those of them which concern the **FM**'s offering advice services and secondly those concerning the **FM**'s offering contracting services (backgrounded in grey color).

As for the first of the mentioned *transaction* groups, we have reflected it in the model, represented in Fig. 7.14. The model concerns the *structural business coMponent* perspective.

As mentioned before, the identification of such a model has been demonstrated, including the identification of *roles* and *transactions*. Hence, we take them directly in building the model, without explaining how we have identified them.

The functionality of **FM** concerns customers and insurance companies (for short, "IC"). Hence, we have two major *role types*: CUSTOMER and INSURANCE COMPANY. As seen from the figure, in the model, they are reflected as the *roles* "*Customer*" (**S02**) and "*Insurance Company*" (**S03**)—those are already ROLES (not role types) because the perspective is case-specific; those *roles* are external with respect to **FM**. The *transactions* **T01** and **T05** concern the **FM-Customer** and **FM-IC** relations, respectively.

Next to that, a number of actions take place within **FM** where we have identified six *roles* (internal as it concerns **FM**). They are **A01 (Advisor)**, **A02 (Match-maker)**, **A03 (Request Processing Unit)**, **A04 (Data Search and Processing Unit)**, **A05 (Subscription Processing Unit)**, and **A06 (Company Profile Builder)**. *Transactions* **T01**, **T02**, **T03**, and **T04** as well as roles **A01**, **A02**, **A03**, and **A04** concern directly the advice delivery: they are about the mere (**FM**'s) delivery of an advice to a customer. *Transactions* **T05** and **T06** as well as roles **A05** and **A06** concern indirectly the advice delivery: they are about the collection and use of information (concerning insurance companies) needed for performing an advice.

As seen from Fig. 7.14, **A01** is to *deliver advice* (**T01**). However, this could be done only based on a realized *match-making*—a matching between what the particular customer requests and what is offered by the insurance companies (registered with **FM**). **A02** is to realize such a *match-making* (**T02**). What **A02** needs in turn in order to realize the match are two things: (1) a complete specification regarding the request of the (particular) customer, a specification presented in standardized notations (the reason is that if such a specification is not standardized, it would be hardly match-able with information concerning insurance companies), and (2) list of candidate-matches. **A03** must *generate the mentioned standardized specification* (**T03**) and **A04** should *provide candidate-matches* (**T04**). In performing **T04**, **A04** is facilitated by two data-banks, namely, **DB01** and **DB02**. These data-banks are claimed to be an essential elaboration concerning the model. Using **DB02**, **A04** gets direction what procedures to apply (and where to find them) in connection to a particular need expressed by a customer. For example, if a customer needs an auto-insurance, following a procedure helps to adequately direct a further searching through companies (in this particular case, searching in their property insurance departments and/or "schemes"). Based on such an orientation achieved, **A04** could effectively direct its search for relevant (insurance-companies-related) information, using the bank **DB01**. It contains information about the (insurance) companies registered with **FM**, the (financial) products offered by them, and also other relevant details. Thus, using those two (mentioned) data-banks, **A04** should be able to provide to **A02** a list of candidate-matches (with regard to the particular (customer) request). Therefore, based on the request specification (delivered by **A03**) and this candidate-matches list, **A02** must realize the match-making. However, this should be done according to a particular criterion (like reliability or quality of service, for instance). It should be specified by the customer. Having received this information, **A02** should apply particular procedures in approaching the "matching" information (this information would be considered in one way if the cheapest (financial) product is the goal and in another way if the most reliable product is to be selected). With respect to this, **A02** is facilitated by the data-bank **DB03**. It allows **A02** to know what procedure (or a combination of procedures) to apply to the "matching" information based on a criterion chosen by the customer. The data-banks and related information will be considered in more detail further on within the current sub-section, when we will address the data *business coMponent* aspects.

Also, it is seen from Fig. 7.14 that **A05** is to realize the subscription (**T05**) of a (insurance) company wishing to use **FM**. Before a subscription could be handled, a company profile is to be built (**T06**) by **A06**. This includes adding data to the data-bank **DB01** which was mentioned already.

As also seen from the figure, the realization of the **T01** *transaction* includes providing (relevant) information to **A02**, **A03**, and **A04** (the dotted lines between **T01** and these roles indicate this). **A02** is to receive the criterion (chosen by the customer) according to which to perform the match-making. **A03** should receive the (full) information submitted by the customer. **A04** should be provided with information featuring the type of the customer need (for instance, "auto-insurance").

Thus, we have done the basic elaboration on the model and will then add further detailisation using *semiotic norms*. This is a logical continuation of the *norm* derivation characterizing the earlier analysis phases (those phases addressed in the previous section have presented the derivation of more general *semiotic norms* intended to "govern" the ones to be identified). Since the role of *norms* and their derivation have already been explained in previous chapters, we will directly go to the content of the identified *norms* attached to the *transactions*. Since they concern the essential level, we will label them as follows: a string consisting of "E" (from "Essential"), "N" (from "Norm") and a number of the particular *transaction*. The derived *norms* are the following:

EN1

> **Whenever** S02 has requested advice.
> **If** A02 has realized match-making.
> **Then** A01.
> **Is obliged to** formulate and deliver an advice.

EN2

> **Whenever** S02 has requested advice.
> **If** A03 has delivered standardized customer specification AND A04 has delivered candidate-matches.
> **Then** A02.
> **Is obliged to** realize match-making.

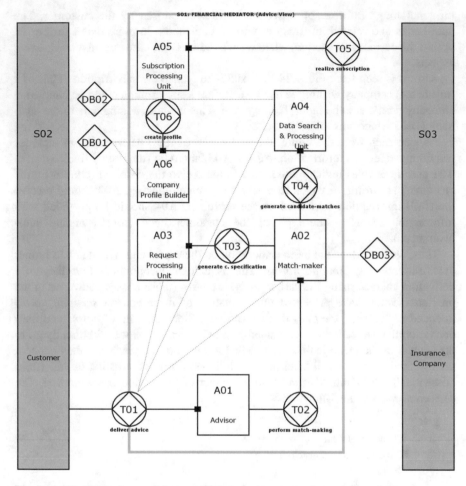

Fig. 7.14 The FM business coMponent (advice view)—structural aspect

EN3

      Whenever S02 has requested advice.

      If A03 has received submitted customer information.

      Then A03.

      Is obliged to delivered standardized customer specification.

EN4

      Whenever S02 has requested advice.

      If A04 has received information about the type of a customer need.

      Then A04.

      Is obliged to deliver a candidate-matches list.

EN5

> **Whenever** S03 has requested subscription.
> **If** A06 has built a (relevant) company profile.
> **Then** A05.
> **Is obliged to** realize subscription.

EN6

> **Whenever** S03 has requested subscription.
> **If** A06 has received submitted customer information.
> **Then** A06.
> **Is obliged to** build a company profile.

Based on the model represented in Fig. 7.14, we derive a model (Fig. 7.15) representing the communicative view on the addressed business reality.

As seen from Fig. 7.15, we have added elaboration (concerning the communicative aspect) by applying the *transaction* pattern (see Chaps. 4 and 6) to each of the *transactions* (see Fig. 7.14).

As seen from Fig. 7.15, two sub-processes are to be considered—one of them relates to the FM's delivering advice to a customer, and the other one relates to the FM's realizing subscription to an (insurance) company. This is indicated by two starting points (on the figure): starting point **001** and starting point **002**, respectively.

As also seen from the figure, the dependence of **T01** on the execution of **T02**, the dependence of **T02** on the executions of **T03** and **T04**, and the dependence of **T05** on the execution of **T06** are all reflected accordingly in the model.

Therefore, we have considered so far the "Advice view" over the **FM** *business coMponent* as far as the structural and communicative aspects are concerned. We continue analogously towards the consideration of the "Contracting view" over the *coMponent*. We proceed analogously and will not offer as detailed explanations as in the previous paragraphs.

The built model (featuring the structural perspective) corresponding to the contracting view is depicted in Fig. 7.16.

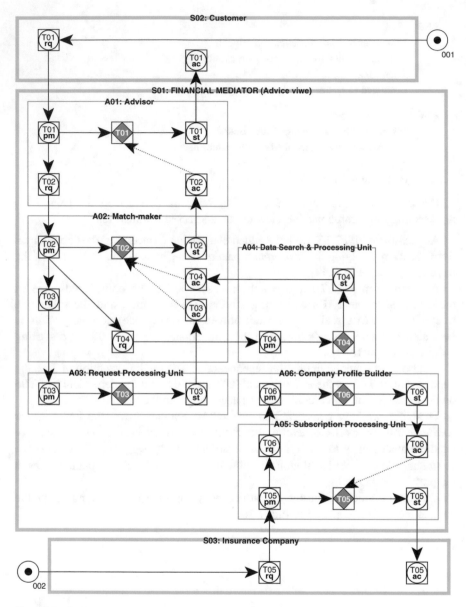

Fig. 7.15 The FM business coMponent (advice view)—communicative aspect

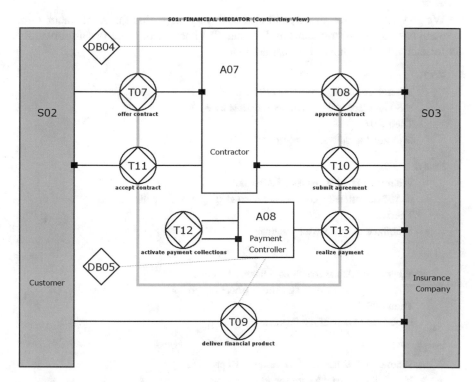

Fig. 7.16 The FM business coMponent (contracting view)—structural aspect

As seen from the figure, the depicted functionality of **FM** concerns also **customers** and **insurance companies**—**S02** and **S03**. There are internal actors as well: **A07** (**Contractor**) and **A08** (**Payment Controller**).

As also seen from the figure, **A07** could offer (**T07**) to **S02** a contract (in doing this, **A07** is facilitated by a data-bank (**DB04**) containing contract templates that concern particular companies). This could be realized only based on an approval (**T08**) of such a contract, from the concerned insurance company.

It could be seen as well from the figure that **S03** could deliver (**T09**) a (insurance) financial product to **S02**. However, this could be done only based on a submitted (to the company) **customer-FM** agreement (**T10**) based on an offer acceptance (**T11**) by **S02**.

It could also be seen from the figure that in some situations, a (insurance) company should realize payments to **FM**. Actually that is about any realized (through **FM**) product delivery. **FM** should be notified about each realized (through it) product delivery. An indication for this is the dotted line between **T09** and **A08**. **A08** has (therefore) the information (it is stored in the data-bank **DB05**) about what each (registered) company owes to **FM**. **A08** is activated by itself periodically. Then it is to handle the payments accordingly.

We go further (as we already did in the above paragraphs) for norm elaboration. We will not do this for transactions **T12** and **T13** because they are straightforwardly understandable. The derived *norms* are below:

EN7

> **Whenever** S02 has requested contract.
> **If** S03 has approved a contract proposed by A07.
> **Then** A07.
> **Is obliged to** deliver the contract.

EN8

> **Whenever** S02 has requested contract.
> **If** A07 has offered a contract not contradicting with the policy of S03.
> **Then** S03.
> **Is obliged to** approve the contract.

EN9

> **Whenever** S02 has requested a financial product.
> **If** A07 has submitted an agreement (about the product) concerning S02.
> **Then** S03.
> **Is obliged to** deliver the financial product.

EN10

> **Whenever** S02 has requested a financial product.
> **If** S02 has accepted a corresponding contract.
> **Then** A07.
> **Is obliged to** submit to S03 the appropriate agreement.

EN11

> **Whenever** S02 has requested a financial product.
> **If** A07 has offered a contract which does not contradict with S02's interests.
> **Then** S02.
> **Is obliged to** accept the contract.

Based on the model represented in Fig. 7.16, we derive a model (Fig. 7.17) representing the communicative view on the addressed business reality.

As seen from the figure, three sub-processes are to be considered: the first one relates to the **FM**'s offering a contract to a customer, the second one relates to an insurance company's delivering a financial product, and the third one relates to the **FM**'s payments handling. This is indicated by three starting points (on the figure): **003**, **004**, and **005**, respectively.

As also seen from the figure, the dependence of **T07** on the execution of **T08**, the dependence of **T09** on the executions of **T10**, and the dependence of **T10** on the execution of **T11** are all reflected accordingly in the model.

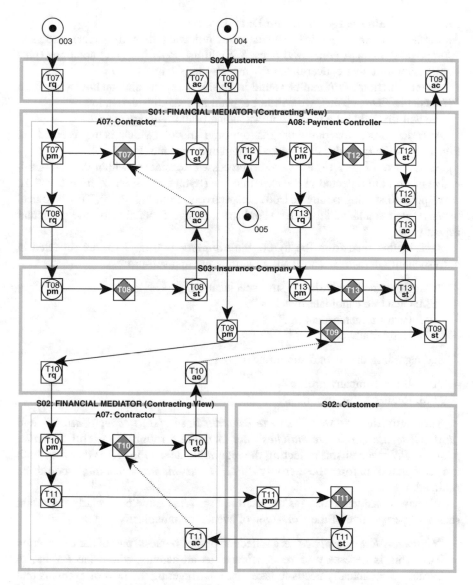

Fig. 7.17 The FM business coMponent (contracting view)—communicative aspect

Therefore, we have considered so far both "Advice" and "Contracting" views over the **FM** *business coMponent* as far as the structural and communicative aspects are concerned.

We continue with consideration of the *dynamic* and *data* aspects.

Financial Mediator: Dynamic and Data Aspects

As for the *dynamic* aspect, it is considered by reflecting the built (so far) models in appropriate dynamic (*work-flow*) ones. We will use *Petri Net* (*PN*) notations (plus *norm* elaboration that concerns the *PN* model—see Chap. 6).

An introduction to *PN* can be found in Shishkov [2] and also on how to derive a *PN* model in *SDBC*. Thus, we will not explain in detail this derivation.

We will firstly build a model corresponding to the "Advice view."

A basic source for building this dynamic model (which is represented on Fig. 7.18) is the (already) constructed communicative one (Fig. 7.15).

As seen from Fig. 7.18, the two sub-processes, considered within the communicative model, are reflected in the dynamic one ("**Start 1**"/"**Start 2**" from Fig. 7.18 correspond to starting points **001/002**, respectively, from Fig. 7.15). This is logical because such fundamental issues should not change depending on the particular aspect view.

As it is also seen from the figure, the *transactions* (Fig. 7.15) are reflected in corresponding *activities*. Those are, regarding the first sub-process:

– "FM: Generate standardized (stn.) specification."
– "FM: Generate candidate-matches."
– "FM: Perform match-making."
– "FM: Deliver advice."

and regarding the second sub-process:

– "FM: Build company profile."
– "FM: Realize subscription."

The activities "*FM: Generate standardized (stn.) specification*" and "*FM: Generate candidate-matches*" are modeled through the useful "*parallel process*" *PN* mechanism, reflecting the requirement (see Fig. 7.15) that they both are completed before the activity "*FM: Perform match-making*" could be realized.

We have considered also (as depicted in Fig. 7.18) some particularly important (from the perspective of the *work-flow* of events) communicative acts:

– "*Customer: Request advice*" is a reflection of the "request" part of the *transaction* **T01**. This is necessary to be considered as an activity within the *PN* model because what actually needs to take place in triggering the flow of events is that a customer requests to receive advice from **FM**.
– "*FM: Process information*" concerns also **T01**; handling an advice delivery should include consideration and processing of the customer information (to be accordingly distributed within **FM**). This has not been modeled as a separate *transaction* because it concerns the "information" level, not the "essential" one (see Chap. 4). However, from the perspective of the flow of events it should be considered.
– "*FM: Realize data search*" actually concerns the execution part of the *transaction* **T04**. Again, because of its concerning the "information" level, it is not considered as a separate transaction although it has to be considered within the modeled flow of events.

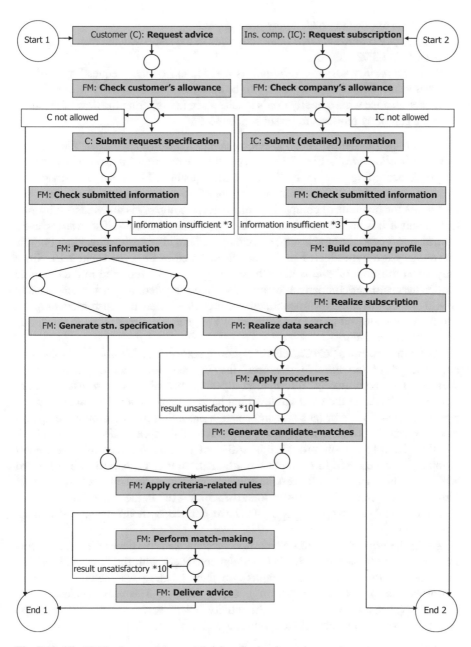

Fig. 7.18 The FM business coMponent (advice view)—dynamic aspect

– The same applies to "*FM: Apply procedures.*"
– "*FM: Apply criteria-related rules*" concerns in the same way the execution of the *transaction* **T02**.
– "*Ins. comp.: Request subscription*" is a reflection of the "request" part of the *transaction* **T05**. This is necessary to be considered as an activity within the *PN* model because what actually needs to take place in triggering the flow of events is that a company requests to be subscribed to **FM**.

As for the activities "*FM: check customer's allowance*" and "*FM: Check company's allowance*" (Fig. 7.18), they reflect a requirement from the business proposal, according to which: "A customer's using **FM** (either for advice, or contract, or product delivery) is to be limited to no more than five times per month. As for (insurance) companies' allowance, a company is allowed to subscribe to **FM** only if it is licensed according to the Dutch financial laws." Those are actually informational (not essential issues) since they concern information checking. For this reason, they are not reflected in the models depicted in Figs. 7.14 and 7.15. Since they affect the flow of events nevertheless, they are to be reflected in the dynamic model: the customer/company allowance should be checked. If a customer/company would not be meeting the mentioned requirements, then the customer/company should not be allowed to use the services of **FM**; hence a direct move to the "**end**" point should take place.

As for the activities "*C/IC: Submit request specification / (detailed) information*" and "*FM: Check submitted information,*" they concern informationally *transactions* **T01** and **T05**, respectively. Information aspects concerning those *transactions* are not to be reflected at the essential level but have to be considered within the *work-flow* of events. This is because the information providing (by a customer/company) is a key activity from a *work-flow* perspective. This applies also for the check whether the information provided is sufficient (if not, the particular customer/company is to be asked to resubmit the information; the "**information insufficient** *3**" means that after **3** unsuccessful entries, the user is "kicked out"—analogous indications are used also in "**result unsatisfactory** *10**" in the same figure).

As for the "Contracting view," we have derived a model (Fig. 7.19) in an analogous way.

As for the *norm* elaboration which is suggested, we have derived several "information" *norms* (attached to the *PN* models) consistent with the "essential" *norms* (identified in the previous paragraphs). In their labeling we include "**I**" (from "Informational"), "**N**" (from "*Norm*"), and a number. The *norm* (below) is an example of such a *norm*, concerning the activity "*FM: Check submitted information*" (we have assigned this activity a number, namely, number **12**):

IN12

> **Whenever** a customer has requested advice.
> **If** she/he has submitted information to FM.
> **Then** FM.
> **Is obliged to** check the submitted information.

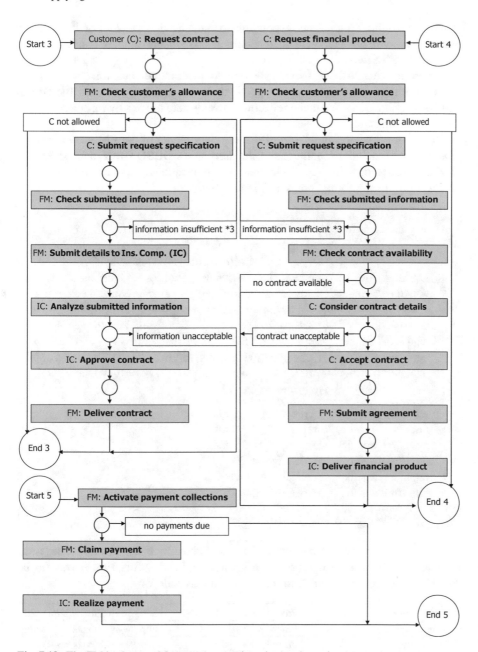

Fig. 7.19 The FM business coMponent (contracting view)—dynamic aspect

And finally, regarding the *validation* of the derived dynamic models, we could apply *discrete event simulation*, as studied in [2].

As for the data aspect, it is considered by reflecting the models built so far in appropriate *data* ones. We will use the *ORM notations* (see Chap. 6) for that purpose.

We will build a model corresponding to the "Advice view". For the sake of brevity, we will not elaborate in the current section the models concerning the "Contracting" view.

Regarding the "Advice view," we turn to the fundamental link between the models (built so far) and the *data* aspect—those are the *data-banks* **DB01**, **DB02**, and **DB03** (Fig. 7.14). We make reflection towards data models by further modeling those *data-banks*.

Hence, our "Advice view" (*ORM*-driven) *data* model of the **FM** *business coM-ponent* should include elaborations of the *data-banks* **DB01**, **DB02**, and **DB03**.

Before proceeding to such an elaboration, we need to add some *data* input to the business proposal information, which is as follows:

> – We have selected for consideration the following seven (insurance) finan-cial companies situated in the Netherlands: *Icomp* (situated in a Dutch city, offering products as follows: **1011001** (those codes will be explained further on)); *OHRA* (situated in Arnhem, offering products as follows: **0001010**); *AEGON* (situated in Den Haag, offering products as follows: **1110111**); *Nationale-Nederlanden* (situated in Rotterdam, offering prod-ucts as follows: **1001110**); *Euro Lloyd Verzekeringen* (situated in Amster-dam, offering products as follows: **0100100**); *Unive Verzekeringen* (situated in Zwolle, offering products as follows: **1111110**); and *AXA* (situated in Utrecht, offering products as follows: **1101001**). Details about those companies have been summarized at:
>
> http://www.sdbc.tk/icomp/detailsicomp.htm
> http://www.sdbc.tk/ohra/detailsohra.htm
> http://www.sdbc.tk/aegon/detailsaegon.htm
> http://www.sdbc.tk/nn/detailsnn.htm
> http://www.sdbc.tk/ev/detailsev.htm
> http://www.sdbc.tk/uv/detailsuv.htm
> http://www.sdbc.tk/axa/detailsaxa.htm

As for the possible *customer needs* (to be addressed by **FM**), they might be "**auto insurance**," "**health insurance**," "**life insurance**," and so on. *Procedures* (to be considered concerning them) and their URLs are as follows:

auto-insurance	Procedure 1	http://www.sdbc.tk/pr/pr1.htm
health-insurance	Procedure 2	http://www.sdbc.tk/pr/pr2.htm
life-insurance	Procedure 3	http://www.sdbc.tk/pr/pr3.htm
. . .		

As for the *criteria* consideration (facilitated by *procedures*), which has already been mentioned, the following *procedures* are to be used, corresponding to the <u>four criteria</u> considered (**pay-back, reliability, quality of service, insurance costs**):

Pay-back	Procedure	PB
Reliability	Procedure	RB
Quality of Service	Procedure	QS
Insurance Costs	Procedure	IC

Regarding the *product codes* (used above already), we would like to make the following elaboration: We have considered <u>seven types of (insurance) financial products</u>, namely, **Life-insurance-related products, Property-insurance-related products, Mortgage-related products, Pension-related products, Travel-insurance-related products, Personal-damage-insurance-related products**, and **Lawyer-assistance-insurance-related products**. We have assigned the following numbers to those types of products:

Life ins.:	*1*
Pr. Ins.:	*2*
Mortg. :	*3*
Pens. :	*4*
Trvl. :	*5*
PersDmg.:	*6*
LwrAsstnc.:	*7*

Then we introduce a <u>string of seven binary digits</u>. Each position there corresponds to the number of a particular type of product.

Thus, the code **0000100**, for instance, should let us know that the particular company (to which this code is attached) offers only *travel insurances* and related (financial) products.

We have presented all this information in Fig. 7.20 concerning the *data* aspect of the **FM** "Advice view."

The top model on the figure concerns the *data-bank* **DB01** (Fig. 7.14); the bottom model concerns **DB03**. The model between them concerns **DB02**.

As seen from the figure, we have consistently conducted *data* elaboration on the model represented in Fig. 7.14, considering adequately the factual case information.

Hence, we have considered so far both the "Advice" and "Contracting" views. Regarding the "Advice model," we have elaborated it in structural, communicative, dynamic, and data aspects. Regarding the "Contracting model," we have elaborated it in structural, communicative, and dynamic aspects.

So, we have demonstrated *business coMponents'* elaboration. In the following sub-section, we will address the reflection of a *business coMponent* in the *specification* of software.

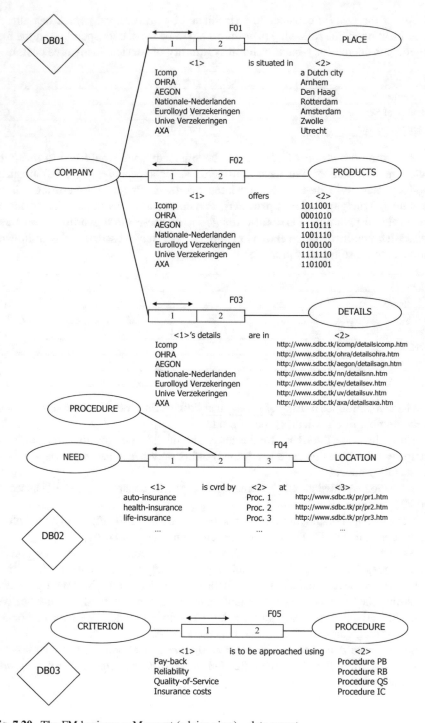

Fig. 7.20 The FM business coMponent (advice view)—data aspect

7.3.3   Towards Software Specification

In the previous sub-section, we have demonstrated the *SDBC*-driven *elaboration* of a *business coMponent*. As mentioned at the beginning of the current section, in this sub-section, we will demonstrate how a <u>UML-driven</u> [3] *software specification model* could be derived on the basis of a *business coMponent* (in this particular case, on the basis of the *coMponent* considered in the previous sub-section). As already mentioned, the software specification model should reflect the *business coMponent*. However, it is necessary that we also consider the *user-defined requirements* towards the software system-to-be. Said otherwise, this model must have <u>two inputs</u>.

1. A *business process modeling* input coming through a *business coMponent(s)*.
2. A *requirements* input coming through the specification of <u>what the (future) users of the software system-to-be require as automation</u>.

We need, therefore, to add a *requirements specification* to the business proposal done already in the current section:

> According to the <u>user requirements</u>, the **FM** must be automated completely, representing an **ICT application** which must be accessible via the *Internet*. The application should have mechanisms for <u>checking the data accuracy</u>, before performing <u>match-making</u>. Also, the application should be facilitated by a <u>database</u> (containing all the information from data-banks **DB01**, **DB02**, **DB03**, **DB04**, and **DB05**), located on a server in The Netherlands.

Therefore, in going through the further (*software specification*) steps, we will consider both the input *business coMponent* (see Sect. 7.3.2) and the user-defined requirements (see the above paragraph).

Use Case Derivation

Use cases are modeling constructs that serve to link the *application domain* (the business world) to the *software domain*, regarding any *UML*-driven *software specification* [4]. Hence, the first step in reflecting the **FM** *business coMponent* into a (*UML*-driven) *software specification model* must be a *use-case derivation*.

According to the SDBC application guidelines [2], a <u>use-case derivation</u> is to go through <u>three phases</u>, namely:

- Derivation of **essential use cases**.
- Derivation of **informational use cases**.
- Derivation of **UDR use cases** ("*UDR*" stands for "*User-Defined Requirements*").

ESSENTIAL USE CASES are pieces of functionality, reflecting actions from a considered *enterprise system*, which are "essential," as according to the *enterprise ontology terminology* [5].

INFORMATIONAL USE CASES are pieces of functionality, reflecting actions from a considered *enterprise system*, which are *informational*.

UDR USE CASES are pieces of functionality added on the basis of a consideration of the *user-defined requirements* towards the software *system*-to-be.

The *SDBC use case derivation* concerning those three types of *use cases* is depicted on Fig. 7.21 and will be followed further on.

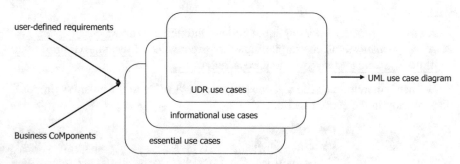

Fig. 7.21   The SDBC use case derivation procedure

Deriving Essential Use Cases

As according to [2], we derive the *essential use cases* (Fig. 7.22) by mapping them straightforwardly from corresponding *transactions* (Figs. 7.14 and 7.16). As for the *UML use case diagram*, the *actors* there reflect straightforwardly the external role types (Figs. 7.14 and 7.16). The reason is that we are to automate **FM** completely. Therefore the **FM** perspective is to coincide with the perspective of the software *system*-to-be.

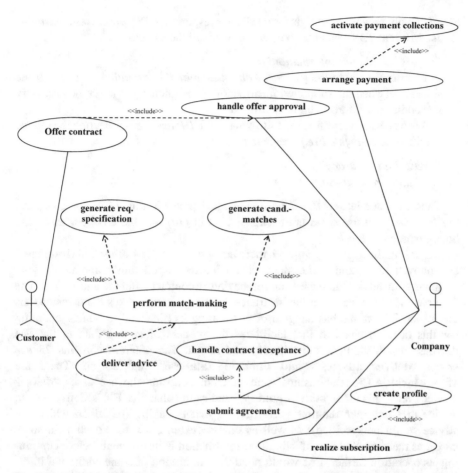

Fig. 7.22 FM: Use case model (identification of the Essential use cases)

Deriving Informational and UDR Use Cases

Based on the identification of the *essential use cases* and having as a source the dynamic (*PN*) models (Sect. 7.3.2), where we have reflected the *informational* issues related to the **FM** *business coMponent*, we identify the following *use cases*:

- *"check allowance"*
- *"check submitted information"*
- *"process information"*
- *"apply search"*
- *"apply procedures"*
- *"apply rules"*
- *"submit information"*
- *"check contract availability"*

all of which reflecting straightforwardly corresponding *PN processes/transitions* (Figs. 7.18 and 7.19). Next to that, we have added the use case:

– *"request additional information"*

as an *extension* to the *use case* *"check submitted information,"* since in some situations (when the submitted information is insufficient), it might be necessary that additional information is submitted.

We have also identified the following two *UDR use cases* reflecting the (above specified) *user-defined requirements*:

– *"check data accuracy"*
– *"add data in database."*

Thus, the complete *UML use case model* is depicted in Fig. 7.23 where, as seen, the *Informational use cases* are backgrounded in *gray* and the *UDR use cases* are backgrounded in *black*.

Regarding the <u>use case diagram</u>, there are two *actors*: **Customer** and (Insurance) **company**. The Customer takes the decision, has the responsibility, and has the goal of having an advice delivered and/or having a contract offered, and so on. The Company (by this we mean the insurance company) in turn takes the decision, has the responsibility, and has the goal of distributing its (financial) products, counting for this on a mechanism that facilitates the process of adding data to the FM database, establishing a subscription, and so on. The diagram contains *23 use cases*: **"deliver advice," "add data in database,"** and so on. There are 15 <<**include**>> relationships (one of them concerns the use cases **"deliver advice"** and **"perform match-making,"** indicating that the **FM**'s delivering an advice to **Customer** requires performing a match-making (based on which the advice would be specified)) as well as one <<**extends**>> relationship (in some cases, as mentioned above, if submitted information is insufficient, before continuing its operation further, **FM** would need the submission of some additional information, so the basic use case is **"check submitted information,"** and it is extended with **"request additional information"**).

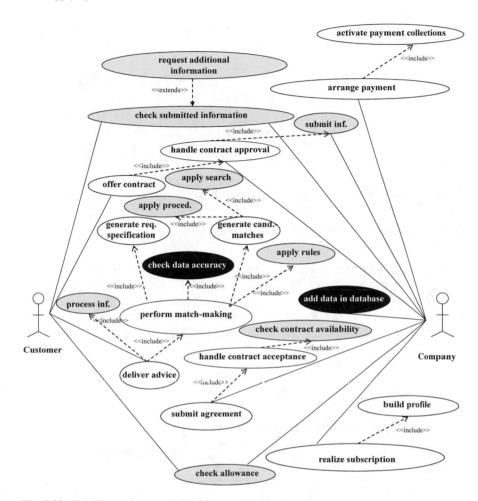

Fig. 7.23 FM: Thorough use case model

Elaboration

Based on the built *UML use case model*, it is possible to make further elaborations concerning either particular *use cases* (specifying them in more detail) or the *model* as a whole.

We will proceed with demonstrating how any particular *use case* of interest could be adequately specified. We follow a *use case* specification mechanism inspired by [6, 7]. Below we will just demonstrate the specification of a *use case* from the *model* already built (see Fig. 7.23).

We have selected, for illustrative purposes, the *use case* "add data in database" and the mentioned investigation is applied to it—see Fig. 7.24 (only those extensions related to Activity 6 are depicted).

The *use case* is written at "system" scope (as opposed to "enterprise" scope) since it describes an interaction with a computer system. The indicated "summary" level means that the *use case* is long running (executed over months or years), showing the context in which the user goals operate.

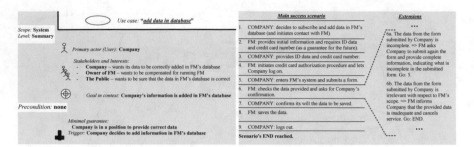

Fig. 7.24 Specification of the use case "add data in database"

For further (dynamic) elaboration (and visualization) of the considered *use case* ("add data in database"), a *UML activity diagram* [3] could be straightforwardly derived based on the *main success scenario + extensions* (see Fig. 7.24). As seen from this figure, there are nine core activities (complemented with extensions), in the mentioned *use case*. Some of them are shown in Fig. 7.25, as an overall *UML activity diagram*.

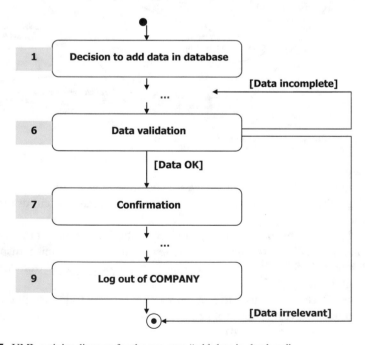

Fig. 7.25 UML activity diagram for the use case "add data in database"

As studied in [2], based on such a dynamic model, it is straightforward to proceed to computer simulation. We will not demonstrate this in the current chapter.

As mentioned above, one might need to elaborate either particular *use cases*, specifying them in more detail, as demonstrated above, or the *model* (Fig. 7.23) as a whole. In elaborating the *model* as a whole, one could take either a *structural perspective* or a *dynamic perspective*.

The PN *business process models* (see Figs. 7.18 and 7.19) can be used as a basis for deriving a *dynamic elaboration* of the overall *use case model* (Fig. 7.23). However, in realizing this, one should add accordingly information concerning the *user-defined requirements* because this information is certainly missing in the *business process models*.

As for the *structural elaboration* of the overall *use case model*, it could be conducted by reflecting both the *structural business process models* (Figs. 7.14 and 7.16) and the overall *use case model* (Fig. 7.23) into *UML class diagram(s)* [3]. We will show below only a partial *UML class diagram* (concerning just the *use cases* "realize subscription" and "build profile"; we reflect also the two profile types, as from the initial case information). The *UML class diagram* is depicted in Fig. 7.26:

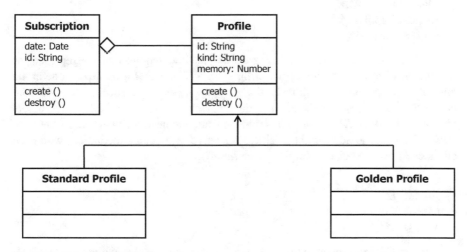

Fig. 7.26 FM: Partial UML class diagram

In summary, so far in the current chapter, we have demonstrated, by means of the Icomp case, how starting from a case briefing and coming through enterprise models software specification could be derived.

7.4 Enabling Service Orientation

The *service-oriented architecture* and its strengths have been discussed in Chap. 5. In the current section, we will demonstrate how the *SDBC modeling* output can be used as a basis for deriving *service-oriented* specifications, such that the resulting software is capable of being delivered to users by means of technology-enabled services. In order to accommodate *service orientation*, we would need partial refactoring of some of the models, presented in the previous sections of the current chapter. Further, we are offering only a partial illustration of the above because the goal is to just demonstrate how *SDBC models* could accommodate *service orientation*.

We firstly take a partial view and do a slight simplification with regard to the *model* presented in Fig. 7.14: We represent the *Customer, Advisor, Match-maker, Request Processing Unit* (we call it "Request handler," for short), and *Data Search and Processing Unit* (we call it "Data searcher," for short), as just entities and put their corresponding labels in named boxes, as follows:

- Customer (**C**).
- Advisor (**A**).
- Match-maker (**MM**).
- Request handler (**R**).
- Data searcher (**D**).

Further, we consider the *transactions* as just interactions that we represent as connections between the boxes featuring entities. The small *gray boxes*, one at the end of each connection, indicate the *executor role* (as according to *LAP* and *enterprise ontology*—see Chap. 4) of the connected entities, similarly to the model represented in Fig. 7.14. The connections indicate the need for *interactions* between *entities*, in order to achieve the business objective of financial mediation; with each connection, we associate a single *interaction* (**i**):

- C-A (**i1**).
- A-MM (**i2**).
- MM-R (**i3**).
- MM-D (**i4**).

Further, **C** is positioned in the *environment* of the financial mediation system **FM**, and **A**, **MM**, **R**, and **D** together form the **FM** system. Through **i1**, **FM** is related to its *environment* (represented by **C**). Thus, from the perspective of **C**, there is no difference between **FM** and **A**.

This all is depicted as a *business entity model* in Fig. 7.27a.

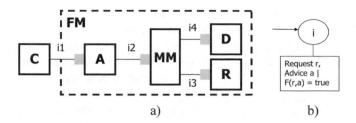

Fig. 7.27 (a) FM: business entity model. (b) FM service behavior represented by a single action (Source: [8], p. 90; ©2006, IEEE, reprinted with permission)

What we have illustrated in Fig. 7.27b is the external behavior of **FM**, at a high level of abstraction, and then we move to the abstraction level which concerns the internal behavior of **FM**. With respect to the *external behavior model*, as already mentioned, it should envision the *interaction* between the customer (**C**) and the system (**FM**) and is represented by a single action (expressed by an *oval*) in Fig. 7.27b. The depicted action has also attributes (put in a *box*) elaborating the result of the *action*.

This single action **i** corresponds to the business objective of the **FM** system: to serve the request (**r**) of a customer, by giving advice (**a**) that satisfies certain criteria (**F(r,a)** = **true**).

Regarding the *internal behavior model*, it should reflect the *interactions* between the *entities* of the *system*, as exhibited in Fig. 7.28. This *model* shows how the *interaction* **i1** between the Customer **C** and the Advisor **A** is made dependent on other interactions (**i2**, **i3**, and **i4**) in the system. Each interaction between two entities (e.g., **C** and **A**) represents a **request** (e.g., from **C** to **A**, of type **RequestC-A**) and advice (e.g., from **A** to **C**, of type **AdviceA-C**), where the **advice** satisfies certain criteria (e.g., as expressed by the truth value of function **FA**).

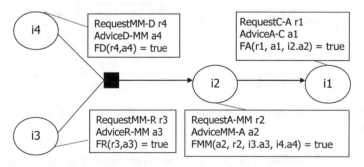

Fig. 7.28 Interactions in decomposed FM system, implementing the FM service behavior (Source: [8], p. 90; ©2006, IEEE, reprinted with permission)

Assuming that the *models* of Figs. 7.27b and 7.28 represent the same *request* from the *customer* (**r** = **r1**) and the same advice to the customer (**a** = **a1**), it follows that **F(r,a)** = **true** iff (**FA(r1, a1, i2.a2)** = **true** and **FMM (a2, r2, i3.a3, i4.a4)** = **true** and **FR (r3,a3)** = **true** and **FD (r4,a4)** = **true**).

We now need to further elaborate this *model*, in order to achieve a better link to relevant real-life enterprise aspects, and we do this by considering the *transaction* concept—as discussed already in previous chapters, this would allow the *modeling* of <u>failure scenarios</u> (not only <u>success scenarios</u>). Further, we acknowledge the essential role of <u>real-life communication and coordination</u> in an *enterprise system*. Hence, we apply the *transaction pattern*, expressing it using a notation well-suited for *SOA*, namely, *ISDL* [8].

Figure 7.29 exhibits the *generic process of an interaction* reflected through the **transaction pattern** (see Chap. 6) and *modeled* at **two different abstraction levels**. At the <u>highest level</u>, the *interaction* is represented by a *single action* which models the *production fact* that is established. Characteristics of the *production fact* are modeled using the *information attribute*. At a <u>lower abstraction level</u>, the *interaction's communication aspects* are modeled conforming to the *transaction pattern* (see Fig. 6.6). *Separate actions* are used to model the interaction's *request, promise, state, accept* and *decline*, and the *production act*. It should be noted that actions **Id$_{Ex}$** and **Id$_{In}$** correspond to the decline of an interaction followed by a unsuccessful negotiation; and actions **Ip$_{Ex}$** and **Ia$_{In}$** represent the promise and acceptance, respectively, which are followed by a successful negotiation.

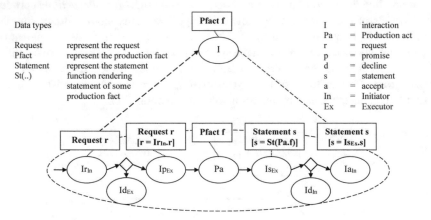

Fig. 7.29 IDSL interpretation of the transaction pattern (Source: [8], p. 91; ©2006, IEEE, reprinted with permission)

Hence, if we would need to go to a still lower abstraction level, compared to the one in the behavior model (Fig. 7.28), we may go for "zooming in" with regard to each of the four interactions, represented in the model, such that we arrive at a detailed behavior aspect model of the FM, as shown in Fig. 7.30:

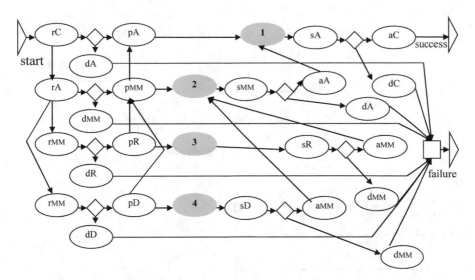

Fig. 7.30 Detailed behavior aspect model of the FM (Source: [8], p. 91; ©2006, IEEE, reprinted with permission)

It should be noted that the number labels of *production acts* (gray ovals in the figure) correspond to the interactions **i1–i4** (Fig. 7.28). Further, following one instance of the behavior, we have *two possible outcomes*, namely, successful and failure outcomes.

Based on the detailed *behavior model* and through simplification, we arrive at a **service-oriented model** (Fig. 7.31): we *group* together *coordination acts* based on their relations to *production acts*. Furthermore, we straightforwardly reflect (from the detailed *behavior model*) the information on how those groups relate to each other; we use an alternative way to model the *decline acts*: a *decline-after-request act* and a *decline-after-state act* are represented by a special value of an *information attribute* (e.g., *Result* **r** I **r** = "**decline**") of the *promise* and *accept* acts, respectively. Information attributes of the act and constraints on the values of these attributes are not represented in the figure. The *model*, presented in this way, defines services rooted in the transaction pattern, consistently with the achieved *modeling* output.

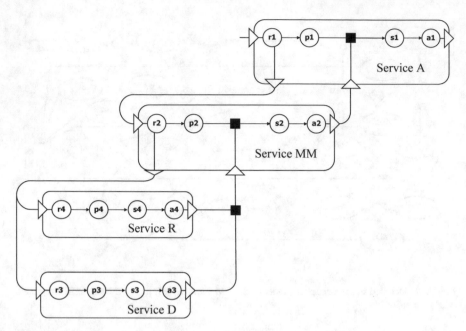

Fig. 7.31 Refined interactions in decomposed FM, implementing the FM service behavior (Source: [8], p. 92; ©2006, IEEE, reprinted with permission)

Thus, the *business entities* represented in Fig. 7.27a point to the (*application*) *components* underlying the *services* represented in Fig. 7.31. This assumes the easiest decision: to do a **one-to-one** mapping between the *business entities* (Fig. 7.27a) and the *application components* (it was implicit that the *business entitiy model* was straightforwardly mapped to an *application components* model where the *application components* correspond to the *business entities*, and this is how we have reached in the end the *service model* represented in Fig. 7.31). Nevertheless, such a one-to-one mapping between the two has the disadvantage that the identified *services* are tightly coupled. This means that there is a dependency of the *service* provided by one *component* on *services* provided by other *components* (as seen from Fig. 7.31). We argue that a solution would be to introduce an additional *application component*, called **orchestrator**, that has the task of coordination— inspired by *service orchestration* (Fig. 5.4).

The *orchestrator* is an application-specific *component*, as the coordination is application-specific. The (subordinate) *services*, however, which are coordinated by the *orchestrator*, may be useful for many different types of applications. Their descriptions may therefore be published through a public or corporate registry, such that they can be discovered and selected for invokation by an *orchestration component*. Related to its coordination tasks, the *orchestrator* could sometimes supply to one service the result of another service, if this is necessary for the service to perform its task.

Figure 7.32a depicts the *orchestrator's* (**O**) desired role. It concerns the interactivities between the "original" *components* (reflecting corresponding *business entities*) as well as *coordination*. The *orchestrator* mediates not only the interaction between the *customer* (**C**) and the *system* but also all interactions between *components* inside the *system*.

For this reason, in order to enable *orchestration*, we need to firstly *refine* the *business entity model* (Fig. 7.27a), by reflecting there the *orchestration entity* (colored gray in Fig. 7.32b) that mediates the interactions among *entities*.

Then in a similar way (see above) we can reflect this in a *behavior model* and in the end in a *service model*.

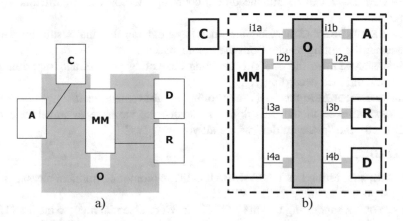

Fig. 7.32 (**a**) Desired role of the orchestrator. (**b**) The refined entity model (Source: [8], p. 92; ©2006, IEEE, reprinted with permission)

Thus, we have conducted an *enterprise re-design* in order to facilitate the accommodation of *service orientation* in the context of *SDBC modeling*.

7.5 Other Examples

Through the *Icomp* case, we have demonstrated how *enterprise engineering* and *software engineering* could be brought together, inspired by *SDBC*, such that *enterprise modeling* and *application modeling* are adequately carried out (and alignment between the two is supported) as well as the (possible) move towards *service orientation*. In this, we have considered *requirements* but not so explicitly and we have assumed a *top-down* approach—starting from high-level business information and moving to lower-level software specifications. Hence, further elaboration is needed with regard to the above and we provide it by considering two illustrative examples, namely, (1) the eVoting example where we explicitly consider *requirements* and (2) the Border Security example where we take a *middle-out* (rather than *top-down*) approach. Those two examples will be briefly considered in the following sub-sections.

7.5.1   The eVoting Example [9]

We consider identifying actor-roles (**AR**) and corresponding relations (**R**) in the context of a typical Voting scenario:

FIRSTLY: ARs

AR1—**CAMPAIGNER**: the one(s) campaigning in favor of a particular policy/party/ vision and influencing the people in that way.

AR2—**VOTER**: the one(s) voting for parliament/president/etc., and thus executing basic rights in the country.

AR3—**PRIMARY COUNTER**: the one(s) counting the votes in a particular voting station.

AR4—**SECONDARY COUNTER**: the one(s) aggregating the final result, by putting together the voting results from the voting stations.

AR5—**ORGANIZER**: the one(s) organizing the voting process and supporting all abovementioned accordingly.

AR6—**CONTROLLER**: the one(s) controlling all abovementioned.

7—**SYSTEM**: even though this is not an actor-role, we have to somehow model abstractly the "place holder" where all voting "goes."

SECONDLY: Rs

AR1-AR2 suggesting that the CAMPAIGNER is promoting political messages that are supposed to influence the VOTER.

AR2-SYSTEM suggesting that the VOTER provides essential input to the SYSTEM, namely, the vote.

SYSTEM-AR3 suggesting that the SYSTEM has impact with regard to each voting station (said otherwise, each voting station has its "own" SYSTEM), by providing the information needed by the PRIMARY COUNTER for calculating the station results.

AR3-AR4 suggesting that the SECONDARY COUNTER needs the PRIMARY COUNTER's feedback from each voting station, in order to aggregate the overall voting results.

AR5-ALL suggesting the ORGANIZER of the elections has relationship with all abovementioned ARs and the SYSTEM as follows: creating conditions for the CAMPAIGNER to do promotion adequately; establishing that the rights of the VOTER are guaranteed; establishing rules and mechanisms according to which the PRIMARY COUNTER and the SECONDARY COUNTER should fulfill their corresponding tasks; and establishing and running the voting SYSTEM.

A6-ALL suggesting that the CONTROLLER should execute effective control concerning all abovementioned ARs and the SYSTEM, as a guarantee that the voting is fair.

This is the basis for our conceptual requirements-driven model; further, we abstract from several issues, such that we do not consider an AR pointing to the one(s) (outside the CAMPAIGNER) who may be somehow influencing the decision of the VOTER—this could have been modeled as an AR by itself but we have not done this because of the lack of technical relevance.

We present our conceptual model in Fig. 7.33, and we use simple and intuitive graphical notations: the labels of the ARs are put inside boxes and the SYSTEM is presented as an oval, while the Rs are represented as lines (the arrows indicate who is ADDRESSED in the relationship—e.g., if the CAMPAIGNER is influencing the VOTER, then the arrow should be at the VOTER end because the VOTER is addressed by this).

As seen on the figure, we have not only drawn arrows at each line (lines representing Rs) but we have also added labels there: the CAMPAIGNER would influence the VOTER, the ORGANIZER would enable the SYSTEM, and so on.

Fig. 7.33 The voting conceptual model (Source: [9], p. 191; ©2016, SCITEPRESS, reprinted with permission)

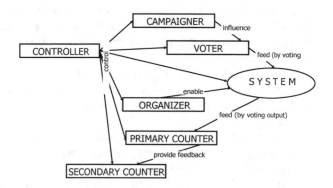

Further, we refer to particular **public demands** with regard to a possible introduction of eVoting, and in this case, the demands are:

- *Secrecy of vote*, possibly achieved through anonymous credentials, such that not even the system "knows" how a person has voted.
- *Cost adequacy*, possibly achieved through smart decisions rather than posh hardware that would generate future "dependencies."
- Guarantee against *violations* with regard to the way the system works.
- Guarantee against *manipulations* of the final voting results.
- Support of *secure communication* between the computers and the servers that is to be possibly cryptography-enriched.
- *Controllability*—any third parties should be able to "verify" that the system is working properly.
- Guarantee that each vote has been counted and that the person who had voted would *not be allowed to vote again.*
- *Fault reaction* is to be established as a guarantee that even if the system (partially) crashes, it would recover and this would not affect its storage and processing functions.
- *Ease of use* even by persons who are not of high computer literacy.
- No need for extra *qualification* of the election authorities.

We then **elaborate those public demands**:

With regard to the SECRECY OF VOTE demand, there are two things: (1) it is to be guaranteed that `nobody can know how a person has voted` and (2) it is to be ensured that the person has been marked as "voted," such that she/he `would not go to vote again`.

With regard to the COST ADEQUACY demand, the only way of avoiding the "big expensive black box" is to conceptualize the eVoting process such that `it is known what technology is needed for what`.

A way to guarantee against VIOLATIONS with regard to the way the system is working is to present the user with `a simple and exhaustive list of options`, with no possibilities to do anything outside the presented options.

A way to guarantee against MANIPULATIONS OF THE FINAL RESULTS is to keep things at two levels, such that the `Primary Counters generate the "raw" results` based on which the `Secondary Counters generate the final results` and this all stays stored with `possibility to check it in the future`.

The COMPUTER-SERVER communication is to be such that there is a guarantee that `a "packet" sent by a computer is received by the server and by no one else`; this is a matter of organization and also a matter of networking protocols.

CONTROLLABILITY can be partially achieved if `all intermediary results get transparent`, and then the only remaining challenge is how are the "raw" results generated.

FAULT REACTION is a matter of `recoverability,` and this is a non-functional concern that has to be addressed from a functional perspective nevertheless.

EASE OF USE is a matter of design.

The issue on QUALIFICATIONS needed for being involved in eVoting is a matter of legislation; as it was mentioned before, sufficient IT literacy among the population is assumed.

We then derive (straightforwardly) *semiotic norms* (see Chap. 4) corresponding to the elaborated demands. We take just for the sake of illustrating this one eVoting public demand, and we reflect it in a specified requirement expressed as a *norm*. We take the SECRECY OF VOTE elaborated demand and we derive the *norm* accordingly:

OS Norm 1:

```
Whenever    John has voting rights
if          John is executing eVoting
then        the eVoting system
is          (1) obliged to mark John as "voted"
is          (2) prohibited from recording the way John has voted.
```

Based on *OS Norm 1*, we derive a *workflow pattern* expressed with the notations of *UML activity diagram* [3]—see Fig. 7.34:

Fig. 7.34 Workflow pattern corresponding to OS Norm 1 (Source: [9], p. 193; ©2016, SCITEPRESS, reprinted with permission)

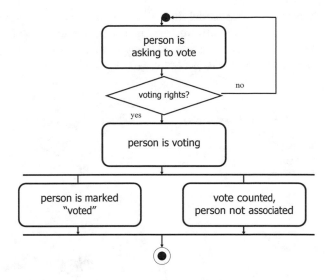

That is how we would methodologically derive *user-defined requirements*, in support of *SDBC modeling*.

7.5.2   The Border Security Example [10]

The Border Security domain is characterized by MANY possible-to-occur situations that concern the monitoring of illegal migration, combatting related crime, and so on, and there is a need for *context-awareness* and better *interoperability* with regard to the existing (national) border security platforms and *systems*. At the same time, we realize that it is not straightforward applying *context-aware solutions* in the Border Security domain. Hence, research is needed on *Context-Aware Border Security* (*CABS*) control since it would be difficult for a country to supply persons and equipment at every potentially risky border point. A *CABS* system would hence guarantee adaptability with regard to the situation at hand—persons and equipment would only be deployed at the spot where they are needed and in the moment when they are needed. In principle, the *modeling* of *systems*, such as a *CABS system*, should not be expected to differ a lot from the way of *modeling* any other *system*, using *SDBC*, as long as *context-awareness* has adequately been addressed (see Chap. 3). Still, the Border Security domain assumes greater complexity because of numerous possible situations and prediction difficulties. Further, what is observed at the border is a "mixture" of personnel and devices, subject to numerous rules and "functionalities", and it is not trivial approaching this in terms of technology-independent models, automation, and so on. This is because some (intuitive) tasks can only be realized by humans while other (surveillance) tasks can only be realized by devices, to give just an example. Hence, we need to "adapt" *SDBC* to the peculiarities of the Border Security domain. *SDBC* goes "top-down" from a "birdview" enterprise model through delimitation with regard to the software system-to-be to technical (software) specifications. Nevertheless, for specifying a *CABS* system, we propose to go "<u>middle-out</u>," as exhibited in Fig. 7.35, and we adapt the application of *SDBC* accordingly.

Fig. 7.35 CABS—way of modeling (Source: [10], p. 209; ©2016, SCITEPRESS, reprinted with permission)

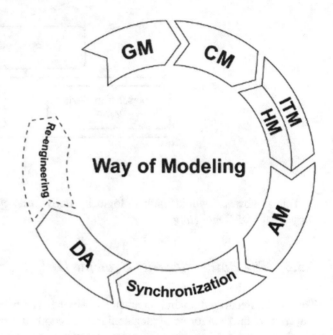

On the figure, "GM" stands for "*general model*", "CM" stands for "*conceptual model*", "ITM" stands for "*IT model*", "HM" stands for "*humans model*", "AM" stands for "*aspect model*", and "DA" stands for "*data analytics*".

We propose to go *middle-out* because in the Border Security domain, it seems most pragmatic to start with modeling "what is there" (a mixture of person-tasks, device functionalities, and so on to be seen at the border)—such a model we call a *general model* (GM). No other model that would inevitably be abstract would allow for grasping everything correctly and also communicating it adequately with all relevant stakeholders—this is claimed to be of great importance particularly for the Border Security domain. Just as an example of GM, we consider a typical land border point and we take an "imaginary" view on things that may be seen at a border point—see Fig. 7.36:

Fig. 7.36 A GM example (Source: [10], p. 209; ©2016, SCITEPRESS, reprinted with permission)

As seen from the figure, there is a border fence and border police officers patrolling along the fence; there are cameras attached to the fence, which realize crowd monitoring and there are mobile cameras attached to drones; there are fingerprint devices that can be used by police officers for personal identification; and there are (networked) computers running and streaming all sensor raw data, and also processing it by applying data fusion algorithms (for example), allowing "higher-level" reasoning, and so on. Hence, we claim that such a model should be the starting point in specifying a *CABS* system.

We use the *GM* as basis for deriving a *CABS*-related *classification* of concepts—this we call a *conceptual model* (*CM*); see Fig. 7.35. This way of "arriving" at the *CM* guarantees that our further *system* development activities would be "grounded." The human agent concept and the device concept appear to be essential within the *CABS conceptual model* (Fig. 7.37). That is because the *CABS general model* suggests that anything that can be observed at the border either relates to a personal (human) role or to a functionality delivered by a device (equipment). Further, among the human agents at the border (besides the persons who are crossing the border and are thus left outside the scope of the CABS system) are customs officers and police officers, while among the devices one could observe at the border are sensors, computers, and vehicles. Sensors in turn could be audio sensors and video sensors, while computers could be servers and personal computers, and vehicles could be cars and drones and so on. This is just as an example on how a *CM* can be derived, based on a *GM*.

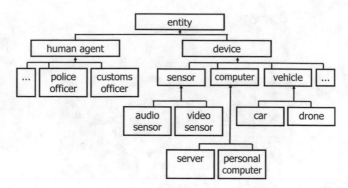

Fig. 7.37 Deriving a conceptual model (Source: [10], p. 210; ©2016, SCITEPRESS, reprinted with permission)

Such a *conceptual model* is the necessary starting point in an *SDBC* software development or just for building an *enterprise model* (see the previous sections of the current chapter).

Hence, we demonstrated that not only *top-down modeling* but also *middle-out modeling* can be supported by *SDBC*.

* * *

IN SUMMARY, in the current chapter, by considering one case study and two illustrative examples, we demonstrated how *enterprise engineering* and *software engineering* can be brought together, supported by *SDBC* and enriched by an explicit consideration of *user-defined requirements*, and also how this can be extended to accommodate *service-orientation* and *middle-out modeling*.

References

1. Yin R (1994) Case study research: design and methods. Sage, Thousand Oaks
2. Shishkov B (2005) Software specification based on re-usable business components. Delft University Press, Delft
3. UML, The unified modeling language. http://www.uml.org
4. Shishkov B, Dietz JLG (2005) Applying component-based UML-driven conceptual modeling in SDBC. In: Proceedings of the 7th International Conference on Enterprise Information Systems (ICEIS), 24–28 May 2005. SCITEPRESS, Miami, FL, USA
5. Dietz JLG (2006) Enterprise ontology, theory and methodology. Springer, Heidelberg
6. Cockburn A (2000) Writing effective use cases. Addison-Wesley, Boston
7. Shishkov B, Dietz JLG (2003) Deriving use cases from business processes, the advantages of DEMO. In: Proceedings of the 5th International Conference Enterprise Information Systems (ICEIS), 23–26 April 2003. SCITEPRESS, Angers, France
8. Shishkov B, Van Sinderen M, Quartel D (2006) SOA-driven business-software alignment. In: Proceedings of the ICEBE'06 IEEE international conference on e-business engineering, IEEE
9. Shishkov B, Janssen M (2016) Towards a service-oriented architecture for eVoting. In: Proceedings of the 6th international symposium on business modeling and software design (BMSD), 20–22 June 2016. SCITEPRESS, Rhodes, Greece
10. Shishkov B, Mitrakos D (2016) Towards context-aware border security control. In: Proceedings of the 6th international symposium on business modeling and software design (BMSD), 20–22 June 2016. SCITEPRESS, Rhodes, Greece

Printed in the United States
By Bookmasters